The Importance
of Average

The Importance of Average

Playing the Game of School to Increase Success and Achievement

Stephen J. Farenga, Daniel Ness,
Bonnie Johnson, and Dale D. Johnson

ROWMAN & LITTLEFIELD PUBLISHERS, INC.
Lanham • Boulder • New York • Toronto • Plymouth, UK

Published by Rowman & Littlefield Publishers, Inc.
A wholly owned subsidary of The Rowman & Littlefield Publishing Group, Inc.
4501 Forbes Boulevard, Suite 200, Lanham, Maryland 20706
http://www.rowmanlittlefield.com

Estover Road, Plymouth PL6 7PY, United Kingdom

British Library Cataloguing in Publication Information Available

Library of Congress Cataloging-in-Publication Data
The importance of average : playing the game of school to increase success and acievement / Stephen J. Farenga . . . [et al.].
    p. cm.
 Includes bibliographical references and index.
 ISBN 978-0-7425-7012-2 (cloth : alk. paper) — ISBN 978-0-7425-7014-6 (electronic)
    1. Academic achievement—United States. 2. Students—Intelligence levels—United States. 3. Educational equalization—United States. I. Farenga, Stephen J., 1958–
 LB1062.6.I66 2010
 370.1529—dc22   2009034482

∞™ The paper used in this publication meets the minimum requirements of American National Standard for Information Sciences—Permanence of Paper for Printed Library Materials, ANSI/NISO Z39.48-1992.

Printed in the United States of America

We dedicate this book to the memory of Dr. Robert Allan Youth—a great teacher and mentor. Bob's hard work, effort, gumption, and élan as a teacher, researcher, and champion for equity and justice shaped average potential into exceptional performance.

Contents

Acknowledgments

We are grateful to many individuals who, without their support, would have made this seemingly interminable undertaking all the more difficult to bring to fruition. At the expense of omitting a name from this list, we take full responsibility for failing to mention any person who has faithfully supported our endeavor.

The authors thank Barbara Hong of Penn State University, Altoona, and John A. Craven of Fordham University for taking their valuable time to read the initial drafts of this book. We are extremely fortunate to have Barbara write the foreword and John write the preface. In addition, we are grateful to those who have reviewed our book, particularly Julie Dangel of Georgia State University and Reese Todd of Texas Tech University.

We are indebted to Jim Borland, professor of education, and Herb Ginsburg, Jacob H. Schiff Foundations Professor of Psychology and Education, both of Teachers College, Columbia University for having supported our scholarly pursuits in the area of intellectual development and social justice. Our dear colleague and friend, Beverly Joyce, aided our research tremendously through her scrupulous reading of our presentation of research methods, especially in our discussion of intelligence in chapter 3.

We also wish to thank several individuals at Rowman & Littlefield who have greatly contributed to the development of this book. We are indebted to Erin McGarvey, our copy editor, for her painstaking care in reading the manuscript and ensuring that the arguments made herein are lucid and transparent to our audience of readers. We also thank Lynda Phung, our production editor, for expediting the publication process and pinning down a foreseeable print date.

On an unfortunate note, we were saddened to learn of the unexpectedly recent passing of Alan McClare, executive editor for sociology and anthropology. Alan successfully oversaw us through some of our earlier projects. With our increasingly routine communication, we got to know Alan on a personal level, and have warm recollections of lunches and dinners with him. Alan was remarkable for his indefatigability in spearheading, sponsoring, and promoting our book projects—including this one—from their nascent stages to the printed products. Alan's passing is a huge loss not only for us, but also for Rowman & Littlefield and the publishing world as a whole. We are grateful to Marcus Boggs, publisher and editorial director of Rowman & Littlefield, for filling in where Alan left off.

Finally, we greatly acknowledge the most important individuals who have inspired us to write this book—the underserved majority of schoolchildren, most of whom would be labeled "average" in contemporary parlance. We particularly acknowledge the multitude of school-aged children who we have taught, and although they were labeled "average," we held them to very high standards and levels of achievement. These very children are now adults who have made exceptional contributions to society. Indeed, our underrepresented and erroneously labeled "average" children deserve recognition and support in their intellectual endeavors—more now than ever before.

Foreword

I am an ordinary person . . . blessed with extraordinary opportunities and experiences.

—Sonia Sotomayor

Why are students reluctant to be engaged in school? Ask them and they will tell you that's because they are bored. In a 2007 study of more than 81,000 high school students across 26 states, two out of three students said they were bored in class *every single day* (Yazzie-Mintz, 2007). Why were they bored? They did not see any relevance or meaning in what they were being asked to do.

How did our nation's schools reach this dismal state? What have the educational policies and teacher education training done to engage our students in learning? Clearly, our nation is at risk not because our students are incapable of meeting challenges, but because schools have somehow failed to challenge them—failed to provide them with an opportunity for authentic learning by boring them with mindless memorization and ritualistic testing.

What is going to become of this nation if our students are raised in an environment where accountability is the name of a game rather than the pursuit of knowledge and lifelong learning? Our efforts to "leave no child behind" should not just be a question of meeting adequate yearly progress. It should be a matter of ensuring that all of our students become proactive, engaged, and self-empowered individuals so that *they themselves do not want to be left behind*!

So far, what No Child Left Behind and high-stakes testing have done is to treat the symptoms of the problems that have existed in public schools for decades instead of treating the causes of the problems of how teachers teach. As the American educator Joel Spring puts it, "The most totalitarian forms of education are those that control students' learning through testing . . . so as to tie learning to state standards, to ensure everyone learns the same thing and no one learns anything" (2007).

A number of ongoing debates about high-stakes testing and playing the test score game have significantly influenced what takes place in schools. These debates have generated more heat than light regarding what's really going on in the classrooms. Schools are *still* not making learning worthwhile for many students. Worse, schools still wait for the child to fail before providing help rather than proactively seeking interventions to prevent failure in the first place.

Teaching may not be rocket science, but reaching every average learner in the class may be close to it. When teachers are so crunched for time in completing the school district's prescribed curriculum, any deviation from traditional instruction to reach an individual learner's needs could mean taking time away from the rest of the class; unless, of course, the student is labeled as needing special services or is enrolled in more advanced programs. But what if a child does not fall into either of these categories? What if a child is just an *average student*, as, by definition, most of us are?

In the language of the U.S. Supreme Court more than a quarter century ago, public schools are not obligated to render additional "educational benefits" to students if they are already "achieving educationally, academically, and socially" (*Board of Education of the Hendrick Hudson Central School District v. Rowley*, 1982). It was never the intent of Congress to go so far as to mandate that schools must maximize the potential of every child, with or without labels, under the statute of "free and appropriate public education" (p. 199).

In our educational system, this means that if students are doing fine, we should continue doing what we have been doing, *even though it does not engage them and they are bored.* From the start, the odds are stacked against this vast majority of average achievers. This is what we are telling our children and future generations: schools are really established to create mediocrity, not excellence. The unfortunate truth is that these average, typical, unlabeled students are those who eventually build our communities, shape our economy, transform our society, and define our civility. If we don't start making extraordinary efforts to meaningfully engage them in school, we will irrefutably be at risk in this globalized, increasingly competitive world. The question is, how do we engage them?

The problem with many schools in the United States is not that teachers don't know *what* to teach, but rather they don't know how to engross students in learning. Think about what we ask students to do when we ask them to perform well in school: Follow oral and written directions. Make logical deductions. Read at grade level. Recall information for tests. Locate answers to questions. Turn in assignments on time. Ask relevant questions. Clearly express ideas orally and in writing. Locate information in textbooks. Participate in discussions. These are not the skills that prepare students to become self-empowered citizens.

Schools have not adequately provided a good basic education that will enhance students' capacity to achieve their desired outcomes. Those who seek a radical change in education characterize schools as mindless, factory-like, bureaucratic institutions, training students to go through the motions of memorizing and the ritual of testing what was memorized. As Linda Conway puts it, "It's not what is poured into a student, but what is planted" (2000). We want our children to be creative and flexible, able to solve problems and regulate their own behavior, but often what we are implanting in the name of standard-based reform is literally shrinking the capacities and stunting the growth of our students.

The literature that succinctly and logically addresses what ought to be done to engage students is unfortunately very limited. Much needs to be done. In *The Importance of Average,* professors Farenga, Ness, Johnson, and Johnson help fill that need by revisiting the purpose of school and showing teachers (and parents) how to rekindle our students' curiosity so that they yearn to discover the joys of learning and growing intellectually. If every highly qualified teacher can do that, then as a nation we can truly say that *all* children have had a chance to grow to their intellectual potential and that no one is left behind.

The authors go beyond providing a framework of what has gone right and wrong with the educational system in this country by deconstructing and reconstructing what learning ought to be in the twenty-first century. Each author objectively selected and crafted model programs that have been time tested to foster true learning outcomes by explaining important benchmarks in the core areas of linguistic development, mathematical thinking, scientific inquiry, and informed citizenry. Together, they combine the signature pedagogies for evaluating curriculum that allow teachers and parents to make a difference in their children's learning.

The Importance of Average is about how to connect teaching to learning so that students find meaning in what they are being asked to do. When you have finished reading this book, be prepared to make changes to your teaching. Be willing to challenge your students, even the average ones. Be ready to savor the moment when one child finally understands what you've been trying to teach and with a spark in his eyes, exclaims, "Aha!"

Barbara Hong
Pennsylvania State University
Altoona College

Preface: Thoughts from a Parent and Educator

> The requirement that . . . child[ren] go to school, for about six hours a day, 180 days a year, for about ten years, whether or not [they] learn . . . anything there, whether or not [they] already know . . . it or could learn it faster or better somewhere else, is such gross violation of civil liberties.
>
> —John Holt

Many years ago, I began my teaching career in the education department of a regionally well-known natural history museum in Memphis, Tennessee. My experiences there had a profound impact on my professional attitudes toward teaching. Our programs centered on science education (biology, ecology, physics, geology) and targeted a wide variety of age groups including early childhood, elementary, secondary, and adult education. Although the museum had fully equipped classroom laboratories, we also took students and adults to field sites to learn about such things as fossil hunting, bald eagle nesting sites, and caving (also known as spelunking). Fortunately, I've learned so much about teaching science content through these experiences. Unfortunately, however, I've learned how terribly unjust schools can be, and to this day, I regret my unwitting role in that process. Let me explain.

Although our science education programs spanned a very wide range, by and large, most of the children I taught were in elementary schools, and most of them were elite students in the talented and gifted (TAG) program nestled in the local, very large, public school district. For a typical TAG-sponsored museum program, a colleague and I would drive a minibus to a school within the district. We'd enter the school and meet up with the TAG teacher who would then escort us to the classrooms. We'd enter the classroom and call out the names of the boys and girls in the gifted program and load them into the bus for a day of museum education. I found those days to be as exciting as the kids. On cave trips, we'd drive about two hours to explore wild caves. To enter the cave we'd have to wade through a waist-high stream and crawl on a muddy bank through a narrow passageway. All the while, we had to make sure our flashlights were kept high, dry, and operational. The next three hours would be spent investigating marvelous geological and biological features of limestone chambers that were hollowed out through chemical processes long ago. During the return trip, the teachers would share their anticipation for seeing the projects or reading the reports and essays the students would write drawing upon the day's experience. We would also use the time spent on the return trip to plan the next trip—perhaps to our fossil site where we would dig up 65-million-year-old marine fossils or to Reelfoot Lake where we would spot hundreds of wintering bald eagles. This was truly an exhilarating experience for the students, my colleagues, and me.

At the same time, it did not take long for a mental image to form that has haunted me since. I distinctly remember the faces of the students left behind—literally—in the classroom. I soon realized that these very students left behind would have greatly benefitted from the experiences given to the "special" (gifted) students. I was told by school authorities that the students who remained could not afford out-of-class time, since they typically had to work on reading and writing skills or mathematics. Ironically, these students weren't really in need of remedial work. They were simply students who were categorized as "average." It seemed to me that none of the school personnel was getting the fact that if these average students had the opportunity to participate in the very same opportunities given these "gifted" students, their motivation to engage in school would vastly improve and their success and achievements would likely move well beyond our expectations.

Yet in schools, students are very clever at picking up the subtle—if not overt—message: *If you are not gifted, you're just not good enough and you don't deserve to engage in motivating activities.* It is the expression of embarrassment, despair, and resignation on the faces of these average students that I cannot, and perhaps never will, forget. After all, in their view, they were not worth the expense to participate in a museum program. Conversely, the TAG students also received the message about their status. I can recall one particular situation that illustrates this point.

For the museum educators, late spring was the season for frog dissections in our classroom laboratories. By far, most of the teachers in the district who booked the programs were the TAG teachers. Each spring, they would take their students to the museum for frog dissections as a capstone experience for the year. I had always hoped that this laboratory investigation would tie together a series of biological investigations, but in reality it was just a fun, if not titillatingly gruesome, experience that the kids knew (through tradition) they would experience near the end of the school year. For this reason, I would always set the stage for the dissection by asking the students, "Why are we here today?" My intent was to evoke both a respect for the life of the frog that we were about to cut open and to transform the students' expectations to a clinical yet educational stance. To this day, I vividly recall one particular laboratory investigation wherein a TAG student answered my question with the response, "Because we are *special*." Out of the mouths of babes, this student demonstrated the awareness of his "special" status. From the student's perspective, he was answering the question quite literally and honestly. They were indeed here because they belonged to the TAG program. And only the "special" or "gifted" kids got to the museum in the spring for a frog dissection. From my perspective, however, I was horrified. We conducted the laboratory investigation for advancement of scientific understanding and certainly not as a reward or entertaining day out simply because these students were perceived as "special." Moreover, as the well-known cognitive psychologist Jerome Bruner would argue, what we did during the frog dissection could be done by *any* elementary student at any level. One did not have to be *special* to participate in a well-constructed, engaging lesson.

Today, many years later, I now consider myself a seasoned teacher. I am a science teacher educator at the Graduate School of Education at Fordham University in New York City. My wife, coincidentally, is also a science teacher educator at another institution in the suburbs of the city. Together, we are raising five special boys of our own (all under the age of eight; no twins). I refer to them as special just as any proud parent would. Naturally, I fully acknowledge that many parents truly perceive a specialness, if not giftedness, of their children; this is, and should be, natural. However, I also can recognize as a teacher that my children are like so many others. They are, at the end of the day, normal, average kids. It's what my wife and I are doing with them that concerns me, for in the words of one of the authors of this book and longtime friend, Steve Farenga, we are likely setting our children up for failure in school. As one might imagine, our home is quite a busy hive with five little boys running—and crawling—around. The backyard abuts a section of the pine barrens on Long Island, so when the kids are not upstairs or downstairs building forts with blankets, pillows, and any other odds and ends in the house, they're mucking around on trails in the woods. I can't always figure out some of the games they play, but I'm certain that their imagination is taking them much further than the boundaries of their own little "hundred acre woods." It's not unusual for me to interrupt their play (sometimes singularly but many times collectively) so I can test out some activities I plan to use in my elementary and secondary (yes, secondary!) science teaching methods courses. Over the course of the recent past, we have (among many other things) built Lego robots, conducted hundreds of investigations of water (plain, soapy, colored, frozen, boiling—you name it and we've played with it), built miniature wind turbines in the backyard, launched all kinds of projectiles into the air using PVC pipes and an air compressor, built zip lines from one level of the house to another for their Webkinz (don't ask), and explored the phenomena of static electricity using a Van de Graff generator. In fact, sometimes I get the kids involved in these investigations to keep them from creating their own version of WrestleMania in the house as much as I do to test out ideas for lessons. For example, following a heavy snowstorm, the boys were playing in the yard. I watched as their friendly snowball fight escalated into nuclear attacks with ice balls. I was about to yell at them to come in when I thought of filling some plastic bottles with water and food coloring. I opened the door and threw colored bottles of water to the four who were outside—one for each boy, with each water-filled bottle a different color. I then closed the door. For the next hour, I watched from the kitchen window as the boys became deeply engrossed in their explorations. Naturally, the boys wanted to know if we could fire up our neighbor's snow blower and feed various colored snow into the mechanism to make a rainbow yard. Fortunately, he wasn't home and his garage was locked.

Thus, as Steve Farenga says, we may indeed be setting up our boys for failure in school. With all of their out-of-school science-related experiences, the manner in which science is taught in most schools will seem so unappealing and even monotonous. At home, the boys participated in inquiry rather than just reading about it from a textbook. From the boys' view, home is where they get to build, design, create, explore, interact, and, yes, even learn. Home is, in fact, a museum, exploratorium, and a place of love, all rolled into one. Indeed, I fully expect my boys to be in school one day when a sixth grade teacher introduces a scientific investigation, only to have them say, "oh yeah, I remember doing this when I was six." Again, I am not at all claiming my boys are special in the sense of "special," "gifted," or "talented." What I am arguing, and what I have come to understand professionally and personally, is that opportunities to engage in intrinsically interesting and experientially enriching activities can move average learners to quite surprising levels in terms of attitude, knowledge, and skills. Failing to provide such opportunities because the average student largely does what he or she is told and is only able to master the curriculum at a sufficient level as to avoid scrutiny by the teacher and administrators is an inadequate rationale.

For these reasons, *The Importance of Average* is a must read for parents and educators alike. I believe that Drs. Stephen Farenga, Daniel Ness, Bonnie

Johnson, and Dale Johnson raise a much-needed flag of concern regarding the meaning and value of the average child. They are correct when they argue that the "average" child is shamefully being left behind. We should not tolerate a system that exploits—through experiential deprivation and economic reallocation—the children who, on average, can function academically and socially in schools well enough to make the school, on average, appear to be functional itself. I only hope that my boys are spared the day in which they have to watch as the "gifted" students leave for a trip to the shore or see the "special" classroom hanging their essays about their trip to the aquarium in the hallway.

John A. Craven
Associate Professor of Curriculum and Instruction
Fordham University

Introduction

The ratio of "nature" to "nurture" remains unresolved. Of course we cannot change genetics, but we teachers can and must conduct ourselves as if "nurture" is the primary determinant in educational accomplishment.

—William F. Pinar (2004, p. 224)

The Importance of Average calls attention to the differential treatment of an entire group of students in our classrooms. This differential treatment in and of itself is not necessarily disturbing. What is disturbing, however, is when an entire group of students is ignored, or worse, subjected to influences that affect their ability to learn and succeed. In this book, we address the policies and practices that discriminate against so-called average students—the silent majority—in the American educational system. We highlight the collateral damage caused to average students through multiple factors. To be sure, legislative mandates, administrative policies, teaching practices, parental beliefs, and adherence to strict psychological constructs are a few of many factors that have contributed to this crisis.

No Child Left Behind (NCLB), although plausibly well intentioned, has not had the overall effect on education as was originally intended. In most instances, students in the middle—the average student population—have been subordinated in an effort to play catch-up with the remainder of the student population. Although some of our colleagues disagree with our assertion that average students are shortchanged, we suggest that they return to schools and classrooms and make contact with teachers, parents, and students whose concerns have been set aside in order to meet the needs of other special interests. Whether this on-hold status of average students is an intended or unintended outcome of education policy at this point is not an issue. What is an issue is that education policy must be changed in order to correct the indifference toward average students in this country. Educational policymakers have sacrificed the education of an entire class of students, indeed the majority, by creating the illusion that underachievement can be eliminated simply by lowering standards and increasing examination pass rates. Even a cursory examination of what many states consider "average" performance would be shockingly disappointing to many parents and others who have not paid attention to the matter. The public would be appalled if it were fully informed of the extreme and grotesque extent that certain school districts take in order for students to pass state tests and subsequently report "acceptable" scores to their communities. One school district whose test scores have been less than stellar recently reported, "Last year, Booklet 3 of the eighth-grade Math Assessment was inadvertently discarded" and "more than 200 student scores will be discounted due to the loss of the booklet." However, the district was sure to inform the public "that this is a direct result of the loss of the booklet and NOT the result of poor student performance" (Mineola Union Free School District, 2009, p. 1). Could discarding more than 200 student exams really be an accident?

Steven Levitt and Stephen Dubner's book *Freakonomics* (2005) exposes how wide-scale cheating occurs in the reporting of test scores. In one example, the authors explain how certain teachers in the Chicago public schools were found to have changed students' answers in an attempt to report higher performance levels. There are a number of punitive measures in place to motivate teachers and administrators to "improve" student performance, ranging from censure, belittlement, loss of promotion, or loss of merit pay. The threat of these measures has not only affected some teachers and administrators' ethical decisions, but has co-opted the instructional time and motivation of many average students. The amount of time spent preparing students to master the vapid content found on these tests is astounding and the collateral damage to average students and their teachers is extensive. Students who score at or above the "average" reference point are ignored. The students who garner the greatest attention as a result of NCLB policy are known as the "bubble students." These are students who are on the cusp of being labeled "proficient" but need additional time and remediation. These students are the school or district's grail, because as soon as they pass into the level of "proficient," the school is then perceived as a beacon of overall achievement.

The impact of NCLB has turned the education enterprise inside out. In a number of circumstances, special education objectives have essentially replaced actual mainstream education objectives as the "new mainstream." In these cases, the actual mainstream itself has been modified radically not to accommodate the needs of students, but to operate with a remedial mind-set. This movement has created standards that are low enough for the majority of students to "succeed." The harm is that average students are succeeding with little effort and few challenges. The difficulty occurs when average students encounter challenging subjects or teachers who are more demanding than what they have previously experienced. The students' prior experiences enable a mind-set that suggests that they have the appropriate skills and knowledge base to successfully continue with their academic careers. Unfortunately for many, this is not the case, for fantasy is no substitute for knowledge. An incongruity exists between the students' perceptions of their abilities and the reality of their abilities. Evidence of this discrepancy is described in research that indicates how average students in the United States generally report higher confidence levels in their mathematics and science abilities than do students in several countries of the Pacific Rim, such as Japan, Taiwan, South Korea, and Singapore. What is interesting is that the U.S. students' achievements in those subjects are lower than their perceptions, while those of their East Asian counterparts score higher than their perceptions of their abilities.

There are a host of reasons to suggest what may cause such a discrepancy in achievement perceptions and actual achievement. Based on our experiences both teaching students from pre-kindergarten through twelfth grade and beyond, along with years of research, we have identified some basics in education that are continually overlooked or forgotten by the education enterprise. Each of the ten points that follow are issues that we emphasize throughout this book that aid in supporting the education of students in the middle—also known as average children.

1. Good teaching is good teaching. A good teacher of English will be a good teacher of science. A good teacher will do what is necessary to become proficient at her profession. In general, good teachers have high expectations of themselves. They are confident and relay those expectations and confidence to all students.
2. Students who are successful learn that with the appropriate effort and assistance, success is possible. They also learn that failure is a temporary situation that is part of the learning cycle and with appropriate effort and assistance achievement is attainable. According to attributional theory, success alone will not increase learning and achievement. Success must be accompanied by student effort, and it must be perceived to be under the student's control, along with the knowledge that effort is responsible for achieving success. It is essential that students develop an awareness of the relationship between effort and success or lack of effort and failure.
3. Teachers must support the development and value of learning goals that emphasize meaning and understanding, which are developed over time and require persistence. Effort cannot be considered the

less-important component of success, where innate ability trumps all other factors. Students require a more practical understanding of the work effort needed for the development of expertise or proficiency. Attitudes that foster the pejorative use of terms such as "overachiever" and diminish the accomplishments of a student imply that innate ability is the only valuable form of intelligence. These attitudes must be dispensed with.

4. Administrators must eliminate the high-profile status of high-stakes testing from the schools. Professional evaluation teams should be established to randomly assess schools throughout the country. A sample of schools in each state should be randomly selected and tested rather than testing every student in every school throughout the country. The evaluation of the school should provide evidence of full accountability that includes a balance of outcomes beyond basic academic knowledge and limited problem solving. The evaluation should include what some might consider outdated, such as evidence of (1) arts in education; (2) informed citizenry through civics and personal responsibility; (3) work ethic and interpersonal skills; (4) physical education and health awareness; (5) careers skills, finance, and technical training; and (6) global responsibility, cultural awareness, geography, and environmental stewardship. The results from the first round of testing should remain private, known only to the evaluation team and local stakeholders. The evaluation team should meet with teachers, administrators, and parents to explain the results and, if needed, to delineate a specific educational improvement plan. The same outside evaluation team should reassess the school. The follow-up evaluation should be unannounced, and at this time, results could be made public.

5. Teachers need to be cognizant that both their overt and covert attitudes form expectations that influence their own behaviors and those of their students. Both overt and covert attitudes influence the direction of achievement in their classrooms.

6. Education policy has to be proactive and place learning goals ahead of performance goals. Students require a rich knowledge-based curriculum that is flexible and addresses problems to which they can relate. The focus of the activity should be on knowledge and skills and not the end assessment that only evaluates a small sample of behavior. Important skills and knowledge in life are not always measurable at a specific point in time.

7. Parents need to be aware that their attitudes and behaviors can—and will—influence the direction of study, careers, and overall achievement of their children. Parents who are unengaged in the welfare of the everyday lives of their children should not expect positive out-

comes. Likewise, highly punitive parents at the other extreme should not expect positive outcomes either.

8. Parents of mainstream students must find their voices and become advocates for their children, and not allow them to fall between the cracks in their academic careers. Find other parents who are encountering similar issues with their children of average academic ability. It won't be difficult! Form an advocacy group. Also, petition local, regional, and perhaps even state legislatures to support the average student majority.

9. Parents and teachers must not be lulled into a false sense of security about their children's abilities based on test scores. The overassessment of student ability, grade inflation, and disdain for persistence and hard work are factors that have worked against the average student. What has emerged is both a feeling of entitlement and a sense of learned helplessness that contribute to student apathy toward school.

10. Finally, as a nation, we can no longer squander our human resources. Regrettably, one of our greatest resources sits and wonders, "What am I doing here?" And this is happening in thousands of classrooms across the country on a daily basis.

All children deserve the opportunity to have an appropriate education. Financial support within our current education system relies initially on funding the general mass of students and subsequently special interest student populations. This method of funding creates adversarial relationships among groups who maneuver to achieve both financial and political recognition. In the education environment, there are numerous organizations that purport to represent constituents, such as teachers, parents, students, administrators, and specialized professional agencies. At some point, we need to examine whether these organizations place their own needs before those of their constituents and, more importantly, ahead of our children. Until now, there has been little concern for the average student in both the popular press and the academic community. In terms of letter grades, this is the student who is usually identified by letter grade with a "B," ranging from B– to B+ (80–89 out of 100 numerically), without expending much effort in academic subjects. We find this problematic because the small number of students with self-initiative or who are fortunate enough to be given the appropriate stimulation by parents, teachers, and mentors are indeed able to exceed beyond what society has inferred from mere grade designations. As a subgroup, these students begin to associate learning goals in school that are parallel to the goals they experience in their out-of-school activities. Playing a musical instrument, reading a Harry Potter novel, perfecting the art of skateboarding, taking acting classes, designing an Intel science project—these informal, out-of-school activities contain embedded learning goals that are powerful because they are often linked to future plans and possibilities that provide students with some relevance and understanding of themselves, others, and their environment. In short, the application of informal activities that promote learning goals to the formal education setting may provide the motivational force necessary for average students to increase achievement.

It is this motivational phenomenon that separates the observed eagerness to engage in many informal out-of-school activities that is sadly absent from many tasks related to formal education. Most formal education is tied to performance goals that are limited to finite academic assessments. For many students, formal education has been reduced to an eviscerated curriculum of closed-ended tasks and test-preparation skills. It is void of creative study, mentors who have the opportunity to inspire students, and open-ended activities. What is left is an environment that requires average students to engage in trite, insipid, and oftentimes specious tasks—tasks that are monotonous, often disengage students from learning and school, and require little, if anything, in academic returns. So, if you expect nothing, you will get it in abundance; unfortunately, our education system lives by this mantra.

We have organized this book on the premise that average intellectual ability is in no way synonymous with mediocrity. Another way to put it: under the right circumstances, average ability can lead to exceptionality in any subject or discipline. The first chapter reveals how society has historically dealt with the "average" label. Most often, the label is a euphemism for the majority of students who simply can be neglected, allowing for the allocation of both social capital and other types of resources to smaller student groups. In the second chapter, we argue that average ability need not serve as a euphemism and can potentially lead to professional excellence. We then study the ways in which students perceive themselves in academic terms and show how rubric use is an obstacle in learning. We continue by recommending the formation of an advocacy group that serves students of average ability—possibly a "committee on the average." In chapter 3, we place the notion of average intellectual ability in the context of the history of intelligence research. We provide an account of a number of psychologists and intelligence experts through the last century who contributed to our current understanding of the role of human intellect and its role and placement within the nature-nurture continuum. This investigation is necessary for the subject of chapter 4 and our discussion of ability, effort, and luck as possible motivational considerations that may be causes of success for average students. In chapters 5 through 8, we change the tone of our discourse by focusing on what teachers and parents can do in the subject areas. More specifically, we investigate the importance of average as it relates to four school disciplines: language arts and literacy, mathematics, science, and history and civics. In these chapters, we identify best practice in each field of inquiry, as well as alternative ways to approach various topics in each of the four disciplines. We also examine a host of factors that seem to be the best predictors of success in the "real world." We outline appropriate practices and questions for any concerned and caring parent, guardian, or teacher to ask in order to obtain the most equitable educational program for the multitude of children who are caught in the middle in terms of ability. We explore methods that provide students of average knowledge in any given area with the appropriate tools necessary for succeeding and becoming an expert in the subject. In chapter 9, we close by positing that although there is a great deal of average curriculum in schools throughout the country, there is no such thing as "average" intelligence.

Our initial goal is to convince readers of the importance in emphasizing society's challenge to even the playing field for students labeled "average" so that they can benefit from the same positive experiences of their "non-average" peers.

1

Average Anyone?

Welcome to Lake Wobegon, where all the women are strong, all the men are good-looking, and all the children are above average.

—Garrison Keillor (2009)

Garrison Keillor, the well-known American humorist, aptly satirizes the state of "average" when he describes the inhabitants of Lake Wobegon: "all the women are strong, all men are good-looking, and all the children are above average." Keillor's description of children who inhabit Lake Wobegon epitomizes the mind-set of the meaning of average in our society. Lake Wobegon taps into the American psyche where no one wants to be referred to as average in a country that values individualism, self-reliance, and, perhaps most important, upward mobility. Unquestionably, then, the term *average* has had a notoriously pejorative history. In particular, generation after generation, people have shuddered with disdain when hearing this term in connection with one's mental faculties, financial status, academic accomplishments, and self-image. Has anyone ever seen a bumper sticker that says: "My child is an average student" or "I'm proud of my average child"?

It is intriguing to note how the American educational system is designed to accommodate each end of the academic continuum but at the same time to devote little attention and few provisions to the average child. Therefore, we examine in detail the phenomenon of sorely limited attention to average students and greater academic emphasis on students who have a recognized classification such as "learning disabled" or "gifted."

Throughout the twentieth century and to the present day, one's academic ability has been measured according to intelligence—that is, intelligence

1

quotient (IQ)—tests that provide educators with a so-called crystal ball for predicting potential achievement. These tests measure some type of ability either by scaling and ranking in terms of mental age or by analyzing correlations among mental tests using factor analysis (Gould, 1996). Although these tests are no longer used en mass in certain areas of the country, other high-stakes tests have replaced them. Further, academic achievement and cognitive ability as measured by high-stakes tests often exclude the contributions related to higher order thinking, creativity, and persistence as factors for success (Johnson & Johnson, 2006).

INTELLIGENCE IS NOT ENTIRELY FIXED

Recently, there has been a need among some researchers to reexamine intelligence beyond the sole criterion of academic achievement. The academic community is only beginning to realize and to take seriously that the goal of education is to produce individuals who can make important contributions to society. With this in mind, researchers suggest that functional intelligence may be composed of numerous attributes that are not fully explained by any single theoretical position. Accordingly, Perkins (1995a) has categorized the numerous theoretical models that attempt to explain intelligence into three broad areas: neurological endowment, experience in a domain, and reflective abilities. Each of these areas appears to account for some aspect of human intelligence (Ceci, 1990; Gardner, 1983; Guilford, 1967; Jensen, 1969, 1983, 1998; Sternberg, 1985). However, researchers are not certain as to how much each theoretical perspective accounts for one's overall intelligence/success quotient. In addition, the relationship between intelligence and brain function is not fully understood. Despite these uncertainties, there is some general agreement in the field that the neurological model, which is primarily indexed to a biological endowment (genetic component), remains relatively stable even after interventions (Brody, 1992; Campbell & Ramey, 1994; Jensen, 1983). Even though researchers have suggested that certain aspects of IQ are highly heritable, it is also important to consider that IQ can also be affected by environmental conditions. In fact, 52 professors, all experts in human intelligence and allied fields, have signed a position statement on the nature of intelligence. They state: "Individuals are not born with fixed, unchangeable levels of intelligence (no one claims they are). IQs do gradually stabilize during childhood, however, and generally change little thereafter" (Gottfredson, 1994). They go on to argue that although the environment is influential in intellectual development, there is a great deal of controversy as to how much the environment plays a role in raising long-term scores in intelligence.

In response to the more classic notions of intelligence, two researchers, Roy Pea (1993) and David Perkins (1995b), have offered the concept of distributed intelligence, which suggests that factors outside the individual help to shape the production of intelligent behaviors. In one's environment, there are physical, social, and symbolic resources that affect cognition. Physical resources can refer to items that are available to the person when thinking about or solving a problem. Social resources refer to the human organizational opportunities available to the individual, such as mentors, peers, families, or teachers. Symbolic systems are the abstract mediums found in culture that individuals use to communicate to express their abilities, such as mathematics, language, art, and music. A notable connection among distributed cognition, Vygotsky's zone of proximal development, situated cognition, and legitimate peripheral participation is that higher levels of thinking can be achieved with some form of scaffolding provided by people, objects, or a culture's symbolic resources. It is thought that one's level of intelligence increases through interaction with physical objects, other people, and symbolic systems found in their surroundings. The concept of distributed intelligence looks at factors outside the individual and supplies a kind of inside-out perspective, suggesting the importance of environmental factors and how these factors support intelligence. Distributive intelligence provides a divergent perspective of cognition; although intuitively appealing, it requires a radical shift in how we conceptualize, measure, and ascertain intelligence. What is most intriguing is that distributive cognition may require us to reconsider the meaning of the average student.

A MATTER OF TIMING

An important point to consider with regard to levels of intelligence is the apparent critical relationship between time and resources—in other words, between the period of time a child spends in primary and secondary education and the quality of any intervention that can promote and foster the child's success and achievement. An individual or organization's provision of unlimited resources after a critical time period may be futile. A cursory investigation of the biological world provides a great deal of support for this argument. Suppose, for example, that a sapling needs water to thrive, and due to weather patterns a long period of drought takes effect. As a result of dry weather conditions, the sapling will undergo desiccation and therefore will likely die in a matter of time. After a certain point in the desiccative process, no amount of water will return the plant to its original, healthy state. The same idea often applies to the child who is not labeled exceptional—in other words, not labeled learning disabled on one end of the spectrum nor intellectually gifted on the other. These unlabeled children who are not labeled are referred to as "average" and are ignored in many classrooms throughout the country.

There is a parallel between the lack of environmental diversity as it relates to intellectual development and children's living conditions. For example, a child living in adverse conditions has a greater possibility of intellectual growth if intervention occurs earlier rather than later. Lack of environmental stimulation toward intellectual growth is also due in part to poor living conditions. Unfortunately, most poor children do not have the luxury to attend quality preschool and professional day care programs. At the same time, cognitive psychology and neuropsychology research has shown that the human nervous system enables all human neonates and young children to respond to environmental conditions in similar ways. That is, assuming a normal gestation period with no complications, one-, two-, three-, and possibly four-year-old children, irrespective of race, ethnicity, or social class, are generally on equal footing in regard to their cognitive abilities and neurological makeup (Gleitman, 1992; Gopnik, Meltzoff, & Kuhl, 1999; Hertzman, 2002). This means that all children have the potential to excel cognitively and intellectually in ways that will lead to success later in life.

Despite a lack of significant differences with regard to cognitive and neurological considerations in the early years, children who are raised in abject poverty do not perform as well as their middle- and upper-income peers. Therefore, children living under these adverse conditions possess certain life experiences that impel them to focus on more immediate concerns—health, safety, protection from crime-ravaged conditions, and other concerns that need more immediate and desperate attention than cognitive development. Research, then, overwhelmingly supports the position that brain development and cognitive development are highly dependent on diverse learning experiences throughout the life span. Given these circumstances, along with research findings showing that a modicum of cognitive and neurological activity is prewired, cognitive and intellectual development is strongly dependent on the diversity of children's actual everyday experiences (Hertzman, 2002; Hertzman & Weins, 1996). The message from the research is clear. It doesn't matter what reason is given for the lack of attention to the average student. By not providing children with the appropriate environmental stimulation and by letting them coast on their own while attending to a perceived greater need among the "bubble students" (those on the cusp of passing high-stakes tests), we guarantee similar results to many of the children who exhibit underperformance, wasted potential, and intellectual apathy. Regardless of cause, depravation is depravation, whether it occurs due to neglect, poorly thought-out educational policies, or poverty. This is our concern for the average child who is not given the benefit of additional attention in the wake of current educational initiatives.

Can the environment affect genetic expression and influence one's potential? It is our bias that the environment can be manipulated so that students who are labeled as having "average" abilities are capable of extraordinary achievement. Some would suggest that this has not been fully supported by federally sponsored Head Start programs. Although this may seem to be the situation at first, further analysis reveals various discrepancies among Head Start programs. It is evident from the research that all Head Start programs are not created equally. Initiatives such as the Perry Preschool Program in Michigan have shown long-term achievement. However, other interventions for the purpose of altering the environment are poorly planned, limited in duration, lack appropriate funding, or are simply implemented too late. In support of our premise, a research field known as epigenetics has demonstrated that environmental factors can differentiate gene behavior or expression (Weiss, 2005). However, the answer to how the environment causes the variation in gene behavior is still under investigation. Given the importance of recent scientific findings in the field of epigenetics, the need for early intervention (i.e., neonatal development) and the importance of conducive learning environments may be more important than once believed in affecting genetic expression. As a prudent response to this information, we suggest that four conditions must be met in order for the interventions to be successful: appropriateness to the learner's ability; early intervention carried out over a long period of time integrating both the home and school environment; quality of the educators carrying out the intervention; and consistency among the providers of the intervention. In short—appropriateness, consistency, time, and quality (ACT-Q).

THE "AVERAGE" PARADOX

Based on the research involving the three broad theories of intelligence, it is important to have at least average intelligence—average "g"—to prime the pump for the experiential and reflective components for increasing intelligence. According to Andrade and Perkins (1998, p. 73), "We can cultivate both experiential intelligence . . . and reflective intelligence." Therefore, the importance of average can become the precursor to achieving above-average achievement and performance. But here lies the paradox: on the one hand, one may require average ability to take advantage of experiential and reflective training; yet, on the other, students who lack a classification or who are not labeled—that is, average—are not entitled to specialized services. It is at this point that being average becomes an indelible referent associated with the average child, so much so that it becomes a disadvantage. In sum, the lack of classification means no extra services provided. It is evident, then, that one's level of intelligence serves as one—and perhaps the most important—of the gatekeepers for receiving special services. Either limited intelligence or abundant intelligence may qualify an individual for federal, state, or district support.

Since the end of World War II, increases in the funding of educational endeavors and enterprises in the United States followed the crisis model: if no crisis exists, then no additional funds and services are provided. In stark contrast, when a particular administration attempts to paint a picture of crisis and emergency as a result of a seemingly so-called lack of preparedness in science and space travel (e.g., the launching of Sputnik) or in general cross-national educational and political comparisons (e.g., the unwarranted conclusions in the infamous publication *A Nation at Risk*), then all organizations that wish to embrace a call to "end" the alleged educational pandemonium receive both federal and private funding and services (Berliner & Biddle, 1995).[1] It is ironic that in many schools across the country students need to be performing below or above their present grade levels in order to benefit from additional monies and special services. The tendency to fund educational services based on one's performance below or above grade level leads us to ask the following questions: Who is ignored by this method of funding? What factors are the best predictors of success in the real world? Why does academic achievement as measured by high-stakes tests often exclude the contributions of higher order thinking, creativity, and persistence? How does intelligence as measured by IQ establish predetermined categories that serve as holding patterns of students throughout the school years? How can parents challenge school policies to help promote their children's achievement? And where does this leave the average student who may require that additional encouragement in order to maximize potential?

Indeed, state and federal governments appear to act only in the presence of a national crisis. Therefore, we call attention to perhaps one of the largest injustices in education: the crisis of the average.

Combined, the authors of this book have had classroom experience from preschool through grade 12, as well as at the college and university levels. We each have independently recognized the plight of the average student, where lack of organized voices, specialized programs, and teacher education cause the current educational system to look down on and past the needs of the average. A call for redirection of educational services is direly needed in order to maintain a competitive workforce in the United States. Average students are the untapped natural resource; if given the attention that their peers at each end of the "intelligence" continuum receive, they can provide the momentum for changing the economic environment. As the United States shifts from a society dependent on other nations for valuable resources to one that is inventive and finds alternative ways to tap new forms of energy, there will be a greater need for highly qualified individuals who, if provided the opportunity, can dramatically improve the level of the workforce. These positions demand us to broaden our notion of intelligence and to realize the importance of the potential contributions of the average individual. Theoretical frameworks that discuss social and emotional intelligences, along with the habits of highly successful people, have just scraped the surface of recognizing the need to maximize human potential. These frameworks emphasize specific life skills and goals that often rely on a variety of traits that are neglected or are not fostered in traditional educational settings and that are measured by high-stakes tests. Even as intellect, persistence, creativity, and practical abilities are valued by the arts, professions, and certain business communities, there are those who still question their relevance in academic venues. In a society that is captivated by numbers, concepts and abilities that evade measurement are circumspect. Therefore, average students who possess an unquantifiable number of various attributes are ignored and the possibilities of identifying their extraordinary accomplishments are lost forever.

2

The Invisible Majority: Making Average Exceptional

Learning is a consequence of thinking.

—David N. Perkins (1995b)

During his leadership in the military campaign against Crimea in 1787, the infamous Russian statesman Grigori Aleksandrovich Potemkin is said to have engineered the development of feigned villages along the Dnieper River. This costly endeavor demonstrated Potemkin's successful attempt to impress Catherine II, empress of Russia, and to make her believe that the Russian annexations of the Crimean region were in the process of colonization. No matter how his rivals may have portrayed this event, Potemkin's actions serve as a perspicuous precedent to contemporary phenomena in education. Two of the more notable phenomena are (1) that average students, the overwhelming majority, are appropriately represented by educational policy and (2) that the notion that high-stakes examinations are substitutes for broad field knowledge.

Accordingly, the term "Potemkin village," and even the word "Potemkin" itself, has been used in contemporary discourse to indicate the implementation of contrived or fabricated events, places, or ideas for one's public support and political gain. We use the Potemkin village precedent as an analogy for the institution of mainstream education and the putative concept of average students. We argue that mainstream education's lack of organizational representation has made average students an invisible majority and has had destructive consequences for average students.

In this chapter, we initially identify the etymologies of certain colloquialisms (for example, "smart" or "average") that are associated with one's level

9

of intelligence. We then argue that, as a society, we need to reconsider the notion of the label "average" as a euphemism for "mediocre," "not bright," "lackluster," "middle of the road," and the like. We follow this discussion with an examination of the ways in which students and others perceive themselves intellectually. Next, we show how the use of rubrics by states and their departments of education have served to thwart the education of average students. Finally, we show that average students—unlike their learning-disabled or high-ability peers—lack representation (such as advocacy groups) as a means to achieve higher status and regard, despite the fact that they represent the overwhelming majority of the population in nearly every demographic that one can think of. We propose the establishment of an advocacy group for the average, such as a "committee on the average," so that all students have an opportunity to learn and to engage in productive endeavors after their period of schooling.

IT'S ALL IN A WORD

One's use of dictionary definitions as a means of supporting an argument might often arouse skepticism because someone who makes a strong claim is generally not concerned with designation, word meaning, or classification. For instance, one might argue that preschool programs and initiatives should receive federal funding because without it, primary school students will lose out on content knowledge that they will need in order to compete later in the global market. The interlocutor might reply: "What is meant by the term 'content knowledge'?" But the individual making the original argument is undoubtedly less concerned about the definition of "content" and "knowledge" and more interested in convincing others about what *should* be done (in terms of policy or value) in this situation or under another set of particular circumstances. But in certain instances, dictionary definitions can be quite fruitful and even appropriate—especially when the meanings of terms have changed at various points in time. This is indeed the case with words like "average," "dull," "smart," and other terms that connote factors or levels of intelligence. Our goal here is to show how these terms changed dramatically in meaning over the years and, in the case of intelligence, were invented by twentieth-century psychologists and philosophers for the purpose of supporting specific agendas—and not always actual evidence in the fields of cognition and intelligence.

When someone refers to someone else as average, there is a lot of explaining that needs to be done. First of all, what is meant by average? Next, how is average defined? Further, how is the term "average" used in context? Answering these questions presents the bare minimum information needed to comprehend the meaning of average. We can examine the term a bit more closely by investigating other terms that place the term "average" and its past and current meanings in context. "Smart," "crafty," "cunning," "pithy," "bright," "gifted," "talented," "creative," "clever," "sharp," "witty," "quick," and "keen" are several terms that connote someone with presumed higher levels of intellectual ability. "Slow," "dull," "thick," "dim," "obtuse," and "dense" are just a few of the terms that connote an individual with presumed low levels of intellect. There is a third group also. We often hear people referring to individuals who possess a skill as crafty, handy, useful, creative, and practical. How, then, are these individuals categorized? Do they fall into the category of "smart"? Or do these individuals fall into the other category? Or perhaps might we need to develop a new category?

It's All Semantics

We often take for granted the words we use every day to describe various conditions and situations. As a brief definition, semantics is the study of meaning or different shades of meaning. A more elaborate definition of semantics would be the following: the intricate relationships of meanings of words, phrases, or text to each another and the ways in which these relationships are brought together into thematic configurations. Let's start by subjecting "smart" to semantic scrutiny. We will follow this discussion by examining the semantic implications of the word "average."

Smart

In *Webster's New Universal Unabridged Dictionary*, "smart" is defined as an adjective in at least 10 different ways, 8 of which have little, if anything, to do with intelligence. In fact, "causing sharp pain" or "quite strong and intense" was the original meaning of the term. Most of these definitions use the words "sharp," "intense," or "severe" as synonyms. From an etymological perspective, "smart," meaning "intelligent," entered the lexicon rather late when compared to its other meanings. "Smart" is an Old English word that was first used in the ninth or tenth centuries to describe severe or intense pain (e.g., a smart pain or a smart lash). The earliest hint of the word being associated with an intelligent person is from the beginning of the fourteenth century (c. 1303), nearly 500 years later, but that meaning had more to do with the way someone crafted words when communicating verbally and nothing to do with actual intelligence—that is, comparisons that are associated with IQ scores.

Average

As the *Oxford English Dictionary* entry on "average" shows, the word "average" can be traced to the Arabic word *arwariya*, which refers to merchandise that is damaged during transit, most often by sea. The Italian and Old

French terms, *avere* and *aveir*, respectively, are similar to *arwariya* in that they refer to one's property or goods but not in terms of physical condition. By the late fifteenth century, the term referred to losses that were incurred as a result of damaged merchandise while in transit. One important question, however, concerns the point in time when the shift in meaning to "medial" or "middle" (let alone its association with intelligence) occurred. The shift in meaning was gradual; although it still referred to goods and capital, it did so in terms of equal sharing among concerned parties. The actual disconnect in association with goods to the more generic meaning of "middle" or "medial estimate" was initially recorded in 1735. Mathematical associations with "average," which were unequivocally linked to notions of "middle," were initially recorded in 1755, and the word was first used in its adjective and verb forms by 1770. The association of the word "average" with levels of intelligence is a late invention, and, as we will show in chapter 3, is a product of the methods used by Lewis Terman, Robert Yerkes, Carl Brigham, and other early twentieth-century American psychologists in the field of intelligence studies.

"Average" Is Not a Euphemism

We might often talk about Joan Smith or Mike Jones as "average" in a number of ways. Incidentally, we note that the names we use in the previous sentence may evoke the aura of average, given that Smith and Jones are the most common American surnames, and Joan and Mike are quite common given names. In his book, *The Average American: The Extraordinary Search for the Nation's Most Ordinary Citizen*, Kevin O'Keefe (2005) examines the idea of average from a sociological lens. He searches for a way that we can identify average in the sense of finding the archetype of an American citizen. O'Keefe asks questions that may demonstrate commonalities among the majority of Americans—for example, if you like peanut butter, do you prefer eating smooth peanut butter or crunchy peanut butter? This is one of several questions he uses to home in on the "plainness" of an individual—how he considers and defines "average." Another way to look at average is to examine it in terms of one's proficiency level of knowledge—that is, in terms of what we know. For example, is a seven-year-old child able to explain the relationship between the ones column and tens column in a multidigit subtraction problem, or is he or she simply able to carry out the problem without identifying the essence of place value? Our primary goal is to investigate the latter—namely, to examine the role of average in terms of intellectual and cognitive development, and how this label has outlived its usefulness. Thinking of average in this way suggests a number of terms that serve as euphemisms: within both popular and academic media, the words "mainstream," "typical," "conventional," "satisfactory," and even "normal" have all been used to describe the intellectual ability of the average individual.

But "average" need no longer be euphemistic. Why must it be the case that society consistently alludes to the notion of average in negative terms? We argue that 68 percent or more of the population who are technically labeled as average (if one were to use IQ measures as a standard frame of reference) represent some of the most productive and potentially successful individuals in any given demographic.

The term "mainstream" is often applied to students who cannot be categorized or do not have an official classification. Classifications might include "gifted and talented" at one end of the bell curve to "mentally retarded" at the other. In between are a host of other classifications that may even include gifted learning disabled, also known as twice exceptional. This should give some indication of the complexity of labels and classifications that may be included in the term "exceptional" that is often used in education. However, nowhere in the term of exceptional will one find "average."

We have found that students who are not labeled above average at the upper end or below average at the lower end are generally lumped together into one large unit and essentially ignored. They are ignored by the popular media. They are ignored by the academic community. They are ignored by our political leaders, public policy specialists, and special interest lobbyists who hold the keys to the coffers that have been earmarked for highly specified groups, such as those labeled "learning disabled" or "gifted." They are even ignored by some parents who do not consider their children to be academically distinguishable.

We are by no means arguing that students at either end of the bell curve should not be given consideration with regard to their group affiliation. Nor are we suggesting that these groups of students give back their hard-achieved gains for an appropriate education. We are, however, arguing that the invisible majority needs to be addressed in an appropriate manner in mainstream education. Greater attention needs to be given to the students who pass their high-stakes exams with the level 3 designation, "meeting learning standards," and who are then left to fall through the cracks. This is a crime: the waste of undeveloped human potential. It exists and it is clearly evident to any teacher who has taught in a mainstream setting. The present educational strategy in many schools is to give attention and effort to students who receive the level 2 designation, "partially meeting learning standards." The tactic of concentrating effort on the "bubble kids," or the kids on the cusp of meeting a standard who demonstrate below-average performance, is discussed by Daniel Koretz (2008). This strategy pays off for school administrators and garners them recognition because a greater percentage of the students will be labeled as "meeting learning standards" or "proficient" if their efforts are successful. Once again, this cloaks average children, rendering them invisible—ignoring their potential to excel. In the interest of equity, we suggest requiring schools to promote equal percentages of students from each category rather than focusing all their efforts on pushing level 2 students to the next level. Why not a national policy to move students designated as a level 3, "meeting learning standards" to level 4, "meeting learning standards with distinction"?

LEVEL 3: THE NEW AVERAGE

In this section, we attempt to make an accurate assessment of the problems that we see affecting education—especially for the large group of so-called average students. Some of the problems stem from educational policies and teacher training, but others stem from lack of involvement in a meaningful way by parents and guardians. To give the impression that a quick fix is available or that others will recognize that a problem exists is to provide a false sense of hope, or more regrettably, to be disingenuous. The fastest way to see change will be one student (and at least one parent) at a time. The best way to affect change is for groups of parents with similar concerns to take more active roles in their children's education. This requires parents to question and to learn about school budgets, class sizes, class compositions, special programs, testing agendas, assessment procedures, curriculum, and educational reform. Without having knowledge of many of these factors, parents will be left in the dark and will have to rely on the perspective of the school district's administration or public opinion.

Case in point: how has No Child Left Behind (NCLB)—a major school reform that engages in social engineering, impacts every school in the nation, and costs billions of taxpayer dollars—affected average students? In our opinion, all recent school reforms have failed the average student. NCLB has not brought about educational change for the average student but has created an environment of mediocrity. In fact, it has created a false sense of achievement, which is not transferable beyond the overpracticed, high-stakes state and local assessments. Sam Dillon (2005), in a *New York Times* article entitled "Students Ace State Tests, But Earn Ds from the U.S." supplies very convincing evidence to cause one to question the relevance of the state examinations. He reports that more than 12 states (some of which include Alabama, Alaska, Georgia, Mississippi, North Carolina, Oklahoma, Tennessee, and Texas) identify students as "proficient" or "meeting the learning standard," although the same students taking the National Assessment for Educational Progress (NAEP) test fall well below the federal level of proficiency or "not meeting the learning standards." For example, Tennessee reported that 87 percent of their students were proficient based on the Tennessee State Math 8 Exam, but only 21 percent of the same students demonstrated proficiency on the NAEP–Math test. This represents a 66 percent discrepancy. Similarly, Mississippi reported that 89 percent of its fourth graders were at or above the proficiency level in reading. However, only 18 percent of the same students demonstrated proficiency on the NAEP–Reading test. This represents a large discrepancy of 71 percent and calls into question the accountability and validity of high-stakes assessments.

The 2007 Trends in International Mathematics and Science Study (TIMSS) reports relatively no change in grade 4 and grade 8 average students' science scores from 1995 to 2007. What is more disturbing is that the scores of minority students significantly declined by 79 points in grade 4 and by 100 points in grade 8 (National Science Teachers Association, 2009). Longitudinal data from NAEP offers additional support that NCLB is a failure and has lulled many average students into complacency. Comparing 10-year trends from the 1970s and 1980s demonstrate a substantial reduction in the achievement gap between minority students and white students. However, for the 10-year period after NCLB (2002) was signed into law, scores for reading remained flat, mathematics scores showed only a slight increase, and science scores were flat for white students and Asian students and plummeted for minorities (Jehlen, 2009; National Science Teachers Association, 2009). Data from the NAEP over the last 10 years do not demonstrate the success that is so often mentioned by some policymakers, educators, and administrators. How can these data be at odds with many state and local assessments that suggest student achievement and growth? The answer is that as a country, we do not prepare for the NAEP. The NAEP is given to a random sample of students throughout the United States, and no individual scores for students, teachers, or schools are provided. Further, the NAEP is an especially telling indicator of educational achievement, because it is a relatively independent measure of students' knowledge in grades 4, 8, and 12.

This is in contrast to the high-stakes state examinations that are used to judge a school's annual yearly progress as required by NCLB. Similar to all tests, the state examinations cover a restricted amount of content for subjects such as mathematics, language arts, science, and social studies (Johnson & Johnson, 2006). These assessments are not comprehensive samplings of student behaviors from a full course of study but rather a small, selected sample of material. After the first couple of years, teachers learn what is on the exams and in many cases can actually use past tests to coach students for upcoming exams. The students are then taught format, content, and timing, and are conditioned regarding how to answer a narrow range of problems. When the following year's test arrives, the scores generally increase. But we ask: what have the average students learned?

For the most part, the students have probably learned how to take a specific test and how to determine the number of hours per day used for drill in language arts and mathematics at the expense of science, social studies, music, art, and physical education (Johnson & Johnson, 2006; Johnson, Johnson, Farenga, & Ness, 2008). However, based on the information above, we question the depth of the content and skills that the students have actually gained. As a result of poor test scores, many schools have been required to adopt new methods of instruction that are supposedly "scientifically based." Scientifically based methods of instruction are strategies that are supported by some type of data to demonstrate effectiveness. Many of these methods are questionable and difficult to replicate on a large scale. Most research in the field of testing, measurement, and evaluation demonstrates that test scores will rise without any special intervention when faced with the pressure of high-stakes tests. Donald T. Campbell (1976), in his paper, "Assessing the Impact of Planned Social Change," argues, "The more any quantitative social indicator is used for social decision making, the more subject it will be to corruption pressures and the more apt it will be to distort and corrupt the social processes it is intended to monitor" (p. 49). The preceding statement is known in social sciences as Campbell's law, and it further asserts that tests can be valuable instruments, but if they usurp or replace teaching and the development of general competence they lose their value as an indicator of educational achievement.

The following strategy is often used to demonstrate achievement, one that mimics what we call the old Test Form A/Test Form B game. The game goes something like this: First, give students Test Form A and see what they can accomplish. Next, drill and remediate any concepts and skills that the students did not understand. It is important to control any possible intervening variables—stated simply, for optimal results, do not change the context or the content. Finally, provide the students with Test Form B and bask in the achievement of gains. This exemplifies a fragile type of rote learning and puts the average student at risk by creating a false sense of ability. This phenomenon is demonstrated by large discrepancies in students' scores on state assessments when compared with outside measures such as college admissions tests or the NAEP, a federal assessment. The test scores cause policymakers, teachers, parents, and students to make widely misleading assumptions about what the students know. Cognitive scientists assert that in order to demonstrate that learning has occurred, students should be able to take what they have learned in one situation and apply it in another. This behavior of using old knowledge or what has been learned in a new context is called transfer. Students' transfer abilities have not been demonstrated by many of the states' high-stakes tests as indicated by their poor performance on comparative exams in which the students were not overly trained (Koretz, 2008). The comparative data suggests that the students have only memorized and parroted the appropriate responses that are taught for those exams. To complicate matters, many of these high-stakes tests are graded using rubrics, which limit the evaluator's grading options, forcing them to place students in categories. This creates a situation where the responses of both the student and the evaluator are limited, which is of no small concern since it causes one to question the validity of the test results.

RUBRICS: A HODGEPODGE OF WORDS HAVING LITTLE OR NO SIGNIFICANCE

Rubrics are the death knell of our average children's education for a number of reasons. First, rubrics either underestimate or overestimate the average student's ability, thus providing both the parent and the child with an inaccurate and distorted evaluation. Second, much of the language that is used in a rubrics design is abstract, fuzzy, difficult to define, and often fails to reflect the appropriate skill level. We believe that state departments of education and their struthious administrative staff avoid transparency by using rubrics to obfuscate the evaluation process. Third, rubrics are often used to quantify either complex behaviors or dispositions—characteristics of academic subjects that simply cannot be evaluated by a single number or term.

In a column entitled "In Lieu of Grades—Applesauce," Linda Seebach (1997) highlights a parent's concerns about the nebulous nature of a new grading system at an elementary school in the Midwest. Sadly, this could be any elementary school throughout the country, and the story would be the same. The parent's primary concern was the fallacy of descriptions of the rubric levels that were used to represent scoring categories. These descriptions added little, if anything, of significance to the assessment process. In general, rubric descriptions muddle reality because they are less informative than the alphanumeric grading system that they have replaced. The rubric to which Seebach refers demonstrates how school administrators in the assessment game attempt to placate parents about their children's academic progress. The levels of this particular school's rubric, from lowest to highest, are: emerging, developing, competent, and strong. In edu-speak, the term "emerging" applies to children who are failing. In the school's words, students who are "emerging" apparently "understand little," possess "no writing" skills, and "show no math" abilities. To most parents, these terms indicate signs of failure. But does the term "emerging" really conjure up the same image in a parent's mind as "failing"? We think not. The term "failing" leaves little room for interpretation. In the same rubric system that is used at this elementary school, students who fall into the average category are identified as "competent." The description for competent refers to a student who "understands most" of the work, has "adequate writing" skills, and "shows some math," perhaps when attempting to solve a problem.

The term "competent" actually sounds much more promising than does the criteria used to define it. When we think of "competent," we generally think of an individual who has the full skill set needed to complete a task successfully, not merely "some math," "adequate writing," or simply understanding most of the work.

A large part of the standards-based assessment movement relies heavily on the use of rubrics. Rubrics are scoring guides that attempt but often fail to operationalize a set of standards or objectives. They have been designed to measure educational activities ranging from content, performance, and outcomes to predetermined specifications. Unfortunately, the way in which rubrics should be developed is seldom, if ever, carried out. If a rubric were to have any instructional value, it would need to be developed using large samples of students, identify context, and provide a developmental continuum for the evaluation process beyond the limited and superficial categories that are frequently described in abstract terms. Proponents of rubrics offer the so-called standardization of scoring as a strength, but we consider it to be a major weakness, since the categories represent gross overgeneralizations. Koretz (2008) argues that separating students into categories, such as "below basic," "basic," "proficient," and "advanced," is a potentially misleading measurement and is "one of the worst decisions we made in testing in decades" (p. 2). This view is supported by Mabry (1999) and others (Delandshere & Petrosky, 1998, 1999, 2002; Hillocks, 1997) who have documented other critical issues in the use of rubrics. They suggest that the use of rubrics as an assessment tool standardizes and homogenizes both the performance of the assessor along with the performance of the assessed. Homogenized outputs can contribute to the restriction on variability of responses and scores. The flaunted strength of the rubric's interrater reliability is almost certainly due to a limited decision range. Mabry (1999) argues that restricting the variability of possible scores may promote reliability but "may simultaneously undermine validity, the more important determinant of quality assessment" (p. 675).

Another concern with the use of rubrics as a measure for the attainment of knowledge is that the process of trying to regiment students' behaviors can adversely affect the rubric's validity. Forcing a behavior into a category can create a discrepancy "between the scoring criteria and the candidate's performance" (Mabry, 1999, p. 675). This occurs when the rubrics are used to quantify complex behaviors into restricted categories represented by numbers such as a "1," "2," and "3," or words such as "unsatisfactory," "satisfactory," and "advanced." In quantifying student behavior, evaluators who use rubrics ignore the context in which the behavior is performed. Cognitive studies have shown that context is a vital component in interpreting students' behaviors. Without context, we run the risk of limiting the ability to generalize from a specific situation to the overall possibility of outcomes. Delandshere and Petrosky (1998) argue, "The context and specificity of the task could be defined as part of the measurement model. And that context would be a fixed condition of the assessment, thereby restricting the universe of generalization" (p. 19).

Research in the field of measurement and assessment demonstrates that rubrics limit potential and creativity by overwhelmingly focusing on predetermined instructional outcomes (Firestone, Fairmen, & Mayrowetz, 1997; Koretz, 2008; Mabry, 1999). What is even more disturbing is the dearth of research in the public domain that demonstrates even the remotest association between children's cognitive development and the behaviors that the rubrics purport to measure. In New York, a child's scale score and performance level on the fourth grade English Language Arts Test can range from a low of 430 (level 1) to a high of 775 (level 4). Within this range are cut-off points that estimate a student's level of mastery of the learning standards. Our average students' scores range from a low of 650 to a high of 715. Within the range of these scale scores, might there be anything that is qualitatively or quantitatively different among the students within level 3? Can we make any cognitive distinction between students who obtain a scale score of 715 and 716? A score of 716 places the student in level 4, "meeting the learning standards with distinction," indicating that "Student performance demonstrates a thorough understanding of the English Language Arts knowledge and skills expected at this grade level." Our average student who receives only one point less (i.e., 715) is placed in level 3, "meeting learning standards" and his "performance demonstrates an understanding of the English Language Arts knowledge and skills expected at this grade level." Although we challenge the use of this method of assessment for instructional purposes and accountability, we have a greater concern for the average student who obtains a score of 652, barely a level 3, but nevertheless marginalized due to obtaining a score at a level of accepted competence.

In support of this example, Finn and Petrilli (2008) draw attention to the proficiency illusion, reporting that proficiency is a moving target that varies by state and grade. They provide a snapshot of a student who has passed Michigan's fourth-grade math exam and is said to be "proficient"—a term that translates as "average." However, the cut-off point in Michigan is so low that this student may have scored below 83 percent of the country when compared to cut-off points in other states. More surprisingly, because the eighth-grade test has more challenging problems and a higher cut-off point to reach proficiency, the student will probably not pass Michigan's eighth grade mathematics test at the same proficiency level. In these situations, students are left in an average wasteland—a place where students are led to believe that their current levels of persistence and effort are sufficient for future achievement and success. Again, here is the transgression on the average student. Students in many states are led to believe that they are average and are left alone for four years or so until the next major assessment. These years are critical for the development of concepts and skills for achievement in high school. In schools with a two-track system, average students have no viable options: they either struggle to keep up in advanced classes during high school or are placed in regular classes that serve as a catchall for all other students.

Patrick Welsh, an English teacher at T. C. Williams High School in Alexandria, Virginia, explains why average students are not well-served by today's educational system. Welsh points out that "today's two-track system shortchanges average students, who have the choice between regular classes, many of which are in fact remedial, or Advanced Placement classes, which they can't handle" (2006). Welsh supports our premise and observations that average students are the most forgotten group in today's education system. His conclusions suggest that these children suffer from inappropriate placements, lack of parental organization, administrative neglect, and a false sense of sufficiency as measured by high-stakes tests.

The new pedagogy of assessment may be more oppressive, limiting the future freedom of opportunity for the average student. Rubrics that are designed to augment the assessment process supply little, if any, additional data to teachers, parents, and policymakers. In reality, many of these rubrics are nothing more than semantic puzzles. Words such as "proficient," "satisfactory," "competent," "sufficient," "good," "adequate," and the like—all terms with almost entirely different meanings—have all been used to describe average students who populate an average wasteland. This is the place where students are led to believe that their current level of effort and persistence will be sufficient in future endeavors. However, we have observed that this is not the case. One need only look at the number of colleges across the country that has a proliferation of remedial courses in reading, writing, and mathematics. Upon the examination of student transcripts, many of these students have B averages and have passed all of their state assessments. Do truly average students need remedial classes in college or at the university level? But fear not: this too shall pass, because rubrics have reached colleges and universities and will ensure that students continue to be average for a while longer or until they have a professor who grades without a rubric. We challenge parents, teachers, and policymakers who are concerned with average students' achievement to reexamine the general educational options available to these students and to reconsider the repercussions from the use of rubrics to provide "evidence" of ability.

COMMITTEE ON THE AVERAGE:
HAVING A COMMON VOICE

Although teachers have a job to do, they are frequently limited by government policies and regulations that may not benefit the average student. Accordingly, all parents must advocate for their children, and parents of the average must find their voice to be certain that their children's concerns are not overlooked by the myriad of bureaucracies that pervade most school systems.

As an initial and crucial step, parents of average students need to protest and organize. Regrettably, many parents of average students putatively believe that mainstream education administrators address their children's concerns. However, after 25 or more years of hearing from and listening to parents of average students, we realize that this is far from reality. Our first message to parents whose children are in mainstream education is that their concerns are not unique and have been consistently addressed by other parents in similar situations. Our second message is that parents communicate with each other, identify and enumerate their concerns, and, most important, *form a social organization*. Since no group appears to succeed without a political action committee, we suggest that this informal group call itself the Committee on the Average, or simply COA. Despite the seemingly radical tone of our recommendation, it is important to remember that all causes need core groups to raise awareness and funding for lobbyists who are able to attract attention of policymakers.

In the present educational environment, the majority—average students—has been marginalized. It has occurred for a number of reasons as already mentioned, but mainly it is due to accountability. The accountability movement, which is dominated by outside pressures, has shifted educational priorities and has reshaped instructional practices. What should be a personal responsibility has turned into an oppressive relationship among outside agencies, schools, and individuals. In many situations, the latest accountability movement has left average students and their parents little control over their own fate. The parents of average students are prevented from questioning appropriate educational placements for their children by being made to feel uneasy or ungrateful about the services already provided. In Paulo Freire's (1996) words:

> If people, as historical beings necessarily engaged with other people in a movement of inquiry, did not control that movement, it would be (and is) a violation of their humanity. Any situation in which some individuals prevent others from engaging in the process of inquiry is one of violence. The means used are not important; to alienate beings from their own decision-making is to change them into objects. (p. 66)

Freire's message is consistent with our argument that average students and their parents have become objects. They are treated as aggregated or disaggregated bits of data to fulfill bureaucratic accountability requirements. These combined useless bits of data are assembled in various ways in order to support superficially based accounts of student achievement. The importance of average students to school officials and policymakers ends as soon as their "proficiency level" is attained.

It is clear that at this point in time, neither the students nor their parents have much control over educational policies. What is unusual about this situation is that it is the student majority that has been alienated from the educational decision-making processes. Present-day policies have been taken over by special interests that do not represent average students. The problem is the widening gap between the haves and the have-nots, which threatens to unbalance public education. Today, the average students are the have-nots, and they teeter on the verge of educational and societal neglect. A great deal of money and resources is spent on public education, but the present allocations do not appear to directly benefit average students. The funding formulas that are implemented have contributed to adversarial relationships among a variety of educational constituents, all of whom vie for a larger allocation of funds. Freire (1996) identifies this phenomenon occurring in education as "false generosity" (p. 26). It starts by recognizing certain groups as "privileged" and part of the haves, or, in other words "those who know," pitting them against all the others who spend their time trying to obtain the benefits of the privileged group. Since resources are limited, the haves fight fiercely to retain all privileges—an unequivocal zero-sum mentality.

The Case of the Montana School

To demonstrate the sorely inadequate allocation of resources to average students, we examine the intriguing case of the Montana School. The Montana School offers students a variety of educational advantages. In this school, certain students can receive extra class periods of instructional time, either every day or every other day, with a teacher who specializes in a particular area. In most instances, this is intense instruction that is conducted in small groups or offered on a one-to-one basis. Students enjoy this privilege because they receive help with their homework, are coached for future exams, have lessons retaught, or work on advanced projects. The Montana School also provides students with pull-out programs in science, mathematics, and technology-related courses, arts and humanities courses, and business courses to enrich their educational experiences and pique their interest levels. Each of these courses is taught by teachers trained in the area of expertise or by outside specialists. This is yet another benefit to students who show academic proclivity in a variety of subject areas.

In tapping the wealth of resources at cultural centers, the Montana School organizes class trips for students to national research centers to work in genetics laboratories, trips to Wall Street to spend time on the trading floor, and trips to various concerts at well-known venues where students work with artists-in-residence. Students who enjoy the arts could also avail themselves of the extended artist-in-residence program that partners with the school. Here, students would have the privilege of being mentored by a professional in the field. Further, the Montana School offers its students many summer programs, which include weekly trips to environmental centers, beaches and lakefronts, museums, aquariums, athletic events, and theater puppetry events. All the experiences that we have discussed here are actual programs and events that are offered in schools at which we have taught, our colleagues have taught, or where we have supervised students. Indeed, the Montana School offers stimulating programs that do in fact enrich the lives of children.

Unfortunately, the only students who are unable to take advantage of these programs are the average. They do not meet the requirements and restrictions that are placed upon the programs. Imagine a trip that was organized for only average students. Should it not be the case that all children have the benefit of such programs? Wouldn't all children's lives be enriched by these experiences? Wouldn't each of these opportunities add some interest and practicality to the mainstream curriculum? Without a voice, these benefits will continue to elude the average student unless someone addresses their concerns.

Taking a Stand

The COA needs a voice. Again, we restate our question: why are average students ignored? We have found that most average students are ignored because no one wants to acknowledge the fact that they have an average child. We have to face the fact that in a country built on the philosophy, spirit, and mentality of individualism and self-reliance, no one wants to be described as nondescript because he or she is like most other people—average. Therefore, parents of average students—and the students themselves—are invisible because they generally do not voice their concerns or convey special status upon the school. Further, average is a label that, by law, does not require any special action by the school. Administrators of schools are more apt to place greater effort and resources on the poorest performing students, so that they can pass exams, as well as the top performing students, who often receive acknowledgement for advanced achievement. Little if any attention is given to average students who can easily pass many states' unchallenging exams. It should be clear to anyone who has worked in a school that the squeaky wheel gets the grease. In other words, no one working in school wants to hear from the parent who calls and complains. So whenever possible, one tries to remedy the situation to avoid the call. Average parents need to start here—make the call to your child's teacher; it is a simple but effective technique to ensure your child is recognized.

But who, in fact, are those being recognized? It is much more common to hear parents say that their child is gifted at one extreme or learning disabled

(LD) at the other—seldom, if ever, do they say that their child is average! Special education or "exceptional" children who fall into either the LD or gifted camps are far from invisible. Hardman, Drew, and Egan (2002) define "learning disabled" as "a condition in which one or more of the basic psychological processes in the understanding and using of language are deficient" (p. 169). Therefore, according to the definition, students indentified as LD usually test below their actual ability due to an impairment that affects their test performance. We suggest that parents of average students take a well-learned lesson from parents of students in special education. Students at each end of this continuum are well-organized and strongly supported by advocacy groups at both local and national levels. They have had an impact on education and have improved the lives of their children. The purpose of these organizations is to make the needs and concerns of the students they represent known to educators, policymakers, and other parents. An example of how politically engaged these organizations are is offered by the Council for Exceptional Children's (CEC) Public Policy Agenda for the 111th United States Congress, January 2009–January 2011 (2008b). The CEC works on policy objectives and is an advocate for the Elementary and Secondary Education Act, Individuals with Disabilities Act, Gifted Education, and Medicaid. The CEC's objectives are to monitor each of these areas to be certain that funding, accountability systems, identification procedures, and intervention programs are available to all who meet the criteria. Such organizations are successful because they have a common voice and have established common goals. The mission and vision statements of the CEC and the National Association for Gifted Children (NAGC) underscore the importance of advocacy for children who they identify as exceptional. The following are the CEC's mission and vision statements.

> Mission: CEC is an international community of educators who are the voice and vision of special and gifted education. Our mission is to improve the quality of life for individuals with exceptionalities and their families through professional excellence and advocacy.

> Vision: CEC is a diverse, vibrant professional community working together and with others to ensure that individuals with exceptionalities are valued and included in all aspects of life. CEC is a trusted voice in shaping education policy and practice and is globally renowned for its expertise and leadership. CEC is one of the world's premiere education organizations. (2008a)

The following is the NAGC's mission statement.

> The National Association for Gifted Children (NAGC) is an organization of parents, teachers, educators, other professionals, and community leaders who unite to address the unique needs of children and youth with demonstrated

gifts and talents as well as those children who may be able to develop their talent potential with appropriate educational experiences.

We support and develop policies and practices that encourage and respond to the diverse expressions of gifts and talents in children and youth from all cultures, racial and ethnic backgrounds, and socioeconomic groups. NAGC supports and engages in research and development, staff development, advocacy, communication, and collaboration with other organizations and agencies who strive to improve the quality of education for all students. (2008)

It is clear from reading the two statements from CEC and NAGC that each association has specific objectives for their specific student population. Nowhere in these statements do we read of a concern for the average student. However, as a caveat, most organizations' mission statements will usually make a reference to improving education for all students in their effort to avoid sounding exclusionary. There are those who would argue that the mainstream education classroom is already geared for the average student. This is an example of a truism based on what the majority of the general public are led to believe—not what is necessarily or actually practiced. In practice, what is not sliced out for either end of the academic continuum is left for the average. This method of portion assignment is analogous to a lion walking away from a carcass after eating, leaving the remains to all others on the savannah. The average students are the others, and this is not equitable for one major reason: it assumes that all average students are equal and are equally balanced in their abilities. Further, it places an unreal expectation on the classroom teacher to either identify multiple talents or abilities by observation or through the use of assessment instruments that are inaccurate or simply do not exist. So what is done to meet the needs of the average student in the general education class? The answer, which is often touted by educational experts, is differentiated education.

DIFFERENTIATED INSTRUCTION: THE NEW PANACEA

Differentiated instruction is not a new educational strategy. W. James Popham and Eva L. Baker (1970) suggest that curriculum can be differentiated by either modifying the objectives or the means of instruction. The authors warn that differentiation is more often discussed than actually practiced, a fact that is frequently overlooked. The field of gifted education has borrowed heavily from techniques that rely on differentiated instruction, and a commonly held belief in the field is that it is well suited for high-ability students. Hardman, Drew, and Egan (2002) reinforce the notion of differentiation for gifted students and define differentiated education as "an education uniquely and predominantly suited to capacities and interests of individuals who are gifted" (p. 550). Kaplan (1981) supports the use of a differentiated curriculum with gifted students but asks the question of what constitutes an appropriate differentiated curriculum. The difficulty in defining what constitutes an acceptable differentiated curriculum is highlighted by Kaplan (1986), who first identifies what a differentiated curriculum should *not* be in an effort to provide clarity for what is an acceptable differentiated curriculum. Instruction may be differentiated by modifying any of the factors affecting a lesson's content, process, or product. There is a dichotomy or continuum of differentiation (depending on one's philosophy) that can be considered when planning instruction. The differentiation dichotomy can involve the following:

1. The rate of instruction, from slow-paced to fast-paced, in order to keep the students engaged;
2. Presentation of content from concrete to abstract;
3. Freedom given in instruction from teacher-centered, less independence, to student-centered, greater independence;
4. Subject matter that is concentrated on a single factor or subject matter that is integrated with other subjects and multidimensional stressing macroconcepts;
5. Lessons geared to convergent closed-ended tasks or lessons that are open-ended and divergent in design; and
6. Lessons that are foundational, covering basic cognitive skills, as opposed to transformational lessons based on experiential activities that change one's perspective and understanding.

Instructional strategies, such as curriculum compacting, independent projects, tiered assignments, flexible skills groups, learning centers, apprenticeships, varied questioning, interest centers, and contract activity packages have all been used to differentiate instruction. The current teaching methodology of differentiating instruction is once again being expanded in practice to serve all students as a way to meet individual needs. What is often forgotten is that these techniques were developed for a considerably more homogeneous group of students with high abilities who generally can work independently on tasks for sustained periods of time. However, we express our reservations about how execution, content, logistics, and talent requirements for differentiation are seldom addressed.

Anyone who has taught or has been in a truly heterogeneous class will realize that differentiating instruction for just three subjects is a laborious task. Differentiated instruction for mathematics, reading, and science at three ability levels can mean as many as nine different lesson preparations for the teacher. Creating, assessing, and managing the multiple assignments can become an impossibility due to logistics and time, and in-depth investigations of content for many of the students can become compromised. The method also can fracture the attention of the teacher who is spending more time managing a lesson than teaching a lesson. Another problem with differentiated instruction that is often not mentioned or recognized is that different levels of instruction produce different outcomes for students. Two common ways to differentiate instruction is either to change the pace of instruction or to manipulate the content taught. In either event, there is still going to be a question of an equal outcome for all students. This concern is often overlooked, and most individuals suggest that students are learning the same concepts either in a different amount of time or in a different way. Based on our experience, we are not so sure that this is the case.

If you change the pace of the instruction, the students of the group with the increased rate of instruction complete their assignment before the other students and are ready for additional work. In some situations, the fast-paced group may be provided with what is considered to be "enrichment." However, in most cases, it is actually busywork or more of the same work that they have already completed. Others present the flexible-skills-group argument as an answer for differences that occur in the pace of instruction. Students who may be in the fast-paced group for one area of instruction will now have time to work on an area of weakness. Although this argument seems reasonable, in an actual classroom, it is quite flawed. Our question is, with whom will the student who has this extra time work to help remediate the so-called deficiency? Is the classroom teacher required to prepare, monitor, and assess this extra work? Any average student in the classroom will not be entitled to a specialist or teacher's aide for assistance in this additional remediation. Again, we ask: is the regular classroom teacher the one who is expected to assist the student and create yet another lesson plan? We think probably not in most classrooms. It would be most difficult and unreasonable, considering the teacher is already instructing, monitoring, assessing, or managing the original differentiated assignment with its three levels of difficulty based on the rate of instruction (slow, medium, fast).

The second concern is the content. Are the same objectives really achieved when we create different assignments? We have noticed that some schools will differentiate assignments based on Bloom's cognitive taxonomy. Some high-stakes state examinations give only the appearance of mastery. In analyzing the assessments, one notices that the cut-off points are relatively low and can often be achieved by answering a number of the low-level questions on the examination. The categories that define the achievement levels are best described as gross approximations of ability. If this is the case, students in the lower or average groups will never be able to convincingly develop critical reading, thinking, and writing skills, especially if they are not sufficiently challenged with the more demanding questions that are designed using the upper levels of the taxonomy. In other situations, the content is modified by giving the groups different tasks. In one observation, the students were working on part of a unit dealing with forces in fluids. All students were asked to describe the relationship among pressure and fluid speed, analyze the roles of lift, thrust, and wing size, explain Pascal's Principle, and describe how drag affects lift. However, the manner in which the students met the objectives was not the same. Some students were assigned direct reading activities with correlated laboratory exercises. Others had to study the wing shape and analyze how the basic shape could have an effect on the air in which the wing travels. This group was also assigned critical thinking exercises that involved the improvement of vehicles to make them less resistant. Although each of the assignments allowed the students in each group to meet the basic objectives in some way, the quality and level of the work was not equivalent. In sum, certain students were reading about Archimedes, Bernoulli, and Pascal, while other students were actually applying the principles of each of the scientists. When schools report the results of what students know, it is usually based on the minimal criteria set by any number of high-stakes tests. The cut-off points are generally made low enough so that a large majority of the students are able to pass the tests, and the district is thus able to report that the objectives have been achieved. Again, we stress that although the objective may have been achieved, it has not been achieved in the same manner or at the same level of understanding. There is a definite qualitative and quantitative difference in what has been learned. We hope that we have demonstrated that equality of the educational experience is not provided for average students. In reality, they are frequently shortchanged and not given the appropriate educational opportunities that would otherwise maximize their potential. A silent discrepancy in ability looms over the educational landscape—one that is kept hidden by inflated grades that subliminally suggest equal achievement by all.

3

Intelligence: That Beguiling Phenomenon

Intelligence is surely not the only important ability, but without a fair share of intelligence, other abilities and talents usually cannot be fully developed and effectively used.

—Arthur R. Jensen (1981, p. 11)

Many of us believe that from birth everyone has an equal opportunity to succeed at anything that we set out to accomplish. Despite the well-meaning intentions of this seemingly pluralistic mind-set of human ability, it becomes increasingly difficult to imagine what life would be like if this were actually true. After a number of years of experiencing the consequences of our actions, we soon find that injustices become increasingly apparent, and the promise of our equal footing becomes nebulous at best or eroded at worst. As we have mentioned earlier, the premise of this book revolves around the social construct of the behaviors that psychometricians attribute to the concept of average. For the most part, these behaviors are skills or abilities that an individual demonstrates at specific points in life in a very narrow environment known as school. Similarly, the labels "below average," "average," or "above average" that an individual receives at school are an invention of the mental testing movement that began in the early twentieth century and are not a discovery found in nature (Borland, 2005; Gould, 1996).

The notion of categorizing individuals from an artistic, intellectual, or physical standpoint can be traced back well before the twentieth century to a time when people began to differentiate and assign tasks within the context of social groups. Since Charles Darwin's time, the literature on conceptions of intelligence and ability in connection with success and leadership roles from a historical perspective has been robust. Five years after the publication of Darwin's *Origin of the Species* in 1864, Frederick Engels (1975) argued that intellectual ability levels were differentiated between those who possessed the skills to create objects (such as axes, knives, and the like) out of raw materials and those who did not. Research in archaeology and historical anthropology has shown that the earliest recorded evidence of conflict among different social groups demonstrated a fairly strong relationship between leadership skills and one's mental and physical abilities in accomplishing particular tasks (Trigger, 2006). We can also appreciate the important role intellectual ability played in history as demonstrated through literary documentation. This is particularly evident in Homer's epic poem, *The Iliad*, where warriors and army leaders are ranked not only for their physical talents and maneuverings, but also for their so-called quick wit as decision makers and military strategists. Homer and possibly other bards who were able to recite this epic poem from memory point to Achilles, for example, as the leading warrior on the side of the Achaeans (i.e., the Greeks), followed by Diomedes, whose name literally translates as "cunning intelligence," and Ajax, a physically powerful warrior but possibly not as cunning as Achilles and Diomedes. On the Trojan side, Hector was the most able warrior, followed by Glaucun and Polydamus.

Centuries later, Plato would argue in *The Republic* that the individuals with the most able minds, regardless of gender, should serve as the guardians of the polis. In other words, heads of state and other political officials should be selected—not elected—based upon both wisdom and intellectual ability; such worthy individuals Plato labeled "philosopher kings." This, in fact, served as the basis that catapulted the role of the "gifted," or the importance of the intellectually able, into full swing in the centuries to come.

We can see, then, that societies through the centuries have placed a very high premium on intelligence. Nevertheless, from society to society, the idea of what intelligence was varied considerably. This can be seen fairly distinctly during the European Middle Ages, a time when intelligence was understood chiefly in terms of how keen one's memory was. It was also a time when the rate of literacy was at an all-time low. So a person with a superior memory was considered a highly intellectually able person and was often thought of as a walking encyclopedia. This individual most likely would have been affiliated with a university in some way, possibly as a rector, tutor, professor, or the like. A person revered during the Middle Ages for having a prodigious memory would be akin to the individual today who would be esteemed for having a high intelligence quotient (IQ).

By the second half of the eighteenth century, quantifying intelligence revolved around methods that would be considered taboo, and therefore obsolete, today. One of these methods is connected to the work of Franz Joseph Gall, the well-known phrenologist of the late eighteenth and early nineteenth centuries. Phrenology, which emanates from the materialist tradition, is the study of knowledge, intellect, ability, and disposition as these traits are related to the bumps, fissures, and general contours of the skull. Accordingly, certain contours would serve as an indication of a certain kind of person—physician, violinist, painter, mathematician, farmer, laborer, and even felon.

Modern foundations of intelligence and the study of what makes people different intellectually are generally attributed to theorists who studied with the first experimental psychologists of the late nineteenth century. A number of these intelligence theorists were influenced by the work of Wilhelm Wundt and the Leipzig school. In the United States, William James attracted a number of students, many of whom studied for a period in Germany. But before the field of psychology emerged as a discipline in the German and American university, much of the foundational work in the field of intelligence was undertaken by Francis Galton earlier in the nineteenth century.

From the historical synopsis above, we identify two important factors that contribute to the meaning of intelligence. First, the meaning of intelligence changes when examining one era and the next and when comparing one society to another. And second, the study of intellectual ability over time and through cultural comparisons has demonstrated the emergence of varying schools of thought with regard to the ways in which intelligence is perceived. In this chapter, we investigate three general paradigms of intelligence that generated a great deal of research—and controversy—from the middle of the nineteenth century to the present: psychometric, developmentalist, and contemporary models of intelligence. We begin by examining the construct of intelligence and how the term's meaning varies depending on context. Next, we discuss Francis Galton's initial program in the emerging field of intelligence research and the key players who shaped the field of psychometrics in intelligence research. We follow with the developmentalist models and then continue with an investigation of more recent theoretical frameworks of intelligence that are central to intelligence research today. Regardless of the school of thought, the problems of deciding how one defines, measures, and manipulates intelligence are still hotly debated.

MODERN FOUNDATIONS OF INTELLIGENCE

The definition of intelligence is constantly changing. At one time, psychometric theory expressed intelligence as a quotient on an IQ test that is obtained by dividing one's mental age by chronological age. Intelligence quotients are no longer used and have been replaced by deviation quotients—such as those used on Wechsler intelligence tests—as a measure of an individual's intellectual ability. What has not changed is our inability to agree on how to measure intelligence and on what behaviors that accurately represent the construct of intelligence. For some, intelligence is a narrow concept represented by an IQ score similar to Boring's (1923) statement in which he argues that intelligence is what the test tests. Yet for others, such as J. P. Guilford (1959, 1967), intelligence may be defined by as many as 150 factors represented by a three-dimensional model that includes the operations used in processing information, the content that is processed, and the resulting product. Even in the psychometric school of thought, whether one posits intelligence as a single, general factor (Spearman) or multiple group factors (Thurstone), it should be evident that the definition of intelligence is an invention. As such, it must be constructed in order to function. A construct in psychology is an idea of what something is and how it is defined. For example, the construct for the word *cunning* might be thought of as someone who displays cleverness. The difficult part of the construct is to agree upon the point-at-able (i.e., clearly observable) behaviors that most accurately represent the term *cunning*. For some it might be a person who is smart, while for others it may be a person who can get out of a difficult situation, and yet for others it may be a person who displays verbal wit. Each of the examples for the meaning of cunning summons a set of different skills and abilities for different people. The difficulty that exists in defining the term cunning is that it is decontextualized. The term in and of itself is void of context, and its meaning is subject to cultural interpretation. A similar argument can be made for other psychological constructs, such as persistence, happiness, love, or intelligence. Given the lack of a universally agreed-upon definition for the construct of intelligence, many tests used in education measure closely related constructs thought to be associated with intelligence, such as school achievement, scholastic aptitude, and a number of other related abilities. The field of intelligence research is filled with numerous researchers with varying theories of intelligence. However, a review of the research identifies some common theorists who are responsible for anchoring specific theoretical positions (see table 3.1).

Early in the history of intelligence research, differences in one's intellectual abilities were tied to how well one could discriminate stimuli. The perception and processing of sensory data from auditory, visual, and haptic stimuli were thought to have a direct relationship on cognitive functioning. The more efficient and refined one's ability to identify various phenomena within the environment (such as perfect pitch, hues in a color palette, or sense pressure from touch), the more intelligent the individual. However simplistic this may sound, reports that "high-g individuals make perceptual discriminations more quickly than average-g people do" (Bower, 2003, p. 92) are still evident in the research more than 140 years since Francis Galton's original claims in 1869.

Table 3.1.   Intelligence Theorists and Their Contributions

Theorist/Researcher	Noteworthy Contributions
Alfred Binet	Credited with developing the first assessment that measures intellectual ability. Scores were based on a comparison between chronological age and mental age.
Raymond Cattell and John Horn	Viewed intelligence as a combination of multiple factors related to fluid and crystallized intelligence. Fluid intelligence was a genetic endowment; crystallized intelligence was related to experience.
Carol Dweck	Examined intelligence in terms of motivation and identified in two groups: individuals who view intelligence as innate and those who view it as a process requiring effort and persistence.
Francis Galton	Used anecdotal evidence of sensory discrimination to infer intelligence
Howard Gardner	Suggested that intelligence was more than the measurement of linguistic, mathematical, and spatial abilities, but included five additional components of intelligence as well.
J. P. Guilford	Developed a structure of the intellect with group factors that identify up to 150 independent abilities.
Arthur Jensen	A proponent of the "g-factor," Jensen found positive correlations between one's IQ scores and reaction times to various external stimuli.
Jean Piaget	Viewed intelligence in terms of knowledge and not as a mathematical ratio, because IQ does not tap one's processes in solving problems.
Charles Spearman	Used empirical methods to test sensory discrimination and correlate it with intelligence as measured by academic ability. Intelligence is a general factor used for all mental tasks. Developed factor analysis and believed that intelligence was based on a single factor called *g*.
Robert Sternberg	Developed the (1) Triarchic Model of Intelligence, which consists of the componential, experiential, and contextual domains, and (2) the Successful Model of Intelligence, which considers analytical, creative, and practical abilities.
Lewis Terman	Combined the Binet Intelligence Test and the Stern ratio of intellectual age to chronological age multiplied by 100 and developed the Stanford-Binet Intelligence Test, which was subsequently administered to school-age children in the United States.
L. L. Thurstone	Argued that intelligence is attributed to multiple factors and not simply a single factor (as Spearman initially suggested).

(continued)

Table 3.1. (*continued*)

Theorist/Researcher	Noteworthy Contributions
P. E. Vernon	Developed a model of hierarchical organization of abilities with specific factors: minor group factors, major group factors (verbal, number, mechanical, spatial, psychomotor), major verbal-educational and practical, and at the apex, a general ability (*g*).
Lev Vygotsky	Argued that intelligence is a sociocultural by-product that cannot be determined without an examination of social factors.

Francis Galton

The earliest attempts at psychometric measures of intelligence as a function of heredity are credited to Francis Galton. Galton's interest in categorizing intelligence emanates in large part from developments in the physical and biological sciences in the early decades of the nineteenth century, particularly with the burgeoning interest in physiological sensation—that is, psychophysics. Foundations of sensation studies began in 1834, when the noted physiologist Ernst Weber noticed that a subject's discrimination of a change in a stimulus is proportional to the magnitude of that stimulus. Take weight lifting (kinesthesia) as an example. The question Weber asked was: when would someone notice a change in weight between two objects that initially were believed to be equal in weight? To answer this question, Weber initially put one 5-kilogram weight in each hand of a subject (two weights, 10 kilograms in total). Weber concluded that nearly all his subjects finally noticed a difference between the weights when one of the weights was increased by 100 grams (0.1 kilogram)—5 kilograms in one hand and 5.1 kilograms in the other. He referred to the subject's initial perception of difference as a "just noticeable difference." To look at it another way, one can perceive a difference between an object weighing 50 units and another weighing 51 units, 100 units and 102 units, 150 units and 153 units, and so on. What came to be known as Weber's law was extended by the work of Gustave Fechner, who quantified sensory perception.

In a similar light, Galton was interested in finding a way to identify differences in intelligence. Galton argued in his book *Hereditary Genius* (1869) that heredity was the essential cause of intellectual ability. He believed that an individual's intellectual ability could be determined by how one responded to and processed environmental stimuli through his or her senses. He proposed a series of nonverbal measures of sensory, motor, and reaction-time tasks to assess intelligence. Galton measured elementary cognitive functions through sensory stimuli, that is, pain thresholds, auditory discrimination, visual acuity, and reaction time. Therefore, according to Galton, intelligent people have more highly refined and acute senses attributed to mental prowess. The criticism of much of Galton's work was that it relied on anecdotal evidence and subjective impressions about relationships between and among variables (Gould, 1996; Brody, 2000). Nevertheless, Galton's work did influence subsequent researchers in the field of intelligence, from Charles Spearman in the late nineteenth century to Arthur Jensen (1980, 1981, 1998) today.

Charles Spearman

Charles Spearman can be credited with advancing psychometric theory of intelligence through the use of statistical procedures to identify individual differences on a series of tests. He attempted to quantify subjective measures used to infer intelligence by Galton and other past and contemporary psychologists by calculating correlation coefficients between variables through factor analysis. In attempting to determine whether relationships existed among sensory tests and academic ability, Spearman concluded that "the common and essential element in the Intelligences coincides with the common and essential element in the Sensory Functions" (Spearman, 1904, p. 269). The correlations between sensory function and academic ability were thought to be a result of general intellectual ability, or mental "energy" known as g, and to a lesser extent, specific abilities. Although Spearman suggested that specific abilities were partially independent of general intelligence, it appeared that many of the specific abilities shared a common variance with g. He suggested that individuals had different amounts of g, and the amount of g a person had would therefore determine his or her performance on intellectual tasks. Spearman's two-factor theory of intelligence is considered hierarchical in terms of factor loadings for specific, group, and general abilities. Additional analysis by Spearman suggests that some of the specific abilities could be combined to form group factors. He explained that any specialized test of intellect would share some common variance, since the mental strength required to problem solve would tap into general intelligence. Inherent in his belief is that discrimination abilities were proxy measures for higher-order cognitive functions. Spearman argued that the statistical procedures he used to analyze test results revealed one's mental power or intellect. Overall, Spearman's view of cognition can be thought of as reductionist because it implies that complex intellectual functioning can be understood or measured by examining an individual's sensory-related behaviors (i.e., the component parts) that are regulated by the brain. However, there is disagreement in the field of intelligence as to Spearman's interpretation—disagreement that can be seen as early as in the works of Wissler, Binet,

Thurstone, Piaget, and Vygotsky, to more recent theorists such as Gould, Sternberg, Gardner, Horn, and McArdle—just some of the theorists who question the existence of *g* as little more than a statistical entity.

Clark Wissler

Earlier in the United States, before Spearman published his work, Clark Wissler demonstrated little to no correlation between intellect and sensory perception. Spearman's suggestion that physiological responses to stimuli correlate with measures of one's intelligence did not go unchallenged. Wissler (1901), one of the earliest critics of Spearman, questioned the value of measuring one's responses to physiological stimuli in a laboratory setting and correlating it to measures of cognitive ability. Wissler's work suggested that many of the correlations between sensory responses and academic achievement were weak at best or nonexistent. The work of Wissler brought to question the measuring of intelligence and its unitary definition. Many years later, Wilson (1953) investigated the relationship between IQ and specific abilities, such as musical memory, artistic ability, and mechanical aptitude and extended the findings of Wissler, reporting no correlations between specific abilities and general intelligence. Even though both of these studies were limited by the restricted range of the samples, each raised questions that once again caused many to rethink the nature and measurement of intelligence. Current critics (Carroll, 1993; Horn & McArdle, 2007; Humphreys, Parsons, & Park, 1979) suggest that *g* is just a statistical artifact that disappears when tests sample a broad range of mental abilities. In addition, other cognitivists disagree with a single-factor or general intelligence that transfers across disciplines. These researchers point to studies in which transfer demonstrates that students with a strong knowledge base in one subject do not automatically use that knowledge base in other subjects.

Louis Leon Thurstone

Also in the psychometric tradition of Spearman, Louis Leon Thurstone proposed that intelligence could be identified by a statistical procedure using factor analysis. However, Thurstone suggested that group factors represented intelligence and therefore analyzed the test data differently than Spearman. Thurstone's interest was in the intercorrelations among groups of tests; the patterns that were found were identified as group factors. Thurstone (1938) suggested that multiple factors or abilities constituted general intelligence. These abilities are verbal comprehension, word fluency, number facility, spatial reasoning, perceptual speed, associative memory, and general, deductive, and inductive reasonings—many of the cognitive areas that we see on intelligence tests today. Spearman's *g* could only be obtained if the abilities that are due to a general intelligence factor are correlated or related in some way. If so, a second-order factor analysis would lead to g if certain primary factors were left out of the analysis (Thurstone & Thurstone, 1941). Thurstone's work led to the general agreement of a hierarchical structure of intelligence with g as the apex. After his death in 1955, Thelma Thurstone (1958), L. L. Thurstone's former student and wife, developed the Primary Mental Abilities Test, which extended her husband's earlier work to include scales that measure a number of specific abilities. These are number ability, verbal meaning, word fluency, memory, spatial relations, perceptual speed, and reasoning ability. The Primary Mental Abilities Test made it possible to profile students' strengths and weaknesses, along with estimates of their IQ scores. However, similar to Spearman's influence on present-day intelligence theorists (such as Arthur Jensen), Thurstone's multifactored view of intelligence seemed to serve as a paradigm for more contemporary theories, such as Gardner's theory of multiple intelligences (as discussed later).

Much of the foundation for the psychometric approach involves statistical procedures relying on correlations from data collected while people perform tasks thought to require intelligence. At this point, we highlight the most basic lesson in statistics: *correlation is not causation.* Simply put, just because two or more things might be related does not mean that one action was the cause of or reason for an outcome. This might be demonstrated by the common example using correlation of the relationship between sales of ice cream cones and thunderstorms. It happens that the sale of ice cream cones is positively correlated with the occurrence of thunderstorms; however, the thunderstorms did not cause the increase of sales of ice cream cones. A more plausible explanation is that thunderstorms occur during warm months, when the atmosphere is more unstable, and individuals seeking relief from warm weather often choose cold refreshments. This raises another important point with any statistical method that uses correlations such as factor analysis. Factor analysis requires a theoretical framework in order to validate and interpret the findings. A number of correlations have been reported over the decades in intelligence research. It is not surprising to find that high correlations exist between IQ and one's economic conditions, career choices, and social standing, since much of the chance factor has been reduced by educational attainment. There is a bit of circular reasoning here in that people with high levels of g, or intelligence, do well in school and that schooling in general appears to support intellectual growth and that higher levels of education are required in a technological society. The key point here is where one gets on the train. Is the person genetically programmed with a fixed amount of g, with relatively little change occurring across a life span? Or is g a malleable factor that is affected by the environment? These questions lead to the nature versus nurture debate, and most modern theorists recognize that some level of interaction exists among genes, the environment, and intelligence. There are a number of conceptual models in the field of intelligence today, but none more widespread than the psychometric approach. Much of the credit in the field is given to Alfred Binet, who developed the first three versions of an intelligence test, the first of which appeared in 1905.

Alfred Binet

Still part of the psychometric tradition, Alfred Binet's response to intelligence was different from that of Galton and Spearman, the former stressing psychophysical responses and the latter, statistical analysis to infer intelligence. Binet's work focused on the manner in which students made decisions or came to conclusions when solving practical problems. Intelligence testing in general and IQ measurement in particular had a humble yet laudable origin, which we can trace to turn-of-the-century France and the work of Binet, a psychologist who introduced psychometric testing in schools. Binet had a more complex concept of intelligence than that of Francis Galton or Charles Spearman. It might be suggested that Binet provided a great deal of practitioner-based knowledge to theoretical laboratory-based work. Binet's tests of intelligence required students to demonstrate memory, reasoning, and social skills. Binet represented intelligence in terms of one's mental age—a construct that was determined by comparing the average chronological age of students who passed the same number of items. For example, 9-year-old student A may have a mental age of 12 because she scored the same on questions that the average 12-year-old would score correctly, while 10-year-old student B may have a mental age of 8 because student B's scores were identical to the scores that the average 8-year-old answered correctly. Binet's objective was to develop an instrument that could identify all students' levels of intelligence—from mental retardation to higher functioning—in order to adequately educate French youth. Although Binet developed the concept of IQ, his primary goal was not to segregate students based on race, ethnicity, country of birth, or even intelligence. Binet did not embrace the idea of a hereditarian perspective of IQ testing; that was an invention of American psychologists, commencing with Lewis Terman and others shortly after Binet's death. In fact, some early twentieth-century psychologists, Robert Yerkes and Carl Brigham, for example, exploited the hereditarian perspective by crafting culture-specific, racist assessments that were biased in favor of Americans of northern European descent (Gould, 1996). Rather, Binet's goal was to help the government of France find a method to educate children of rural families who migrated to Paris and other large urban areas. Since rural children, due to lack of schooling, were unable to compete intellectually with urban children, it would have been implausible to school rural children in the already existing educational establishment in France. Schools at the time were not equipped to educate children who did not have the same experiences as urban middle-class children. After Binet, however, the primary use of intelligence testing drastically changed over the course of time. Nevertheless, Binet's test was the prototype of modern tests, and it contained items that were grouped by order of difficulty and were given an age/grade equivalence. This test evaluated a variety of abilities and was conducted in schools rather than in a laboratory.

Lewis Terman

In 1912, approximately a year after Binet's death, the German psychologist Wilhelm Stern reinterpreted the way in which an individual is scored on the Binet-Simon scale as being the quotient of the ratio of one's chronological age by the mental age that is subsequently multiplied by 100—a term that Stern coined "mental quotient." Three years later, the American psychologist Lewis Terman extended the work of Binet by improving the psychometric properties of the Binet-Simon intelligence scales and replacing the term "mental quotient" with "intelligence quotient" (IQ). Terman developed a new test based on Binet's contributions, called the Stanford-Binet Intelligence Test, published in 1916, that was standardized across a larger population. The subscales measured an individual's skills in arithmetic problem solving, vocabulary, inductive reasoning, spatial visualization, and social judgment. The work of Terman gained credibility for the use of psychometric testing in schools due to the test's ability to make simple comparisons of students using a single score—the IQ score. Although the test required the individual to complete a variety of tasks, the composite score gave the impression of intelligence being the single factor.

Terman's overall rationale for the use of the IQ test was to find a way to classify and sort students into grades by rank and to make decisions regarding one's promotion to the next grade level and school transfer. The appropriate training or educational programs could then be made available to students as soon as they are classified by ability. However, after a number of years, the Stanford-Binet Intelligence Scale's validity and reliability were questioned due to a nonrepresentative sample and revisions of test items that relied on outdated norms. Today, the most widely used intelligence tests in education are the Wechsler intelligence tests, which include the Wechsler Preschool and Primary Scale of Intelligence (WPPSI), the Wechsler Intelligence Scale for Children (WISC), and the Wechsler Adult Intelligence Scale (WAIS). These tests contain subtests that measure verbal and nonverbal abilities. In general, most intelligence test scores are scaled scores, where a score of 100 is the mean and 15 is the standard deviation, which is the measure of variability in a set of scores. This is visually represented by a normal bell curve (see figure 3.1). The bell curve is constructed

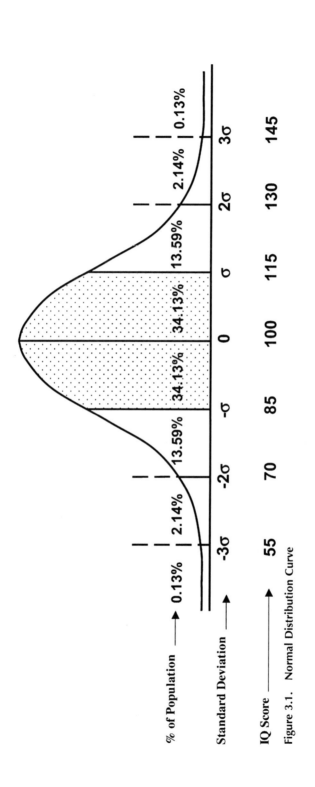

Figure 3.1.   Normal Distribution Curve

where approximately 68 percent of the population scores within one standard deviation of the mean. IQ scores between 85 and 115 would fall in this range. IQ scores between 70 and 130 are two standard deviations from the mean and include approximately 96 percent of the population. Beyond two standard deviations is a small percentage of the population, which displays extraordinary abilities (for an extended discussion of the Wechsler intelligence test, see Sattler, 2001).

COGNITIVIST SCHOOL OF INTELLIGENCE RESEARCH

Is intelligence really something that can be interpreted by a single score? Theorists in the cognitive school of intelligence research most likely would not agree. To the cognitivists, the meaning of intelligence differs greatly from the psychometric perspective. Intelligence is not merely a measure of individual differences that arise from a testing situation. Rather, the cognitivists place an overwhelming emphasis on the processes and contextual conditions that influence intellectual abilities. Our discussion of the cognitivist school of intelligence research revolves around Jean Piaget and Lev Vygotsky—two theorists whose work has greatly influenced the trajectory of the intersection of educational research and intellectual ability from the late 1960s to the present day.

Jean Piaget

Piaget's theory of intellectual development answered two questions in the study of intelligence. The first had to do with the capabilities with which infants were endowed, and the second had to do with how infants progress beyond genetic endowment to advanced cognitive abilities. Piaget's view of intelligence provided more of a theoretical perspective of intellectual malleability than Binet had posited in his work a decade or so earlier. Similar to earlier work on intelligence, Piaget argued that intelligence was a unitary construct that controlled specific abilities across all domains. Unlike earlier work on intelligence, Piaget provides an explanation of intellectual development that can account for the entire life span and not solely school-age children. Early in his career, Piaget worked at the Binet Laboratory on the development of intelligence tests. Unlike his fellow colleagues, however, Piaget was interested in error analysis—in other words, the errors the children made and how these errors seemed to fit specific patterns at different points during childhood. More specifically, Piaget was interested in the tacit knowledge that children demonstrated while completing a task. Through the clinical method (i.e., adult interviewer and child interviewee), Piaget learned what each child could do without any assistance from other adults or peers. This led to his conclusion that children's thinking was not equivalent to that of adults but was nevertheless organized and had a form of logic of its own. Interestingly, one might notice common themes between Piaget's emphasis on tacit knowledge and the procedures that contemporary psychologist on intelligence Robert Sternberg and his colleagues have undertaken in understanding practical intelligence or action-oriented knowledge (Sternberg, Wagner, Williams, & Horvath, 1995). There are a number of variables that may promote a child's levels of analytic and practical intelligence. Here is a place where a child's average performance can be either substantially increased or decreased over time, depending on the child's interaction with caregivers in his or her environment. Differences in parenting style that may be caused by differences in education levels can determine how the parent responds to the child. Parents who communicate by explaining and elaborating on their children's questions add to the child's level of understanding, as opposed to parents who do not have the ability or the disposition to engage in this form of communication. This argument can be made for teachers and their level of engagement with their students. Indeed, a teacher with a poor disposition for various knowledge bases will not perform as well as a teacher who engages students with a rich knowledge base and incites their motivation to learn.

Unlike the nativist tradition embraced by people like Galton and Spearman, Piaget followed Rousseau's belief that children who were allowed to follow their own course of development achieved optimal abilities. Piaget was an organismic thinker; he looked at the human as an organism that acts on the world, not simply a passive entity. Unlike the empiricist-reductionist model, he thought of the organism functioning as a structured whole entity, in which the whole is greater than the sum of its parts.

Piaget argued that children went through a sequence of reorganizations of their mental structures. This sequence of reorganizations, or systems of processing information, were qualitatively distinctive from one another and led Piaget to think of development in terms of stages, a point of contention brought up by a number of his critics (see Flavell, 1982; Gopnik & Meltzoff, 1997; Siegler & Ellis, 1996). Piaget rejected the basic behaviorist traditions of thinking, which were put forth primarily by American psychologists (e.g., E. L. Thorndike and B. F. Skinner). For Piaget, sensory motor development, as well as the maturational patterns during childhood, precedes learning and intellectual growth. Piaget's answer to the possibility of speeding development was unequivocal: there is no purpose for hastening development; anything you tell children (as most teachers do) will prevent them from the process of discovery on their own terms. If a child developed more slowly, thinking things through, that child would develop more adaptive, scientific, and logical abilities (see chapter 7 for a modified Piagetian perspective in science education).

Piaget's theory of intellectual development is founded on a basic developmental process that he posited was at work throughout the life cycle. Piaget called the basic unit of knowledge a "scheme." A scheme is a context that developed from a pattern of behavior. It is the most basic structure in Piaget's developmental theory and composes our frame of reference. According to Piaget, it is impossible to know anything without a frame of reference or structure that serves as a means of processing incoming information. The difficulty in understanding decontextualized information has been demonstrated in numerous studies in cognition (see Kirschner & Whitson, 1997; Rogoff, 1990). Piaget suggests that as humans we are equipped with some basic schemes that are the foundations of future knowledge. Infants are born with three schemes that are forms of reflexive actions when encountering the world: looking, grasping, and sucking. The infant uses these schemes in an automatic and reflexive manner. These basic schemes, however, are modified over time and develop and expand into newer and more complex schemes.

The development of schemes throughout the life span unfolds through two key cognitive processes: assimilation and accommodation. Since we only know what we can process through prior knowledge (basic structure of constructivist philosophy), we apply our current schemes to a new piece of information from the environment and incorporate it into our existing scheme. This is the process of assimilation—the new piece of information assimilates into the preexisting knowledge base for purposes of constructing generalizations. Assimilation also allows us to generalize between different phenomena and to develop a sense of classification. Although assimilation allows individuals to generalize and apply knowledge to many different conditions, it distorts reality and does not adapt to it because assimilative processes defy restructuring and modification of schemes. Accordingly, the process of accommodation takes over and serves as a complementary process to assimilation.

Given that no two situations or entities are the same, young children are constantly in the process of modifying their schemes. Accommodation, then, is the process of reorganizing or modifying our current schemes in order to handle new information or changes with regard to an object or idea. In this respect, we adjust to reality instead of distorting it. Accommodation allows us to alter our existing schemes for the purpose of applying the modified schemes to more varied situations. For example, infants must adjust the way they look at something, the way they move their lips, or the way they hold something when encountering a different object or discrepant event (such as sucking a small toy rather than a thumb). However, accommodation is not completely the process of modification of existing schemes; it can also involve the elimination or creation of new schemes as well. For example, the infant who makes a fist may encounter a rung of a crib. The infant may initially make contact with the rung by tapping or hitting it. He will create a new scheme as soon as he grasps the rung of the crib instead. This is evidence of an entirely new scheme. Likewise, the older child who refers to a dolphin as a "fish" because "it has fins and swims in the ocean" will be told by an adult, "No, the animal is not a fish; it is a mammal." This is a critical point in development; when the child questions this, he can be answered with encouragement and additional information about what characteristics make the dolphin a mammal. The child at this point must reorganize his knowledge of animals in such a way that he differentiates between fish and mammals, in essence creating a classification system with rules based on an organism's characteristics. The complementary processes of assimilation and accommodation refer to the system of equilibration.

For Piaget, as living organisms, people desire equilibrium. As a result, we are always motivated to assimilate and accommodate objects and ideas in our environment. Doing so leads to a state of equilibrium. The inability to assimilate or accommodate new objects or ideas completely leads to a state of disequilibrium. Through the ongoing cycle of assimilation and accommodation, Piaget argued that human beings do not acquire intellectual capabilities through thousands of successions of stimuli and responses (a behaviorist position), nor do they possess innate modules that one can characterize as locations of intelligence in the brain (a nativist position). Rather, Piaget argued that intellectual levels were attainable through time because one's maturation and growth were inextricably tied with intelligence. He thereby identified four stages of intellectual development—commencing at birth with the sensorimotor stage, followed by the preoperational stage (approximately between the ages of 2 and 7), the concrete operational stage (approximately between the ages of 7 and 11), and finally the formal operational stage (from approximately 11 or 12 years to adulthood) (see table 3.2).

Piaget utilized two prominent forms of data collection for the development of his research program: systematic observation and the clinical method. Despite his vast body of literature, Piaget discusses the methods of systematic observation and the clinical method only briefly in the introductory chapter of his book entitled *Origins of Intelligence in the Child* (1953). For Piaget, the method of observation was perhaps the only way to tap into the development of organisms that do not possess any form of language capacity (i.e., speaking, reading, or writing). Infants, of course, would be categorized in this manner. Piaget developed a thorough progression of the cognitive development of infants and subsequently discovered the six substages of the sensorimotor period of intellectual development. Piaget's motivation for using the clinical method was to identify specific cognitive attributes that children possess during the preoperational, concrete opera-

Table 3.2. The Four Stages in Piaget's Theory of Intellectual Development

Stage	Characteristics
Sensorimotor	Schemas—which emerge from the innate processes of sucking, grasping, and looking—are associated with the development of motor skills. Learning initially takes place locally and through bodily functions and subsequently becomes externalized. Development of language ability in the second 12-month period. Semiotic ability is developing.
Preoperational	As the child matures, learning takes place externally (i.e., learning is not primarily based on bodily functions or interest in an activity through happenstance). Rapid development of language. Concepts of "past," "present," and "future" can be communicated. The child is unable to succeed in tasks involving conservation and seriation. Two substages: In substage 1, the child fails to conserve; in substage 2, there are intuitive regulations, but the child cannot reason with two variables simultaneously.
Concrete Operational	The child has the ability to succeed in tasks involving conservation, seriation, and some aspects of order relationships involving logic. The child, however, is unable to make abstractions about concrete situations. For example, the child might be able to determine the next number in a sequence, but he or she might not be able to generalize about the sequence as a whole. More specifically, in the sequence 2, 4, 8, 16 . . . , a concrete operational child might know that the next number is 32 but more than likely will not know that the general rule has to do with the power of 2. The child can generalize to a greater extent from conservation tasks involving matter, weight, volume, and length. The child will be able to decenter—that is, deal with more than one variable when problem solving. Transductive thinking becomes more intuitive.
Formal Operational	Thinking appears more systematic. The individual is able to control and manipulate variables in an experiment and think abstractly. The individual is able to make generalizations when given specific tasks. For example, when A is older than B, C is younger than A, and C is older than B, the individual will be able to generalize that $B < C < A$.

tional, and formal operational stages. The clinical method, which was in the format of an interview, entails a number of elements. First, the interview is a form of assessing one's knowledge and not a means for instruction. Therefore, hints or leading questions are not used, for this would prevent the researcher from tapping a child's intellectual abilities. Second, a specific organized structure or protocol is used to investigate the child's intellectual abilities. In addition, Piaget used countersuggestion as a means of confirming an individual's genuine understanding of a specific task. Countersuggestion is when a child produces a correct response to a problem, but the interviewer does not verify the response in any way (Ginsburg, 1997). For example, in the problem 37 + 14, the child might point to the 7 and 4 as the ones column and the 3 and 1 as the tens column. The interviewer will subsequently ask the child if the 7 and 4 is the tens column and the 3 and 1 is the ones column as a form of countersuggestion. The child's subsequent response will then determine whether he or she has genuine knowledge of the ones and tens labels.

Piaget's theoretical framework has had a tremendous impact on educational programs throughout the world. Many past and present scholars and practitioners consider him the pioneer of constructivist philosophy—in brief, the idea that the ability to solve problems is based on one's preexisting knowledge base. Piaget was one of the first theorists to support the organismic perspective with empirical data. The organismic perspective led to the view that children are not born as blank slates; rather, their experiences with the environment foster their cognitive development. The constructivist approach altered American education from a primarily behaviorist model prior to the 1970s to a more developmental approach in recent decades.

Lev Vygotsky

Lev Vygotsky, whose research program became accepted only in recent decades, and subsequently became part of the psychology canon in posterity, was interested in the sociocultural implications of cognitive development. Vygotsky's work suggests that knowledge is transferred through the interactions among individuals within a cultural context. As an expert in the psychology of art as well as an early proponent of Soviet policy, Vygotsky was strongly influenced by the two intellectual thinkers who served as his early models—Georg Wilhelm Friedrich Hegel and Karl Marx. Their philosophies strongly emphasized the importance of society and the value of labor as a means of increasing the potential of human ability. Vygotsky believed that the Marxist perspective, in which technology and tools (defined as any object or idea that allows a human being to act on something) transform society and help humans to evolve socially, could be the foundation for a new theory of human development that would account for human functioning in a more progressive context. One aspect of the intersection between the Hegelian and Marxist perspective on human development that Vygotsky embraced was a dialectic view of change. Vygotsky was one of the first psychologists to introduce Hegelian dialectic in psychology, particularly in cognitive development. In dialectic reasoning, one begins with an argument (thesis). Another individual presents a counterargument (antithesis) as a challenge to the original argument, and as a result of the interaction, the two (or more) individuals construct a synthesis—a new level of argument or understanding. For Vygotsky, this dialectic was between two or more individuals. In synthesis, the arguments are combined to develop higher levels of thinking and functioning. These principles became the foundation of Vygotsky's theory known as cognitive mediation.

Vygotsky's primary interests in human development were on the early stages of language, intelligence testing, principles of education, and "defectology"—the study of severe physical disorders that affect learning and intellectual abilities. Vygotsky's interest in intelligence testing was similar to the paths of Binet and Piaget, namely, identifying levels of intelligence for the purpose of maximizing the cognitive potentials of individuals, regardless of level of performance.

Vygotsky's general theoretical framework is referred to as cognitive mediation for a number of reasons. First, Vygotsky believed that we share our lower mental functions with animals. We differ greatly, however, from animals because we possess mental, psychological tools that enable us to think. It is important to consider Marx's influence here, as Vygotsky believed that tools are the mediators of progress. According to Vygotsky, we acquire tools from our culture and the prior learning of our species. In comparison with learning theory, external stimuli elicit responses from individuals; however, when we acquire a psychological tool, like language, the tool itself mediates between the external stimuli and the subsequent responses. Our psychological tools help us compare, classify, and even plan events; that is, psychological tools create intentionality. Therefore, humans, unlike nonhuman animals, learn to avoid direct response to external stimuli and instead employ the cognitive process of thought as a mediating device between stimulus and response.

Culture is passed on to us through society, which is passed on to us through the adults in our society. What we identify in our culture is what we incorporate into our cognitive structures, which determine the psychological tools we use (e.g., if we are born and raised in an English-speaking country, we will develop knowledge of speaking, reading, and writing English as a means to various ends).

What are psychological tools, where in culture do they come from, and why are they so important for the development of what Vygotsky refers to as higher cognitive processes? First, psychological tools are symbols (e.g., spoken and written language). Language, play, art, writing, and mathematics, for example, are Vygotsky's primary tools for cognitive development. These symbol systems differ from Piaget's in at least two ways: (1) they are derived from society—the people around us—and not necessarily from within ourselves, and (2) these symbol systems are not merely the means by which we think, but rather they can completely reorganize the manner in which we think.

For Vygotsky, language is the primary psychological tool. Vygotsky outlined the process by which children internalize language as a personal tool. At first, adults in our culture provide the child with a particular language and set of symbols. As the child masters the use of language, he or she begins to use language both to communicate with others and as a form of egocentric speech—talking to oneself, usually out loud. As time progresses, the child is able to eliminate the overt nature of speech and internalize egocentric speech. Vygotsky referred to this internalization as inner speech. The child is still talking to himself but only mentally. Adults do this as well, as a mechanism for regulating their actions. In time, the inner speech becomes the mediating tool for the child's thinking. He or she begins to use automatic and truncated speech to think and plan. Although language is the primary tool, other symbolic tools become internalized as well, like mathematical thinking or spatial thinking.

Curriculum experts and educational psychologists have promoted Vygotsky's view that society, through the aid of adults and one's peers, helps children regulate their actions until they have internalized the symbol systems that mediate their behavior. This process of internalization of egocentric speech does not carry the connotations of conditioning or behavior modification. Vygotsky rejects outright the stimulus-response framework of learning theory because the behaviorist model is reactive and focuses solely on external properties. Instead, to understand the essence of someone's behavior, overt response is not important.

Vygotsky makes the distinction between spontaneous, or everyday, concepts and scientific, conceptually systematic concepts. Spontaneous concepts are concepts that children develop within their everyday environment. These concepts are like reflections, accurate representations of the situational, empirical (what the child sees with her own eyes), and the practical but often distorted if applied to certain situations. In contrast, scientific concepts, also generally identified as conventionally systematic concepts, refer to a hierarchical system of interrelated ideas. Scientific concepts are highly organized and systematic. Given its emphasis on the learning of formal procedures and algorithms, school instruction, for example, makes a child self-conscious of particular concepts.

Rudiments of systematization enter the child's mind through scientific concepts. Vygotsky argued that instruction in scientific concepts is very helpful because it provides children with broader frameworks in which to place their spontaneous concepts. For example, a five-year-old boy might have developed the spontaneous concept of fish, but his concept is primarily based on his pet betta, a Siamese fighting fish. If we ask him to define the term, he might reply, "It's bright red and blue with long fins and stays alone in a bowl." Formal instruction, in which the teacher categorizes aquatic life (including concepts such as freshwater, marine, tropical) can give the child a broader framework in which to place his spontaneous concept and help him understand what a betta really is (Vygotsky, 1978). Vygotsky suggests that spontaneous concepts moved in an upward manner while scientific concepts had a downward movement: "The upward everyday [spontaneous] concept clears a way for a scientific [conventionally systematic] concept and its downward development. Scientific concepts provide structures in turn for everyday concepts by making them conscious and deliberate" (see figure 3.2).

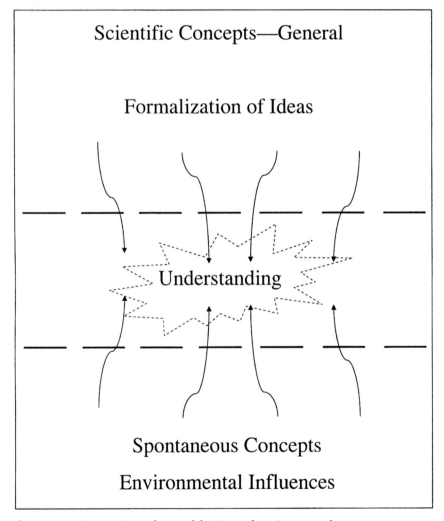

Figure 3.2. Concept Formation Model: A Vygotskyan Interpretation

One of the most significant contributions of Vygotsky's theory of cognitive mediation has been the concept of the zone of proximal development (ZPD). According to Vygotsky, the zone that covers an individual's current developmental level stretches from the level at which the child has already completely mastered, lower-level skills and knowledge, to the level at the upper limit of the individual's capacity, where the child can use a skill or knows something only in the best of circumstances. Vygotsky defined the lower level of the zone as the actual level of development. Everything below this level has already been mastered—prior knowledge, or what the child can do now. Everything above this level is as yet unachievable by the child and beyond his or her limits (the future). Everything between these two levels is in the zone and is potentially achievable by the person (the present). This area is called the zone of proximal development because this range covers the problems, challenges, and tasks that are proximal, or next to, the person's last fully developed level of abilities.

Vygotsky proposed a zone rather than a distinct point in the course of an individual's cognitive development because whether a person can perform a task or successfully solve a problem depends on many environmental factors—for example, whether a problem is written clearly, whether a problem has a simple solution or a complicated one, whether there is another person serving as a facilitator, or whether aids, cues, or hints are provided. Vygotsky's concept of ZPD is to intelligence testing as derivatives and integrals are to measuring functions in calculus. Each of the techniques or methods provides a more precise measure. The ZPD is a dynamic environment and the examiner attempts to pinpoint the child's maximum ability with the appropriate prompts.

It is important to note that traditional tests of intelligence do not address Vygotsky's concept of potential mastery. These tests fail to measure the individual's maximum performance level with appropriate intervention. Feuerstein (1979, 1980) argues for dynamic testing protocols, which the examiner can mediate and modify the child's cognitive functioning by providing the appropriate feedback through the testing session. The idea of increasing a child's cognitive potential by providing the appropriate scaffolding during performance-based assessment has continued to emerge in the literature (Brown & French, 1979; Pascual-Leone & Ijaz, 1989).

CONTEMPORARY VIEWS IN INTELLIGENCE RESEARCH

Thus far, we have seen earlier conceptualizations of intelligence that possess strict interpretations of definition. These conceptualizations are categorical for the most part and are more or less rigidly defined within the nature-nurture continuum. Contemporary positions, however, suggest the possibility that intelligence is malleable and expand the definition of intelligence beyond academic achievement alone. These positions tend to be interactionist, accounting for both genetic and environmental influences as factors of intelligence. One of the most pressing current questions under investigation is: can environmental conditions foster a predisposition to increase ability? Possible answers to this question will depend on the field of epigenetics, the study of environmental factors and their influence on gene expression and variability. At the core of epigenetics research is how environmental influences such as diet, space, hormones, exercise, pollutants, and emotional experience affect a person's DNA profile and possibly their cognitive ability. A simple explanation suggests that certain environmental conditions deactivate a gene or activate a dormant gene, making an individual susceptible or resistant to certain conditions. Much of epigenetics research is based on studies of twins, which demonstrate slight changes in the copy number of genes during gestation. At a young age, monozygotic (identical) twins have very similar genetic profiles, but with time, the profiles begin to transform. Further, identical twins who shared similar lifestyles and environmental conditions have similar epigenetic profiles while twins who did not share common lifestyles and environments have more divergent epigenetic profiles. Epigenetics appears to support an interactionist approach to human development, bridging the nature versus nurture argument, and suggests that some academic interventions are time sensitive in relation to genetic expression. The concept of sensitive genetic blocks of time for child development is reminiscent of Maria Montessori's (1966) theoretical position in which she concluded that these genetically sensitive periods lead development. Thus, an individual's genetic predisposition in conjunction with appropriate environmental stimulation can avoid the short selling of ability. This is an area of interest for educators and parents who advocate for the average student. Still, what has not been demonstrated is how and when to manipulate the environment to influence one's genetic disposition and modify intelligence.

The two contemporary views of intelligence that are often discussed in educational settings are Gardner's multiple intelligence theory and Sternberg's successful intelligence theory. The educational implications that arise from each theory cause one to reconsider the meaning of average, since each suggests certain areas of intelligence can be modified. Supporters of multiple intelligence theory posit the existence of domains of intelligence. The range of intellectual ability can be limited to one domain, as with a savant, or can carry across several domains (art, science, mathematics), as demonstrated in the intellectual contributions of Leonardo da Vinci. The successful intelligence theory highlights the processes in intelligence behavior. It includes analytic thinking, practical experience, and creative ability. On the surface, the range of behaviors that are identified by the theories

and the individuals who demonstrate those behaviors are suggestive of a
"Renaissance man," where one's actions may have been less compartmen-
talized than they are today and where a more fluid thinking style integrates
intellectual, practical, and creative abilities. It is quite intriguing that we are
still discussing and examining what Aristotle recognized over 2,300 years
ago: that one's intellectual abilities represent more than solely an academic
form of intelligence (episteme) but also include practical experience and
everyday intelligence (phronesis) as well.

Howard Gardner

Howard Gardner's work on multiple intelligences spans three decades
and has attracted much interest in the fields of education and cognition.
Gardner, like others before him, defined intelligence as a complex set of
behaviors that extend far beyond what is measured by paper-and-pencil
tests and the general work of psychometricians. Gardner's (1993) theory
of multiple intelligences identifies a variety of distinct abilities in a number of domains that represent the complex capabilities of an individual.
Gardner suggests that everyone has some level in each of these domains
that make up intelligence. His eight basic domains include bodily-
kinesthetic, interpersonal, intrapersonal, linguistic, musical, naturalistic,
spatial, and logico-mathematical (see table 3.3). For Gardner, intelligence
goes beyond the linguistic, spatial, and logico-mathematical skills that
are measured by most traditional intelligence tests. He argues that our
conceptions of intelligence should reflect what we know from the studies
of gifted students, virtuosos, individuals who have brain damage, experts
from a variety of domains, and savants. Gardner asserts that each of these
individuals can demonstrate extraordinary talents in a select domain,
suggesting a specific ability rather than a general ability of intelligence.
Further, it is also possible that individuals can possess extraordinary ability in multiple domains, especially where skill sets overlap. This is evident in the linguistic and logico-mathematical domains that rely heavily
on analytic abilities. Moreover, the most conducive academic setting for
Gardner's framework is one that promotes project-based learning, where,
for example, students may work in collaborative groups to complete an
activity. With a variety of skill sets or multiple intelligences within a particular group, the task required to accomplish the activity may be assigned
by levels of talent found in the group. The proposed advantage of multiple
intelligence theory is to recognize students' areas of intellectual strength
and to use those strengths in remediating any areas in which the child
might be deficient. Therefore, learner-centered instruction can provide the
required experiences that are needed to increase one's level of intelligence
in a deficient domain.

Table 3.3. Outline of Gardner's Theory of Multiple Intelligences

Domains of Intelligence	Examples of Professions	Demonstrated Skills
Bodily-Kinesthetic	Athletes, Dancers, Surgeons, Watchmakers	Profession/career where dexterity is important; body sense and muscle sense
Interpersonal	Clinicians, Teachers, Sales, Politicians	Empathy to sense other people's feelings
Intrapersonal	Any field—however, people who understand their own abilities make effective use of their skills	Self-awareness
Linguistic	Communicators, Writers, Lecturers, Speakers	The ability to communicate either in writing or orally; multilingual ability
Musical	Composers, Musicians	Ability to either compose, read, or perform music
Naturalistic	Biologically related fields —Conservationists, Naturalists, Ecologists	The ability to recognize patterns in nature, interrelationships within and among similar and different species
Spatial	Surgeons, Engineers, Artists, Designers, Architects	The ability to abstractly recognize the proper placement of objects
Logico-Mathematical	Mathematicians, Actuaries, Engineers, Physicists	The ability to reason with quantities and learn complex mathematics

Gardner's multiple intelligence theory, however, is not without criticism. One major argument against it is that the theory is considered too broad to be operationally defined or tested. The inclusion of some domains that Gardner considers as intelligences (such as music) is thought of by many scholars in the field of intelligence as a skill, ability, or talent. Second, each of Gardner's intelligence domains is comprised of a number of skills for which a hierarchy of prerequisite subskills has not been established. Individuals may possess some of these subskills for a particular domain, while lacking other subskills thought to engender that particular intelligence. For example, in music, an individual may be an exceptional composer but need not have perfect pitch. Two monumental examples of this phenomenon are the eminent nineteenth-century German composers Robert Schumann and Richard Wagner (Sacks, 2008). Third, it has been suggested that much of the basic framework of multiple intelligences is similar to the earlier work of Thurstone (1938), who believed that multiple group factors more accurately explain the complexity of intelligence, rather than a unitary general ability (Morgan, 1996). In a similar argument, Bouchard (1984) posits that a common thread exists between linguistic and logico-mathematical intelligences and Cattell's (1963) and Horn and Cattell's (1966, 1967) crystallized and fluid intelligences. Fourth, Sternberg (2001) and Plucker, Callahan, and Tomchin (1996) raise concerns regarding the psychometric properties of the instruments used to assess multiple intelligences. The problem is that no tools other than self-reporting inventories, which rely on introspection or naturalistic observations, are available that accurately identify each student's intelligence or measure of it. The poor psychometric properties from self-reporting instruments or inventories that use naturalistic observations can also be a cause of concern for educators. Despite these criticisms, multiple intelligences theory has expanded the contemporary view of intelligence beyond analytic ability, which has traditionally emphasized solely verbal and quantitative thinking.

Robert J. Sternberg

Robert Sternberg's research has had a great impact on changing the way in which we view intelligence. Two of his models on intelligence, the triarchic theory of intelligence (1985) and the more recent successful theory of intelligence (1996), also expand the definition of intelligence by including behaviors that are not measured by conventional tests of intellectual abilities. The triarchic theory contains three subtheories: componential, experiential, and contextual components. In this model, a component is a psychological construct that is thought to operate on abstract symbolism. In an information processing paradigm, "a component is an elementary information process that operates upon internal representations of objects or symbols. . . . The component may translate a sensory input into a conceptual representation, transform one conceptual representation into another, or translate a conceptual representation into a motor output" (Sternberg, 1985, pp. 97–98). The componential component controls the manner in which individuals process information. It includes the analytic abilities used in knowledge acquisition, performance components, and metacomponents. Knowledge acquisition is comprised of three subskills that are utilized during cognitive activity: selected regulating processes of encoding, combining, and comparing information. Performance components are the learning strategies that are employed at the onset of a task. They are the actual actions on the knowledge acquisition subskills of encoding, combining, and comparing of information in response to the stimuli that initiated the action. The metacomponents are the metacognitive processes that involve planning, monitoring, and evaluating one's thinking.

Students who employ metacognitive strategies engage in active learning by using strategies to make sense of information, self-assess, and reflect on the quality of their performance. For example, as an initial step, the learner may incorporate the "survey question read recite review" (SQ3R) method when faced with learning new material. The SQ3R method teaches students a procedure to access the executive cognitive functions that will enable them to utilize and improve metacognitive strategies by fostering an awareness of their own cognition and learning. Metacognitive processes have been linked with the ability to apply what has been learned in one context to another. It has been demonstrated that students who practice metacognitive strategies can increase the level of transfer when learning new material. The important educational implication is that these strategies can be taught, resulting in an increased level of intelligence (Palincsar & Brown, 1984; Schoenfeld, 1984, 1991; Sternberg, 1985; White & Frederickson, 1998). Each of the components that comprise componential intelligence can be demonstrated through task analysis and is associated with analytical skills. Students with strong componential skills generally do very well in traditional scholastic environments that emphasize critical thinking in verbal and quantitative domains.

The experiential component explains how an individual deals with problems that are novel in performing a task and understanding the nature of that task. This component integrates a hierarchical and nonhierarchical approach to information processing. The model accounts for the manner in which experts and novices solve problems. Experts benefit from a more localized processing system that enables them to complete a task, thus freeing up global resources for other situations, while novices depend on a more global response utilizing additional cognitive functions in order to solve the task. The experiential component lends itself to creative abilities, possibly through the process of automatization of routine mental processes, and is strongly influenced by factors found in one's environment and culture. Take learning to play the piano as an example. The novice piano player focuses primarily on the mechanics of playing, such as fingering, the amount of pressure exerted on the keys, coordinating both hands, and playing in rhythm. These skills require most of the novice's mental energy while playing the piano. In contrast, the expert pianist automatized many of these mechanical processes at the local level and instead is able to free up other cognitive functions in order to develop artistic, creative, and aesthetic qualities of piano performance. Horn (1998) argues that since everyone's experiences are different, the experiential component can demonstrate significant variability among individuals. The experiential component also reflects what Horn and Cattell (1966, 1967) identify as crystallized intelligence, G_c. Later, Horn (1979) elaborated that crystallized abilities "are the breadth of knowledge, sophistication, the intelligence of experience, one's appropriation of intelligence of his culture" (p. 62). Crystallized intelligence, G_c, is therefore a relative concept dependent on the context in which it occurs, thus making it difficult to generalize about intelligence among individuals.

The contextual component has to do with one's ability to select, adapt, and manipulate environmental conditions to one's benefit. Since activity does not occur in a vacuum, all behaviors are contextually bound, and our performance is relative. How individuals select, adapt, or modify their environment can differ from person to person. The contextual subtheory of intelligence "implies that, because what is required for adaptation, selection, and shaping may differ across persons and groups, as well as environments, intelligence is not quite the same thing from one person (group) to another, nor is it exactly the same thing across environments" (Sternberg, 1985, p. 47). The contextual view requires one to evaluate behavior in terms of a variety of personal attributes and environmental conditions. Due to practical and cultural implications, both the experiential and contextual components of the triarchic theory expand our current knowledge on the nature of intelligence by integrating implicit and explicit theoretical approaches in the description and analysis of cognitive ability.

Sternberg's successful theory of intelligence modifies the triarchic theory by stressing the experiential and contextual components that expand into creative and practical abilities. Successful intelligence theory identifies three areas of intellectual ability: analytic, creative, and practical. Analytic intelligence relates to componential components used in information processing. Students possessing keen analytic skills excel in the areas that Benjamin Bloom (1956) identified in his cognitive taxonomy of educational objectives as knowledge, comprehension, application, analysis, synthesis, and evaluation. All of these are the prerequisites for critical thinking. Creative intelligence consists of the ability to think in novel ways, generate ideas, and work beyond rejection. In this respect, Sternberg (2005, pp. 330–33) identifies 11 attributes that are required of creative individuals. A creative person can redefine a problem, question and analyze assumptions, realize that creative ideas do not sell themselves, recognize that knowledge is a double-edged sword, surmount obstacles, take risks, tolerate ambiguity, achieve self-efficacy, find what he or she loves to do, delay gratification, and possess courage.

Practical intelligence involves the skills or abilities to solve problems that are situated in a real context. Problems situated in an everyday context are often unique and possibly poorly defined, requiring the problem solver to first identify the problem before strategizing ways to solve it. This intelligence is readily apparent when a person takes his or her car to an auto mechanic for repair after hearing a strange noise. When asked what is wrong with the car, the person describes a noise that could be caused by a loose bolt on an exhaust hanger, worn brake pads, or a leaky water pump. The mechanic may ask for a description of the sound but will more likely take the vehicle for a test drive. While driving the car, the mechanic has the opportunity to listen for any noises and can discern minor from major concerns. Integrating analytic ability and practical knowledge, a master mechanic can identify the problem and repair the vehicle. Within the successful intelligence theory, the mechanic possesses what Sternberg calls practical intelligence and has the tacit knowledge of automotive maintenance to diagnose and repair the problem. Practical intelligence requires the study of tacit knowledge, which is the unspoken, intrinsic ability of situated expertise that originates from prior experiences (Sternberg & Kaufman, 1998).

A combination of analytic, practical, and creative intelligence can often be seen in children's play activities (Ness & Farenga, 2007). In one situation, two four-year-old boys who work on a block construction demonstrate analytic intelligence when they discuss the number of blocks needed to serve as the walls of a block building. One child says, "we're gonna need eight," basing his statement on the process of multiplication, whereby two times four equals eight. In another example, when the children exhausted the quadruple blocks (a larger block), they made use of two double blocks in its place. Their practical intelligence involves the general knowledge of building constructions, such as the realization that rooms generally have four sides for the four walls. Also, students use informal mathematical and scientific thinking to demonstrate symmetry, balance, and stability in their constructions. Their creative intelligence is evident in terms of their use of blocks in creating various geometric and spatial designs—such as symmetry, foundations of block buildings, trabeated construction (i.e., post-and-beam construction), and construction involving enclosures.

Children's cognitive behavior (as in the example above) demonstrates a number of limitations with current methods in assessment, measurement, and evaluation. First, a novice interviewer might interpret the child's play as just that—play or participation in trivial, nonsensical activities—and miss the advanced display of behaviors that represent a high level of cognitive ability. Second, the language used by the children embodies the tacit knowledge of their mathematical and scientific thinking that requires an attentiveness to be organized and quantified. In order to accurately assess the tacit knowledge, a degree of expertise is required that is not possessed by all individuals. Third, practical and creative intelligences are sometimes difficult to quantify but can be recognized when they occur. However, Tannenbaum (1983) reports on the difficulty that some scholars have in discussing creativity objectively and suggests that "they tend to approach it projectively, as if to a Rorschach-type figure, and respond with all kinds of protean images. Occasionally, the sentiment is so florid that it borders on hyperbole" (p. 241). Our concerns reflect Tannenbaum's position when making a decision to include or exclude creative and practical abilities in the construction of students' cognitive profiles. From the psychometric perspective, the inclusion of creativity and experience is subjective, and there is no way to compare students because it is difficult to operationalize creativity and quantify experience. Conversely, the exclusion of creativity and experience may eliminate two-thirds of a person's cognitive potential in assessing ability. The cognitive skills that rely on crystallized intelligence G_c, and to a much smaller extent fluid intelligence, G_f, can reduce the measure of potential.

Sternberg's view of intelligence differs from Gardner's in that he does not consider multiple intelligences as distinct forms of intellectual ability. Rather, he considers the mechanisms that are used in regulating, processing, and interpreting information in the areas of analytic, creative, and practical thinking. In these three areas of intelligence, his fundamental components for human cognition involve performance, retention, and metacognitive components of human information processing. He used componential analysis to investigate the different processes that individuals employ to solve complex problems. Similar to Piaget, Sternberg is interested in the tacit knowledge children use during problem solving. Unlike Piaget, who essentially inferred understanding of a participant's cognitive ability without assistance from the interviewer, Sternberg's work helps to distinguish intellectual ability from what a participant can do both with and without assistance.

SUMMARY OF CONCEPTIONS OF INTELLIGENCE

The testing industry grew from the premise that in order to provide school- or grade-appropriate placement for all children and to improve student achievement, there must be a way to measure intelligence. It should come as no surprise that most well-designed achievement and IQ tests are able to measure some level of school performance, considering that test questions reflect content from the school curriculum. These tests typically measure some degree of memory, one's ability to recall an answer, for example, and analytical ability, which refers to inquiry-related behaviors, such as comparing and contrasting, critiquing, analyzing, and evaluating information. Cognitive studies have enhanced the psychometric model of intelligence by demonstrating that an important factor in how well an individual can recall or analyze information is highly dependent on the context in which it is placed. So the context can have as much to do with getting a correct response as the level of intelligence, *g*, that a person possesses. In general, all disciplines, careers, or hobbies have their own "language" and a level of tacit knowledge required for someone to excel in a particular area.

Individuals who enter the workforce are not surprised that much of what is taught and learned in school is out of context in their lives and selected careers. Students often look for opportunities to match their analytical knowledge with their practical skills. In fact, the purpose of internships, field placements, and apprenticeships is to provide context for what is taught in school. The internship's purpose is to bridge the gap between what one has learned in a formal setting and the ability to apply that knowledge in the real-world context. This is the test that is important in life to both the individual and society. Most employers and recipients in need of a person's abilities and skills want to know whether the person has the capability to deliver exceptional performance. More often than not, this exceptional performance is delivered by an individual who may have been labeled "average" but is motivated and has a good deal of practical intelligence to be successful.

The problem here is that a label based on a narrow definition of intelligence can create a glass ceiling and a leveling of ability, or worse, a decrease of human potential. As educators and parents, our primary function is to maximize potential. This may require manipulating a number of factors within young children's environments. Factors such as teachers, schools, curriculum, and out-of-school experiences can all contribute to the expression of one's potential by increasing the level of crystallized intelligence.

Clearly, there are numerous definitions of intelligence, but most suggest that an intelligent person can problem solve, think abstractly, memorize information, and work with complex ideas. Intelligence is a general mental construct that is represented by behaviors such as reasoning, planning, understanding, learning from experience, and speed in processing information. A review of intelligence research in professional journals, textbooks, and encyclopedias reveals that some ideas and practices that are promoted in education are not fully supported by research. However, a narrow band of intelligence can be measured, and mainstream IQ tests are valid and reliable assessments for measuring academic achievement. Intelligence tests vary in their construction, but all appear to measure the same general ability, which is useful in traditionally scholastic environments. It is clear that psychological tests of intelligence do not measure traits or aptitudes such as creativity, character, or personality, nor do they attempt to do so. Some intelligence tests have verbal and performance scales and require cultural priming, while others purport to be language-free (i.e., nonverbal) and use universally recognized concepts. Intelligence tests, according to a number of researchers, are not seen as culturally biased. Rather, the tests measure, and are sensitive to, societal inequities that are exacerbated by poverty, lack of opportunity, and differences in experiential background (Borland, 1986; Lorge, 1953; Tannenbaum, 1965). Sternberg (1985) concludes that no test can be culture-free because "all tests require a degree of acculturation for successful completion" (p. 77).

The most influential theory of intelligence used in school settings is the psychometric model, whose basic premise is that ability is equally distributed in the population. In this model, the range of individuals' test scores forms a bell curve where most individuals cluster around the average score of 100 with a standard deviation of 15. Contemporary views seem to conclude that intelligence is something of a global attribute that may be thought of as being culturally defined and that extends beyond tests, scholastic achievement, and the individual's capabilities. It reflects the ability to manipulate and adapt to an environment in order to create optimal conditions for the individual to succeed. The neural functioning that underlies the concept of intelligence is still unknown. Current research examines how processing speed, rate of neural transmission, glucose use, and patterns of electrical activity among brain cells relate to intelligence. Perhaps future research in brain behavior and cognition will shed new light on these physiological processes and their direct effects on intellectual development.

4

Success for the Average:
Effort, Ability, or Luck?

Genius is nothing but continued attention.

—Claude Adrien Helvetius (n.d.)

In chapter 1, we emphasized the need for society to devote more time and resources to students in the middle. In the following chapter, we pointed out a number of factors as to why average students comprise the invisible majority and what should be done in order to improve the conditions of this enormous student population. We then followed in the third chapter with a treatment of different theorists' conceptions of intelligence within the last century. Within that chapter, we argued that a new conception of intelligence must be considered in order for average students to succeed in school and beyond. But there is at least one additional component to this complex interplay between student academic placement within the intelligence continuum (i.e., the bell curve) and academic achievement—and that is the question of how success in school and beyond can be possible for average students, given the lack of attention they receive from local, state, and federal bodies. Further, does success involve ability or some other innate characteristic? Or does it involve effort and one's will or desire to succeed? Or can it possibly be simply a matter of luck? These are some of the many critical questions we raise and grapple with in this chapter. We begin with an examination of motivation and how it contributes to success. We then show how students think of their own intelligence and knowledge of the world through the principles of attribution theory. Our next objective is to introduce specific factors and models of success that can serve as a starting point for students who are described as average.

MOTIVATION AND SUCCESS

Cognitive scientists and education researchers generally concur that motivation is the force that drives persistence and is used to explain an individual's sustained effort in deciding whether to continue a task or to embark on it in the first place. The difficulty that most researchers have is their agreement on the nature and source of motivation. Researchers have essentially embraced one of three general models to explain the source of motivation: stimulus-response, social cognitive, and the general cognitive models.[1] Stimulus-response theory explains motivation as the result of consequences of one's actions (Skinner, 1968). According to the learning theory perspective, students' behaviors or actions are shaped by what has been reinforced in the past, and their motivation is based on these actions. A contrary point of view is offered by the social cognitive perspective that focuses on the anticipated, rather than past, consequences of behavior. That is, a person's source of motivation is explained by expectations of future consequences and also the principle of self-efficacy (Bandura, 1986, 1994; Dweck & Leggett, 1988; Pintrich & Garcia, 1994). For example, certain students imitate sports figures, older siblings, or perhaps a teacher who they view as competent or perceive as having prestige or power. These students model behavior based on their observations of the actions of mentors or famous figures and are motivated by the idea that they themselves have the potential to achieve a similar status at some point in the future. Unlike the stimulus-response and social cognitive perspectives, the cognitive perspective of motivation helps to explain individuals' efforts, how people think, and how thought is modified over time (Piaget & Inhelder, 1975). In this perspective, motivation is contextual in the sense that it is circumstance-specific, and the particular circumstances affect behavior. This is also known as situational motivation, where an individual may be inclined to engage and remain involved with a task based on conditions within the immediate environment. There are a number of factors found in a student's surroundings that can affect a particular level of motivation, such as teachers, curriculum, lesson format, level of difficulty, relevance of a topic, attitude, aptitude, and the overall class environment. But the main concern now is not whether one adheres to any one of these three models, but how average students perceive success, particularly their general attitudes toward success, as it relates to school and overall academic achievement.

Recognition of Differences between Ability and Effort

When do students develop a realization of effort, ability, and success? Associations, let alone causal relationships, between effort and achievement or ability and achievement do not appear until later in the child's life. Young children do not generally have a sense of the differences among ability, effort, and achievement (Nicholls, 1978, 1979, 1990). Before the age of seven, children generally cannot distinguish among these three characteristics of success. In fact, many children in this age range overestimate their ability at certain tasks. This has been documented by Piaget and Inhelder (1975), who noted that children evince greater belief in their ability to control elements in their physical surroundings than they actually do. In another example, Nicholls (1979) found that many first graders overestimate their reading abilities, believing themselves to be better readers than they actually are. At about seven or eight years of age, children begin to realize a causal relationship between effort and achievement but not ability and achievement. Between 9 and 11 years, children have an understanding of the relationship between ability and achievement but see no causal relationship between the two. Nevertheless, they still believe that effort accounts for the greatest factor of achievement. By 11, however, most children distinguish between effort and ability and realize that each can separately affect success. Some 20 years later, Eccles, Wigfield, and Schiefele (1998) have corroborated Nicholls's earlier findings and support the conclusion that as children get older, they generally have a more realistic notion of their abilities in relationship to their classmates, and they have a more established view of their abilities. Moreover, these evolving explanations given by students for their successes and failures are referred to as attributions. It is evident from this information that students make a number of observations about why they are or are not successful. Equally valuable is the knowledge of the general cut-off ages for the developmental phases of students' explanations or perceived reasons for their success, as we consider whether the source of motivation comes from within or comes from some external set of factors that can be modified to benefit the average student.

Motivation: Intrinsic or Extrinsic?

Motivation is generally considered as intrinsic or extrinsic, depending upon the reason for the behavior. That said, what specific signs of a student's behavior will help us identify how to differentiate between the two forms of motivation? We can recognize intrinsic motivation by noticing a student's level of curiosity, long-term interest in a particular subject, desire to know, or demonstration of effective metacognitive abilities—or efficient learning strategies. Intrinsic motivation is driven by an internal cost analysis where the individual weighs either direct or indirect benefits of their decisions—in other words, "What do I enjoy doing for me?" From a psychological perspective, Feather (1982) argues that motivation is a combination of perceived value of a goal and the probability of achieving that goal. However, Atkinson (1964), who recognized the complexity of explaining motivation and attribution, cautions us about the possibility of an interaction among three factors: expectancy, value, and attribution. For example, interaction can be understood when considering a student who believes he or she has a high probability of doing well on an examination and thus puts forth little effort. In this situation, the student's motivation to prepare for an examination diminishes, while another student who has moderate (rather than low or high) expectations of performing well on a test tends to expend more effort on preparation for an examination. Therefore, a student will exert little, if any, effort when a task is perceived to be either extremely easy or arduous to accomplish.

Motivation and Success

Students develop an expectancy of task difficulty either by self-estimation or through interaction with others. The result is that student motivation is not always increased by success alone. This is an important consideration, for students must recognize that a cause-and-effect relationship exists between the level of effort expended and the level of success achieved. Given the causal link between effort and success yet the lack thereof between ability and success, we have noticed two contributing factors that lead to the state of "learned effortlessness" for average students. The first factor is the establishment of an academic climate that is performance-centered, where performance is valued over knowledge. In a performance-centered environment, the actions taken to achieve a successful outcome are more important than the knowledge learned. This is evidenced by the adoption and use of assessments with extremely low skill levels needed in order to achieve a passing grade. A performance-centered climate is created with an overemphasis on test preparation, whereby average students can put forth little effort in order to be rewarded with a degree of competence. The second occurs when teachers and parents give positive feedback to students in the form of false praise for their minimal achievements. However, according to federal data (see chapter 2 for an extended discussion), average students are not in actuality reaching appropriate levels of achievement. In this situation and in others that follow a similar pattern, adult role models are inadvertently inflicting and thus fostering mediocrity upon a whole category of students. As a result, the use of false praise as positive feedback will have deleterious effects on student success, because it contributes to a decrease in motivation and in turn encourages average students to focus overwhelmingly on ability level with nearly entire disregard for effort. In examples like this one, teacher and parent praise for a "nonaccomplishment" may cause students to question their actual ability.

Deci (1992) and Deci and Ryan (1985, 1992) consider two additional factors in determining levels of motivation, namely, competence and self-determination. The components of competence and self-determination can be integrated with Sternberg's contextual subtheory of intelligence and can also work in conjunction with attributional theory of motivation and achievement to explain successful behaviors. You will recall in chapter 3 that according to the contextual view, behavior is evaluated in terms of a number of personal attributes and environmental conditions. The level at which students are able to solve problems that are situated in real contexts is determined by their ability to adapt, select, or shape the environment in order to increase the probability of a successful outcome. Students who are able to shape their environments demonstrate a sense of competence and are able to manipulate and work within the conditions found within their individual contexts. They display a sense of self-determination and perceive that they have control over the events that occur in their lives, even those that occur in school.

In many respects, we can think of school as a game where students learn the intricacies and subtexts of how the school system works and how to succeed in the classroom. Students who are successful learn the rules early and are able to manipulate and adjust to the classroom and school environment. Each teacher has different rules and procedures, and these procedures change as frequently as period to period or as seldom as once per year. However, most people would agree that students are generally quite successful—and even clever—at identifying what each teacher wants and adapting to that situation. The current system of education has been designed around external rewards, and most students have learned to do just enough work to get through the grade. In today's educational milieu, few opportunities are available for setting learning goals; rather, most schools set performance goals (Dweck, 1989; Dweck & Leggett, 1988; Elliott & Dweck, 1988). These two types of goals both benefit and foster the development of two very different kinds of learners. Learning goals are encouraged when teachers are concerned about increasing student confidence. In doing so, they emphasize a rigorous knowledge-centered curriculum that addresses student failure by teaching students the importance and value of appropriate effort in working toward success. Students who hold this belief view success as a journey and failure as only a temporary detour. In contrast, performance goals are encouraged when teachers tailor the curriculum to avoid demanding topics, thus sending a message that even with a degree of effort and assistance, the probability of success is poor. In this mind-set, students are taught to avoid challenges unless they think that they can be successful and receive positive feedback. Performance goals lend themselves to the "carrot-and-stick" mentality, where the carrot might be seen as grades, tokens, or some form of approval by others. It has been identified that the longer students remain in school, the less intrinsically motivated and more extrinsically motivated they become. Perhaps this change in motivation is more a function of cultural tendencies toward external reward systems that promote performance goals than one of the length of time spent in school.

Along with changes in motivation, students' interests and abilities become more stable over time, and there appears to be a change from intrinsic motivation to a perception of practicality or usefulness in reaching long-term goals. For example, a student might develop good study habits in mathematics, because a good performance on college entrance examinations will increase chances of college acceptance. In this case, the student has internalized the benefit of studying hard for a long-term future reward. This example demonstrates delayed gratification, in which the student is able to forgo smaller rewards in order to reach a higher goal at a later time. However, many average students are conditioned to accept a silent contract that internalizes the relationship between success and conduct rather than success and effort. In this situation, practicality and usefulness are exhibited by students who remain in their seats, behave cooperatively, and exhibit a taciturn and quiet disposition. The average students have learned that these behaviors are what are necessary to get an acceptable grade. Unfortunately, the grade received has probably been inflated and holds little value, but it is nonetheless the reward for adhering to the terms of the silent contract and responding with the expected behavior. In reality, what is learned in many situations by many students is how to please the teacher. The students perceive what is valued by the teacher and respond accordingly. Deci and Ryan (1995) suggest that this type of behavior is reinforced not by intrinsic or extrinsic motivation but by a third category—internalized motivation.

Internalized motivation is set by adapting behaviors that are important or valued by others, regardless of the consequences. These behaviors can evolve as a result of external regulation, introjection, identification, and integration. In external regulation, students' behaviors are guided by external consequences that may follow as a result of their actions. For example, a student may decide to attend an "extra help" class in order to avoid parent or teacher discontent. The introjection phase is exhibited if the student attends such a class in order to seek parent approval and remains for the entire session motivated by guilt rather than leaving early to seek other forms of enjoyment. If the student personally values attending the class and views it as an important part of academic success, the identification process is in control. Finally, if the student thinks that it is truly beneficial to attend the class because it is believed to raise college entrance scores, actions become integrated with academic goals. As we progress in school, our motives and goals in participating in certain activities may be more complex, and the actions themselves may constitute a hybrid of both intrinsic and extrinsic forms of motivation.

Intrinsic motivation is an important cognitive component to develop in average students. At the same time, the task of providing appropriate feedback to help students identify their effort attributions for either their failures or successes poses many challenges. It involves an awareness of the student's potential in order to provide appropriate feedback to reinforce the likelihood of sustained effort. Teachers need to assess the assignment's level of cognitive intrigue, task difficulty, the developmental level of the student, and the nature of the effort exerted by the student to complete the task. Ideally, teachers should model suitable strategies to use to complete the task in order to increase the motivation of the average student. Regrettably, many classroom environments are not conducive to support the development of intrinsic motivation, because the teacher's time is diverted from the main activity of teaching to other tasks, such as an emphasis on meeting external standards, raising test scores, socialization, and attending to too many ill-defined demands. We now turn to attribution theory to help us identify the origins of these attitudes and general beliefs about intelligence and school success.

ATTRIBUTION THEORY

Attribution theory is rooted in the work of Fritz Heider (1958), who argued that attributions are ways to explain how people perceive themselves and others. They are also a way to interpret how people make causal explanations about behavior, which may be determined by internal or external factors. Attribution theory is concerned with one's beliefs about self and others. It is posited that effort, ability, task difficulty, and luck are four factors that affect expectancy and value. Expectancy is what one anticipates as an outcome, and value refers to the personal level of importance that is placed on the task. A basic tenet of attribution theory is that nearly all students want to sustain a positive self-image. In order to maintain a positive self-image, students may create a distorted view of a situation. At one extreme, students may self-impose impeding behaviors that hinder their achievement, such as acute apathy, drug abuse, clowning, selective mutism, truancy, or absenteeism. Each of these behaviors helps to protect students' self-image, and academic failure can be attributed to these impeding behaviors. In general, success can be attributed to their own abilities and efforts, and failure can be attributed to factors that protect self-image, such as bad luck or situations that are deemed as unfair. A student's own perceptions or attributions for either success or failure influence the amount of effort the student will expend in future activities. This is an explanation for what drives motivation. Motivation, then, is more dependent on perception than on reality. This is a key concept for attribution theory and motivation. What an individual perceives as the value and expectancy of success in a given situation determines the amount of effort he or she expends in the future.

It is critical that teachers recognize that students have the ability to evaluate their surroundings and do what is necessary to protect their self-image.

There are a variety of ways to tap into the various attributes that students offer as causes for their successes and failures. The use of analogy is a common way to identify a general idea of one's self-appraisal. To this end, we provide the following analogy, which encapsulates an individual's core beliefs about the meaning of success and failure. Based on your own feeling about success and failure, select a word or phrase for each of the blanks from the list that follows.

SUCCESS is to _____ as FAILURE is to _____.

Ability
Lack of ability
Luck
Misfortune
Effort
Lack of effort

This simple analogy provides insight into one's beliefs and values regarding success. It helps us identify whether some people consider hard work and effort to be the reason for increased success and whether these individuals are willing to exert the effort to make it happen. For others, success is based on ability, an innate attribute. Those who believe that ability is responsible for successful achievement are more likely to give up as soon as difficulties or increased challenges begin to arise. The work of Bernard Weiner and Carol Dweck will add greater insight into the nuances of the words selected to complete the analogy and their meanings.

Weiner (1974, 1976, 1986) is credited with the concept of attribution theory of achievement motivation. According to Weiner, success or failure is attributed to degrees of locus of control along a three-dimensional, dichotomous model: (1) causality (internal or external); (2) stability (stable or unstable); and (3) controllability (controllable or uncontrollable). Within this three-dimensional model, there are four factors that influence motivation in educational settings. These factors are effort, ability, task difficulty, and luck. Effort is considered to be an internal and unstable factor in which students have a great amount of control. It is said to be unstable because one can increase or decrease the amount of effort in a given situation. Ability is considered as an internal and stable factor over which students do not possess very much direct control. It is the potential that students possess from their genetic makeup or innate ability. The level of task difficulty is beyond students' control and is perceived as an external and stable factor. Task difficulty is thought of as a stable factor, because the control of the task is external to the individual since they are usually derived by others. Luck is external and unstable, and obviously beyond the control of the students. The degree to which students internalize and recognize control over effort, task difficulty, ability, and luck determines their level of understanding of the reasons for success or failure.

In terms of causality, students who believe that they are responsible for and can control the outcomes of a situation have high levels of internal locus of control. In contrast, those who believe that the outcomes are a result of external factors in the environment possess higher levels of an external locus of control. In each circumstance, it must be determined whether the control of the cause rests within or outside the individual. The relationship between locus of control and the development of self-regulatory behaviors is often overlooked in educational settings in gauging student intelligence. Students who self-regulate report higher levels of internal locus of control than students who do not possess the ability to self-regulate. These students who demonstrate self-regulatory behaviors believe that they can control their effort to achieve desired results and can be recognized by their task persistence, their willingness to engage in error analysis, and their keenness for challenging assignments. They show a great deal of motivation in which they demonstrate a high degree of control over effort, realize that task difficulty is an external factor that is not under their control, and have stable sense of their abilities. Given similar circumstances, these students believe that the causes of their successes or failures are stable and anticipate future success or failure under similar conditions. These behaviors are usually what separate children who possess higher levels of self-regulatory behaviors and persistence from children who do not. An interesting research finding suggests that a stronger correlation exists between school achievement and students' measures of locus of control than with other measures of intelligence (Nowicki & Strickland, 1973; Reid & Croucher, 1980). However, there has been reluctance in the assessment community to integrate these findings with standard measures of assessment in order to create a holistic student profile. Descriptions of locus of control can be recognized as an integrated part of contemporary intelligence theories that discuss practical or creative abilities. But to date, none of these theories offers a practitioner-based motivation achievement model that is fully applicable to the general education community.

INDIVIDUAL FACTORS FOR SUCCESS

Carol Dweck's (1999, 2006) concept of intelligence, which explains in part why some individuals are successful and others are not, moves beyond the external factors in the environment to the internal factors that form the basis of one's belief system. Dweck extends attribution theory and suggests that a dichotomy exists in how individuals view their abilities. One group of individuals is composed of entity theorists who believe that the outcome of success is due to innate ability. The other group, incremental theorists, believes that varying degrees of effort lead to success. Although environmental stimuli can help reinforce an individual's mind-set, it is not the sole cause of achievement. According to Dweck, mind-sets are learned and can be altered to foster success, even beyond that of academics.

The Entity Mind-Set

For the entity theorists, intelligence is viewed as innate and immutable. Dweck identifies students with this mind-set as those who believe that their intelligence remains constant across the life span and demonstrates intellectual ability through performance or product. Entity learners believe that they absorb the whole learning experience in its entirety; one either understands what is learned or does not. A student who understands what is being taught in a relatively short amount of time may consider it due to innate ability. In contrast, a lack of understanding indicates that the academic content is beyond the student's ability, and there is no need to pursue the content further because it exceeds one's academic limits. This ability-driven self-concept limits the role of effort in achievement that can cause educational difficulties at some point in the future. In some cases, what is missing is the students' ability to recognize the connection between effort exerted and success achieved in current and subsequent acquisition of knowledge. Generally, we notice an increase in this problem at three critical points in students' academic careers where the ability-driven self-concept leads to academic difficulties. The problem initially surfaces in grades 3 or 4, resurfaces at grades 7 and 8, and finally reappears during freshman year in college. At each of these pivotal points, the workload begins to increase beyond the amount of effort put forth, and what is being taught is increasing in cognitive complexity beyond basic memorization. Our observations indicate that three common factors are present in many of these students: (1) a lack of appropriate study habits; (2) little educational stamina; and (3) inappropriate skill sets for their current situations. Due to the underdevelopment of these three factors, the concept of sustained and appropriate effort, along with the needed metacognitive skills, escapes these students. Students in this situation with high average ability or even above-average ability share a common outlook. They believe that they do not have to work hard and diligently to succeed. Until this point, all of their successes have come to them without much effort. These students have been lulled into a false sense of ability-driven success by limited academic demands.

It is often surprising to hear about the number of students who believe that they should automatically understand a topic—as if all areas of study can be intuitively understood after a lecture or a cursory reading of a text. This attitude exemplifies entity learners as described by Dweck. In one discussion, a student explained to us that he was deeply disappointed with his grades on a science and mathematics assignment. He was equally disappointed with his teachers' responses when they suggested that he needed to work harder and allocate some time for homework. Even more troubling to him were the responses by his parents who implied that he was lackadaisical and not working to his full potential. To our student, this did not make sense. In his estimation, he studied a great deal. The student also believed that if his teachers and parents knew that he studied diligently and still performed poorly, they would reason that he does not have the ability to succeed. The very idea of being labeled incapable was a threat to his self-image. The student told us that he prepared for a test by cramming for at least two days, for a total of at least five or six hours. Based on the outcome of his efforts, the student felt both disappointed and inept. The student's developing perception is that the content of science and mathematics is beyond him. After all, he studied hard but still failed.

It is crucial to realize a dynamic at work among effort, expectancy, and value of the task that can increase or decrease future chances of success. Neither the teachers nor the parents helped the student make the appropriate effort attribution for his poor performance. The teachers and the parents believed that the student put forth little or no effort. Clearly, the student did study, but he did not study in a manner that maximized his efforts and improved his chances of success. What is of interest to us is the student's comments. He insisted, "I studied like we do in class before a big test." He further explained that "before all big tests, we forget whatever is being taught, and just focus on what's on the test—only the important stuff." This scenario is repeated countless times in every subject by a large percentage of the average student population. The aspect of learning that is often neglected is the value and significance of active studying over an extended period of time and its link to proficiency. Many students believe that if there is no written assignment, then there is no homework, either. In addition, long-term projects in which students become engrossed in the content have been eliminated for other assignments that stress superficial mastery. In doing so, we have neglected to inform our students that there is no real shortcut to obtain expertise—or at the very least, proficiency—in a particular subject. It is clear that students, teachers, and parents are focused on performance goals, not necessarily learning goals. The student's philosophy is more aligned with an entity mind-set that is being reinforced by environmental and sociological factors.

As entity learners, many students see no benefit to studying diligently and putting in long-term effort, because they believe it is their innate ability that makes success possible. A mind-set exists for these students who think that if they have to work hard, then they must not be very intelligent. When students with the entity philosophy or mind-set do not succeed, they need to develop a way to preserve their self-concept. Some students simply stop trying in order to blame their failure on their lack of effort rather than lack of ability. These students may also fall victim to learned helplessness, a belief that can occur with repeated failure due to misapplied effort or developmentally inappropriate curriculum. Attribute theory reminds us that all excuses and actions are designed to preserve the student's self-concept, even if the actions are counterproductive to achievement.

The Incremental Mind-Set

The second category, the incremental mind-set, refers to a belief in intelligence as something that can be increased through effort. This may be carried out by studying, practicing, and working hard. These students are learner centered and will seek out challenging tasks in order to improve their skills. Dweck identifies students with this mind-set as incremental theorists and suggests that they will have the best chance at overall success. Incremental learners are more inclined to establish what are recognized as learning goals and exert reasonable effort in an attempt to master the objectives of a particular activity. They believe that competence is the outcome of working through difficult problems in a variety of activities, and they exhibit a positive disposition toward effort and achievement. Incremental learners attribute effort as the cause of success or failure and are aware that increasing their effort usually improves their chances for success. Students with this mind-set can be recognized by their can-do attitude, and they use this determination to set mastery learning goals when engaging in a task. They also learn from their mistakes and continue to work beyond occasional obstacles, aware that a degree of failure is a part of learning. The attributes of the incremental learner are aligned with students who participate in Intel science competitions, world piano competitions, competitive athletics, mathematics and science Olympiads, writers' workshops, political science clubs, or debate teams. The vast majority of these students who engage in long-term projects due to self-interest and initiative usually have some kind of a support system. The external support may come from parental encouragement, school services, mentorships, or internships. The skills and abilities of the incremental learner closely align with students who are identified as high ability and who already have the additional option of specialized academic services.

Current research has demonstrated the deleterious effects of ignoring learning goals by fostering achievement based solely on performance goals. Although this method supports the achievement motivation of entity learners, no educational reforms have yet addressed the advancement of the more stable, effort-based incremental learner (Dweck, 1986, 2006; Dweck & Elliott, 1983; Perkins, 1992). We wonder whether the schools are prepared to foster incremental learning strategies for the average learner. Is the U.S. Secretary of Education ready to put learning goals before performance goals in order to change the attitudes about learning, knowledge, and success? It is evident from the research that performance goals are more closely aligned with entity learners and that the type of understanding that performance goals foster is fragile, as it is based on perceived ability, and misapplies the role of effort, expectancy, and task value on long-term success.

THE AMERICAN SCHOOL MODEL OF SUCCESS: CONFRONTING SELF-FULFILLING PROPHESIES HEAD-ON

Unquestionably, the belief that student ability is the primary means of success constitutes the overall philosophy of the American school model. Accordingly, this philosophy places the average student at a great disadvantage and even at risk. In order to benefit average students, American society must reconsider ability as the primary means of success and shift to student effort, along with average ability, as the primary means of success. Unfortunately, in many educational circles, effort is considered a secondary or even an inferior cause of success. In fact, numerous constituents of school districts use the term "overachievers" pejoratively to describe average students who demonstrate above-average success. The term "overachiever" is edu-speak for students who are perceived as not being innately smart but who work extremely hard to achieve success. The underlying message is that success should be easy and that the persistence attribute that promotes a work ethic somehow devalues the achievement. We argue that the myth of overachievement as an endeavor only suited to average students must be dispelled immediately if we are to improve students' levels of expertise in all the subject areas.

Researchers in cognitive psychology and creativity have often alluded to what is known as the 10-year rule: the idea that expertise in any specific academic domain requires students to engage in intensive practice and study in that domain for at least 10 years—or more than 10,000 hours—in order to reach "expert" status. The 10-year rule seems to be supported by research on the works of lifelong composers such as Bach and Mozart, whose music ranged from "excellent" during the formative years to "outstanding" or "sublime" during the apex years (Hayes, 1981). This rule also applies to expertise in academic subjects, such as mathematics (Gustin, 1985), chess (Chase & Simon, 1973), medicine (Patel & Groen, 1991), as well as expertise in various types of sports. It should be clear, then, that the well-known 10-year rule for honing expertise should call attention to the outright fallacy of construing overachievement as a sign of intellectual weakness and so-called innate intellectual ability as an asset.

Further, the ability philosophy does not benefit the average student, because it suggests that success is predetermined and establishes a self-fulfilling prophesy, implying that success is not possible without above-average ability. Research has demonstrated that teachers, parents, and students form, communicate, and respond to expectations (Alexander, Entwistle, & Thompson, 1987; McLoyd, 1998; Rosenthal & Jacobson, 1968). Powerful examples of the effects of individuals' preconceived beliefs on the outcome of an experiment has been demonstrated by the Westinghouse Study, Pygmalion in the Classroom, and countless others. A classic experiment by Robert Rosenthal (1966), a former professor of social psychology at Harvard University, demonstrated how a self-fulfilling prophesy can be established. In one particular assignment, Rosenthal's students were asked to train rats. However, one group of students was told that it was working with "bright" rats, and the other group was told that it was working with "dull" rats. Students were not told that both groups of rats were essentially the same in terms of their cognitive levels. Despite this, the outcomes in the experiment were quite different. The group with the "bright" rats spent more time with the rats than did the group with the "dull" rats. The group working with the "bright" rats reported better performance, found their rats to be more pleasant, and treated their rats better than the group working with the "dull" rats (Rosenthal & Fode, 1963). This finding mirrors the results of investigations of middle-class teachers and their treatment of students from lower socioeconomic situations. Similar to the actions and attitudes of the students working with the "dull" rats, the teachers' actions and attitudes were manifested in behaviors that alienated students under these circumstances by also providing little attention, less challenging work, and less overall interaction (Alexander, Entwistle, & Thompson, 1987; McLoyd, 1998; Rosenthal, 1994). From Rosenthal and others, a number of general principles have been observed regarding expectations. It seems natural that people form expectations. However, as soon as they are formed, expectations appear to be self-sustaining and take on a life of their own. In cases such as with overachievers, teachers needed to create a term to justify their inaccurate initial perception of average students' abilities. These students did not conform to their teachers' expectations. Rather, they exceeded them. In short, people do not like to be wrong. There is a sense of comfort in being right, and it has been reported that teachers enjoy students more when they meet our expectations. In fact, teachers report liking students more if they match their expectations, regardless of whether those expectations were high or low.

There is an extensive body of research on the self-fulfilling prophesy and how teachers both overtly and covertly communicate their expectations to students. Work by Jere Brophy (1982, 1983, 1987) and others have reported on the differential treatment of students based on perceptions of the students' abilities. Brophy reports that students who are not perceived as academically advanced are given less attention, fewer opportunities to answer questions, inappropriate feedback, praise for lower-level work, less constructive follow-up to correct failing situations, less wait time (pausing after a question to allow students to formulate an answer), highly critical evaluations, and are seated farther from the teacher. Although a degree of controversy still surrounds some of the original work in the self-fulfilling prophesy, it is difficult to be skeptical of the results achieved in the lower elementary grades. Teacher expectations may not always come to fruition, but the "existence of a teacher expectation for a particular student's performance increases the probability that the student's performance will move in the direction expected, and not in the opposite direction" (Brophy, 1982, p. 8). Other researchers have demonstrated that more positive performance can be obtained by increasing expectations and providing the appropriate support to reinforce the effort put forth by students in lower socioeconomic situations (Midgley, Eccles, & Feldlaufer, 1991; Midgley, Feldlaufer, & Eccles, 1989; Phillips, 1997).

When teachers and others expect little or nothing, they will usually receive it in abundance. Therefore, a better fit for the average student is to exchange ability for effort, placing ability as a secondary cause of success. The effort philosophy suggests that a good dose of effort and persistence combined with average ability can produce extraordinary performance. This is possible and has been demonstrated in a number of contemporary examples such as Jay Matthews's *Escalante: The Best Teacher in America* and the work of Marva Collins at the Westside Preparatory School in Chicago. In each of these examples, the teachers had high expectations, confidence, and work ethic, which they conveyed to their students.

From School to Home

Parents are children's first teachers and as such must convey the appropriate messages regarding learning to their children. Their attitudes and beliefs can have an incredible impact on students' school achievements (Eccles, Adler, & Kaczala, 1982). Parents often have many ideas regarding why their children succeed or fail. Parents with average children often attribute their children's successes to ability and effort and failures to task difficulty and luck. Later work in attribution theory suggests that parents recognize a stronger separation between ability and effort, but many parents still believe that the reasons for their children's failures are due to task difficulty and, to some extent, luck. These attitudes have remained relatively stable over the years and do not promote an effort mind-set. Parents who hold these beliefs instill a message in their children that success may be beyond their control and that success is more a function of chance.

Although it is often difficult to generalize about cross-cultural comparisons, findings from studies between the parents of Japanese students and American students are important in understanding attributional theory and its relationship to success. Japanese parents and teachers believe that with enough effort, all students will succeed, and if a child is not achieving, he or she is not trying hard enough. American parents and teachers believe that if a child is not succeeding, it is either due to the difficulty of the subject or the child's lack of affinity toward the subject. In the United States, we look at ability as the cause of success or failure, where in many other nations, the cause of success and failure is more closely associated with effort.

The literature is replete with differential expectations of parents for their children. Parallel to the attitudes and expectations of teachers, parental expectations can also limit or increase the success of their children. The greatest differences in parental expectations are by gender, and different educational goals are established for sons and daughters. Eccles, Adler, and Kaczala (1982) write that "children's attitudes are influenced more by their parents' attitudes about their children's abilities than by their own past performances" (p. 320). In support, Eccles, Adler, and Kaczala (1982) also report that "parents of sons compared with parents of daughters felt that math was more important than other subjects for their child. . . . Parents of daughters felt that their child's general school performance was better than parents of sons, and fathers of daughters rated both English and American history as more important for their children than fathers of sons" (p. 316). Again, a self-fulfilling prophesy may be at work between parental attitudes toward a daughter's ability and the daughter's perceptions of appropriate success in a particular subject. Attribution research maintains that girls think that they have to try harder than boys to succeed in quantitative subjects, even though they spend equivalent time and effort on such tasks (Eccles, Adler, Futterman, Goff, Kaczala, Meece, & Midgely, 1980, 1983). The effect of parental bias appears to have a clear impact on young girls' perceptions of appropriate courses to take and the difficulty of those courses (Farenga & Joyce, 1999). Parental values and expectations for success may serve to mediate the indirect influence of other factors such as self-concept and career choices. The effect of the stereotype that emerges for average young girls is double that of young boys, for girls may fall victim to the general bias against average students as well as a gender bias, which is well documented by a number of research findings. This is readily observed in subjects such as mathematics and science, where some parents still foster a double-standard in regard to the importance of studying mathematics and science for their sons and daughters.

5

The Right Start in Reading and Writing: The Development of Language and Literacy

And so to completely analyze what we do when we read would almost be the acme of a psychologist's achievements, for it would be to describe very many of the most intricate workings of the human mind.

—Edmund Burke Huey (2008)

Learning to read and write may be the single greatest intellectual achievement of anyone's lifetime. Acquiring the ability to make sense of printed symbols and to use those symbols to make meaning and to communicate has its beginning in the home, and the parent or caregiver is a child's first teacher. Between the time of their birth and their entry into first grade, children gain significant facility with language. By age six, a child has developed control over a complex system of communication.

LANGUAGE

Language exists to convey, expand, and comprehend meaning; it exists so that humans can communicate. Language has been studied, researched, and debated by the great minds of science, among them linguists and anthropologists Edward Sapir and Benjamin Lee Whorf, psychologists Rudolf Arnheim and Jean Piaget, and linguist Noam Chomsky. Chomsky's work showed that every human has an innate capacity for language learning—a language instinct. Eve Clark, David Crystal, Stephen Pinker, and M. A. K. Halliday continue to inform us about language and how it is acquired.

Language may be best defined as a formal system of sounds and symbols and the rules that govern them for the formation, expression, and comprehension of meanings, thoughts, and feelings. Every major language has five component systems: the phonological system (speech sounds), the orthographical system (written symbols), the morphological system (words and word parts), the syntactic system (sentences), and the semantic system (meaning).

The phonology of a language is comprised of the speech sounds used to communicate. English is thought to have about 40 distinct phonemes depending on one's dialect or accent. Is the vowel sound heard in *Don* the same as that in *Dawn*? In some dialects, it is. Do you hear one, two, or three different phonemes in the first syllable of *Mary, marry,* and *merry*? Contrasted with our use of about 40 phonemes to conduct all communication, some languages use many fewer and some many more. Crystal (2005) found that "Rotokas, in the Pacific Islands, has only 11. By contrast !X in southern Africa has 141" (pp. 66–67). So languages vary as to which speech sounds matter.

Spoken language in one form or another has been in use for at least 50,000 years. Recent research suggests that the first human language began with the Hadza and Khosian people of eastern and southern Africa (Wade, 2003). Writing systems are much more recent inventions. Altmann (1997) wrote, "The advent of the written word must surely rank, together with fire and the wheel, as one of mankind's greatest inventions" (p. 160). There are more than 6,000 distinct languages spoken on Earth, but only about 10 percent of them have writing systems, and 95 percent of the world's population speaks fewer than 100 of these languages. Twenty percent of the world's population speaks one language—Chinese.

The orthography of a language—the writing system—relates to the phonology of a language but not directly. English uses 26 letters to represent in varying ways the 40 phonemes. In addition, our writing system uses 11 different punctuation marks plus a space and several logograms (e.g., $, @, &, %, #). It is through these letters, punctuations, and logograms that written language represents oral language. English lacks uniformity in the relationship between letters and sounds. Some letters represent several sounds (e.g., the letter *a* in *at, tale, call, father, away*), and some phonemes can be represented by several letters or letter combinations (e.g., the *a* sound in *play, pain, stake, steak, neighbor, gauge, they*). The hundreds of letter/sound relationships add to the difficulties children experience learning to read and write English. This can be seen with such word pairs as *break/speak, paid/said, five/give, how/low, though/enough.*

The morphology of a language involves the structures of words and word parts and includes how words are formed. Thousands of English words are created through morphological rules that give us compound words (e.g., *blacktop*), words with prefixes (e.g., *rewrite*), words with suffixes (e.g., *helpful*), grammatical conversions (e.g., the noun *paper* becomes a verb in "to *paper* a room"), inflections (e.g., *faster*), possessives (e.g., *Deanna's* car), word blends (e.g., *infomercial*), clipped words (e.g., *burgers*), abbreviations (e.g., *CPR, FEMA*), and other types of word formations.

The syntax or grammar of a language helps us know that "The dog ran down the hill" makes sense, but "Hill dog down the ran the" makes no sense. The syntactic system of a language, once internalized, enables us to create sentences we never have spoken before and be understood by others. Syntactic rules enable us to understand what others say. By age 18 months, most children begin to utter two-word sentences, "Bring blankie"; by age 2 the sentences are three or four words in length, "Ebony hide ball"; and by age 3, questions are formulated as well as sentences with more than one clause, "That more better cause the water warm." For most children, acquiring grammatical constructions continues until about age 10 or 11, the intermediate grades.

The semantics, or meaning system, of a language embraces its vocabulary and morphology but also the nuances and variations of words used in particular situations. Semantics includes such figurative language as similes, metaphors, personification, idioms, slang, and catchphrases. Semantics incorporates the different functions that language plays for different purposes (e.g., to satisfy needs, to influence others, to explore and find out, to inform, to interact with others, to express oneself, to imagine). All five systems of language are developing during the preschool years with parent or caregiver.

Oracy is the spontaneous process of learning to listen and speak, and literacy is the educational process of learning to read and write. Oracy is acquired naturally, but literacy must be taught—even though the two are inextricably intertwined. Every physically and mentally healthy child learns how to speak, but a great many children and adults never master written language. As early as 1874 in *The Descent of Man*, Charles Darwin stated that humans have "an instinctive tendency to speak, as we see in the babble of our young children; while no child has an instinctive tendency to write" (cited in Pinker, 1994, p. 20). In summary, parents or caregivers who want to help their children acquire language will have the greatest challenge with the development of literacy—the ability to read and write—the major focus of this chapter.

LANGUAGE DEVELOPMENT

Children do not wake up on their first birthday and begin speaking. The groundwork for language skills starts to be laid practically from birth. Consider the monumental tasks children must accomplish in the five or six years before they enter school. They need to recognize and eventually produce all of the phonemes of their first language. Young children must learn hundreds of ways of combining these sounds to form the words they utter and to comprehend the words they hear. Estimates of the number of words children learn before they enter school at age 5 or 6 average about 14,000 (Clark, 1993).

Young children hear and utter hundreds of syntactical (i.e., grammatical) constructions, and they internalize the rules that permit these constructions, although they are not aware of those rules. Children learn the elements of phonology, morphology, and syntax simultaneously and naturally. As they acquire the semantic system of their language, children learn that many words have more than one meaning—some words have many meanings (e.g., *set* has 464 meanings, *run* has 396 meanings, *take* has 343 meanings, and *stand* has 384 meanings) (Ash, 1995). They must learn that some meanings are represented by different words called *synonyms* (e.g., *thin, skinny, lean*). Children learn ways to initiate a conversation, to listen to another person, and to hold a person's attention. Children learn that some words that parents and adults use are taboo for them. Beginning with uttering their first word at about age 1 and learning about 10 new words a day by age 2, many children have developed surprisingly sophisticated conversational skills by the time they enter school.

The important role of parents, caregivers, siblings, and others in the language development of preschool children cannot be overstated. The verbal interactions between adult and child affect the quantity and rate of vocabulary growth, speaking ability, and syntactic sophistication. The existence of a human predisposition to language learning—the natural instinct—is nurtured by plentiful and rich oral interactions. The essentiality of adult-child verbal interaction to language development is well documented (Snow, Burns, & Griffin, 1998).

The window for easy "natural" language acquisition, especially syntactic development, may begin to close by early adolescence (Lenneberg, 1967), and there is evidence that in a few unusual situations in which children *were not* exposed to language before their teens, the children never learned more than fragments of language (Ingram, 1992).

After children begin to absorb and produce their first words at about age 1, the pace picks up rapidly, and they may produce up to 200 different words by 18 months and 500 different words by age 2, but this pace varies from child to child. Some infants produce only one word at a time for several months, but others seem to use two-word utterances shortly after their first words.

In a research study conducted by psycholinguist Eve Clark (1993), a two-year-old child was able to produce 477 words, of which two-thirds were labels for objects. The array of words learned by this child included 18 words for people (e.g., *baby, boy*), 25 words for animals (e.g., *duck, mouse*), 18 words for vehicles (e.g., *bike, sled*), 14 words for body parts (e.g., *toe, nose*), 35 words for toys (e.g., *block, doll*), 14 words for clothing (e.g., *sock, button*), 12 words for furniture (e.g., *rug, bed*), 18 words for utensils (e.g., *spoon, bowl*), 31 words for food (e.g., *egg, carrot*), 24 words for attributes (e.g., *big, wet*), and 74 words for activities (e.g., *go, fall*). The child also used words for locations, routines, and responses. Children gradually progress from naming and categorizing to differentiating words within and across categories (e.g., *dogs and horses have a tail and four legs, but dogs bark and horses neigh*).

FAMILY FACTORS THAT MAY INHIBIT LANGUAGE DEVELOPMENT

Language development continues in the home and in the early and later school years as children acquire the ability to read and write and to comprehend and produce language in ever more polished and mature ways. There are a number of family-based factors that can delay language development, and among them is a family history of difficulty with language. Children whose older siblings or parents have had problems with reading and writing often have the same problems.

The literary environment of the home is a major contributor to language development and, in particular, the development of literacy skills. Jennings, Caldwell, and Lerner (2006) cite research showing that in comparison with poor readers, good readers are much more likely to have a favorable family environment. The most important factor in the home is the quantity and quality of verbal interactions between parents or caregivers and children. It is through these interactions that vocabulary and oral language facilities develop. Shared conversations and reading to and with children contribute to subsequent literacy development. Children reared in homes without such verbal interactions and without a value placed on literacy (e.g., reading materials in the home, trips to local libraries, parents or caregivers who are readers) are at a disadvantage throughout their school years (Jennings, Caldwell, & Lerner, 2006).

A major home-based factor that influences language development of children is the socioeconomic status of the family. Children whose families have low incomes are more likely to lack proper medical care, dental care, and adequate nutrition. Low-income families have limited resources for such items as books, children's magazine subscriptions, electronic devices that facilitate literacy, and other types of support enjoyed by children from families with higher incomes. Low-income families often are one-parent families—usually headed by the mother—who have less time for verbal interaction because of the stresses of coping with poverty and the demands of working two or more minimum-wage jobs. As a result, low-income children typically learn fewer words and language conventions than children from middle- or high-income families. Vocabulary, spelling, comprehension, and composition skills lag behind those of more affluent children (Johnson, Johnson, Farenga, & Ness, 2005).

READING AND WRITING: WHAT THE RESEARCH SAYS

In the century since Edmund Burke Huey published his observations about the complexity of the seemingly simple task of reading, tens of thousands of research studies have been conducted that examine aspects of reading and writing. From the mountain of research data, research analysts have been able to reduce the major findings to a large handful. Braunger and Lewis (2006) identified 13 "core understandings about reading." They are:

1. Reading is a construction of meaning from text. It is an active cognitive and affective process. (p. 59)
2. Background knowledge and prior experience are critical to the reading process. (p. 60)
3. Social interaction is essential at all stages of reading development. (p. 62)
4. Reading and writing are reciprocal processes; development of one enhances the other. (p. 64)
5. Reading involves complex thinking. (p. 65)
6. Environments rich in literacy experiences, resources, and models facilitate reading development. (p. 67)
7. Engagement in the reading task is key in successfully learning to read and in developing as a reader. (p. 72)
8. Children's understandings of print are not the same as adults' understandings. (p. 75)
9. Children develop phonemic awareness and knowledge of phonics through a variety of literacy opportunities, models, and demonstrations. (p. 77)
10. Readers learn productive strategies in the context of real reading. (p. 90)
11. Students learn best when teachers employ a variety of strategies to model and demonstrate reading knowledge, strategy, and skills. (p. 94)

12. Students need many opportunities to read, read, read. (p. 123)
13. Monitoring the development of reading processes is vital to student success. (p. 129)

Daniels and Zemelman (2004) also analyzed the research and drew 10 "major conclusions from six decades of reading research" that pertain to adolescent students in middle and high school. They are:

1. Kids should read a wide range of materials in all classes.
2. Students should read for the same purposes as literate adults, both for information and pleasure. A sense of purpose is key to reading success.
3. Students need to read a lot; volume, quantity, and practice count.
4. Students should read plenty of books and articles written at a comfortable recreational, not frustration level.
5. Kids need genuine choice of reading materials: at least half of what they read should be self-selected, based on interest and curiosity.
6. The classroom should become a reading community, a group of people who regularly read, talk, and write together.
7. Teachers must help students develop a repertoire of thinking strategies to handle challenging texts and guide students to be increasingly aware and in charge of their own thinking processes.
8. Students should engage in frequent interdisciplinary inquiries, projects, and, where possible, entire interdisciplinary courses to explore topics in depth.
9. Students of all ages need to hear powerful writing in performance— reading aloud by the teacher and other students, dramatic interpretation, audio books, and so forth.
10. Adolescent students need opportunities to connect with the adult literate community, starting with teachers as readers who generously share their reading lives with kids. (p. 252)

The overlap in the two interpretations of what constitutes "core understandings" or "major conclusions" from the research is apparent. Both lists cite the need for rich literacy environments with a lot of material to read, reading materials of all kinds and on all topics. Reading improves through reading, so plentiful reading is encouraged. The importance of building communities of readers and writers to read, write, and talk together is advantageous. Any type of learning, including reading, requires the learner to relate new knowledge to prior knowledge; therefore, building experience and prior knowledge is critical with all learners. Reading and writing are supportive processes, and the development of one enhances the development of the other. Components of the reading process such as being able to hear the differences in speech sounds (phonemes) and to understand the relationships between print and speech are essential.

WHAT YOUNG CHILDREN KNOW

Preschool

Preschool children acquire an enormous amount of language. They understand and use in their speech a rapidly increasing number of words. In their first three or four years, they develop all systems of language at an astonishing speed. Development continues during the preschool years and into elementary and secondary schooling, "but they will never again acquire language at such a dizzying pace as during their first three or four years" (Barchers, 1994, p. 33).

Most preschool children, however, do not learn to comprehend or produce the written forms of language, except for very common words, such as the names of people they know, words on signs and buildings, and a few others. Learning to read and write for most children does not get fully under way until they enter school. There they may be taught using a "top-down" approach that begins with children's stories and focuses on meaning from the start, teaching words and phonics in the context of real stories. Or they may be taught with a "bottom-up" approach, which begins with building speech sounds and spellings into words and words into sentences and stories. Most elementary teachers pick and choose from both methodologies to meet the needs of their students. Regardless of the type of instruction provided in the school, the accomplishments listed below are achieved by most children at the grade levels indicated. Research reviewed by Snow, Burns, and Griffen (1998) and Johnson and Johnson (2005) suggests that these abilities may be considered benchmarks against which parents or caregivers can compare the performances of their children.

A Checklist for Parents

Kindergarten. *Kindergarten children*

- follow a line of print when being read to;
- notice when pages have been skipped by the reader;
- listen attentively when someone else is reading;
- retell stories in some detail;
- make predictions while listening to stories;
- recognize and name some letters of the alphabet;

- use unconventional writing and invented spellings to express meanings;
- write their own names;
- answer questions about stories correctly;
- identify differences in speech sounds; and
- know some books by their titles.

First grade. *First grade children*

- read age-appropriate books aloud;
- recognize—in print—300 or more words;
- understand simple written instructions;
- spell some short words correctly;
- use some punctuation and capitalization;
- answer questions about materials they have read; and
- write readable short sentences and short paragraphs.

Second grade. *Second grade children*

- comprehend age-appropriate fiction and nonfiction;
- read voluntarily;
- reread sentences to clarify meaning;
- contrast characters and events in stories read by others;
- attend to spelling and punctuation when revising their writing;
- compare information from different sources;
- read irregularly spelled words; and
- pose answers to *why, how,* and *what if* questions.

Third grade. *Third grade children*

- correctly spell previously misspelled words;
- point out words or phrases that cause difficulties in comprehension;
- read aloud with fluency (i.e., accurately and expressively) from grade-appropriate books;
- distinguish between facts and opinions;
- write paragraphs with clarity after revision;
- share writing with others;
- infer word meanings from surrounding context;
- make inferences about unstated information; and
- read longer chapter books and nonfiction works.

Intermediate and upper grades (4–8). In the intermediate and upper grades, listening, speaking, reading, and writing become increasingly more integrated and mutually reinforcing. Language and literacy development centers on four broad purposes. Older children use language for:

- gaining information and understanding;
- literary response and expression;
- critical analysis and evaluation; and
- social interaction.

Based on reviews of research and analyses of the expectations of state standards in literacy, Johnson and Johnson (2005) prepared a summary of intermediate and upper-grade children's language and literacy development related to the four broad purposes. They wrote that intermediate and upper-grade students:

- develop skill in note-taking, summarizing, categorizing, and organizing information;
- distinguish between relevant and irrelevant information;
- acquire facility with the writing process;
- learn to identify important literary elements such as foreshadowing, symbolism, metaphor, and irony;
- read aloud with expression to convey the meaning and mood of a work;
- write poems, stories, and essays that show increasing sophistication;
- become adept at presenting personal interpretations of literature;
- learn to evaluate information, ideas, and language usage in advertisements, editorials, documents, and reviews;
- come to understand bias and propaganda used in speeches and writings;
- present clear analyses of ideas, events, and issues, and support their positions through reasoning;
- learn to express themselves clearly in group discussions and conversations;
- learn to use language and style that are appropriate to the situation and audience; and
- develop skills in writing personal letters, invitations, greetings, and electronic messages to acquaintances, relatives, and friends.

STRATEGIES FOR PARENTS AND CAREGIVERS

Most children develop proficiency in oral language before entering school, and that development continues to be refined and expanded throughout the school years. Literacy does not come so easily, and sizeable numbers of children—and adults—learn to read and write with great difficulty. This highlights the importance of parents or caregivers working closely with their children's teachers. Parents might offer assistance when their children are experiencing problems with reading and writing at school. This could include helping their children learn words important to understanding their schoolbooks, helping with sentence constructions, asking comprehension questions, helping with expressive oral reading, and other tasks identified by the teacher or the parent.

Together with conversation, discussion, and other oral engagement with their children, one of the most important things parents can do to help their children with literacy is to make books and other reading materials available in the home. Children's books can be costly, but there are alternatives to buying them. Taking your child to the local library frequently and regularly can provide a steady flow of age-appropriate books into your home. We recommend that you introduce young children to the resources of the public library at an early age. We have great respect for librarians; they are knowledgeable about all kinds of books and reference materials, and they can help you locate almost anything you or your child might want. As soon as possible, each child should have his or her own library card, and as they get older, children can visit the library on their own or with friends. The school library can be a valuable resource as well.

What kind of materials might you look for to help with literary breadth and depth? Dahl (1984) prepared guidelines for selecting children's books based on her many years as an elementary school teacher. The guidelines are as relevant today as they were then.

Guidelines for Selecting Children's Books

Infants and Young Preschool Children (Ages Birth to Three Years)

- Bright, colorful picture books with simple designs and books with sturdy bindings are good choices.
- Counting books with simple objects are often favorites.
- Alphabet books with large, colorful illustrations encourage early recognition of letter shapes and names.
- Short stories about animals and people help children learn values, manners, and good behavior.
- Books with definite rhythm and repeated lines are excellent choices.

Older Preschool and Kindergarten Children (Ages Four and Five Years)

- Wordless picture books offer opportunities for creating stories.
- Fairy tales with excellent illustrations appeal to these children.

- Poetry, nursery rhymes, and Mother Goose should be used frequently.
- Pop-up and other toy books with corresponding puppets, dolls, or other items are favorite selections.
- Books with repeated lines encourage memorization helpful to the development of reading ability.

Primary-Age Children (Grades 1, 2, and 3)

- Easy readers help the child to develop skills being learned at school.
- Riddles, jokes, and nonsense rhymes appeal to children at this age.
- Picture books must have solid story developments and strong characters.
- Nonfiction titles are useful as children begin to develop reference and research abilities.
- Books on "things to do" gain popularity: magic, cooking, drawing, building.
- Books to be read to these children should be above the child's current reading ability level.

Intermediate Children (Grades 4, 5, and 6)

- Each child's individual tastes, hobbies, and interests dictate selections.
- Newspapers, magazines, and paperback books become popular.
- Titles under the heading "modern contemporary realistic fiction" appeal to older children.
- Books that accompany movies or television shows may appeal. (p. 309)

School and public librarians as well as children's booksellers can help you find appropriate materials.

Two books that we recommend for every home with children are age-appropriate, recent editions of both a dictionary and a thesaurus. A good dictionary is used by a reader or listener who wants to look up a word to find its meaning, pronunciation, or usage. A thesaurus is used by a writer or speaker who is looking for a more novel way to express an idea. Dictionaries can rather quickly become dated because of our ever-changing language. A 50-year-old children's dictionary may contain words no longer in use (e.g., *hight*) and would not include words that have entered our language since the dictionary's publication (e.g., *condo, cell phone*).

Research has shown that we grow and learn by relating new knowledge to prior knowledge—but many young people have minimal prior knowledge. By reading to your children, they can visit other lands and cultures; they can learn how other people think; they can visit other periods in history; and they can sample words from other languages. All of this builds their prior knowledge and experience.

All language is oral; therefore, being read to helps a child build understanding of the varied language patterns of English. These patterns become part of a child's subsequent spoken and written language. Read aloud to the child in your care daily or as often as possible. This includes adolescents as well as younger children. There are many reasons to do so. Reading aloud is an effective way to get close to someone. Stories show feelings and emotions—love and dislike, fear and anticipation, sorrow and elation—that we do not always express to our children, but through a common story, we can talk about life and some of its joyous or painful aspects.

Being read to permits the imagination to soar through thoughts of what was, what is, and what could be. It helps expand horizons of good and poor readers by stimulating them to explore the world of literature. There is no better way to introduce children to poetry than through oral reading. Poetry embodies the "melody of language" as Bill Martin Jr. (1966) expresses it, with the rhyme and rhythm of poetic expression.

Reading to children can have a positive impact on writing development. Through listening to oral reading, new vocabulary is learned within context; figurative language (e.g., idioms, similes, metaphors, personification) is experienced; new sentence structures are encountered. These exposures can help children develop into better writers and readers.

It often is said that we learn to read by reading, and we learn the joy of reading by listening to someone read aloud. Throughout this chapter, we have highlighted the value of oral interaction between parent or caregiver and child. What better way to achieve those verbal interactions than through talking about the story being read, its characters, settings, problems, and solutions? What better way to discuss connections between a story and the child's own life experiences than through the medium of a read-aloud story?

To produce oral language and to understand it are the most natural of human activities. But learning to read and write is surprisingly unnatural and difficult. Yet we who can read and write take these feats so much for granted. A child's parent or caregiver, sibling, relative, and friend can play the most important role in nurturing the natural language development that emerges into fluent reading and writing.

6

The Right Start in Mathematics: The Development of Mathematical Thinking

> I thought I am not good enough for physics and I am too good for philosophy. Mathematics is in between.
>
> —George Pólya (2008)

Mathematics is perhaps the first academic subject that we immediately associate with intelligence. As the saying often goes, you're either good at it, or you're not. Unfortunately, many people avoid this subject like the plague. Why such an overwhelmingly negative reaction? There are so many reasons that it is almost impossible to provide an answer within the scope of a book, let alone a single chapter. The body of research on the very broad topic of mathematical avoidance is enormous and comprises a number of subtopics. Some of these subtopics include mathematics anxiety (Richardson & Suinn, 1972; Tobias, 1993), attitudes and conceptions about mathematics (Fennema & Sherman, 1976; Hembree, 1990), learning disabilities in mathematics (Geary, 2004; Macaruso & Sokol, 1998), and mathematics as the filter discipline for career success (Steen, 2004). Indeed, each one of these subtopics can be a single theme of an entire book in its own right.

But people make math out to be a terrifying subject when it is not. Math does not have to be such a dreadful area of study. In this chapter, we argue that with a little ingenuity and perseverance, your child, who you may have subconsciously believed was mediocre at best and below average at worst when it comes to calculation and computation, can actually succeed in math—and even enjoy the subject, too. To show the ease with which one can succeed in mathematics, we start by providing a general overview of the development of mathematical thinking and the emergent cognitive processes by which young children acquire mathematical ideas. We then discuss important math habits that will instill a sense of triumph when your child encounters mathematical topics. Although these habits are crucial during the early years of formal schooling (i.e., kindergarten through fourth grade), it is never too late to practice them in later school years. We then explain the importance of pattern detection and identification as an indispensable activity in succeeding in math. We show this through examples that require thinking (i.e., cognitive) abilities as opposed to the more rote, mechanical pencil-and-paper procedures or algorithms. Without identifying and recognizing patterns and relationships in mathematical problems, it is difficult to inculcate the motivational component of the subject—something that usually demonstrates a challenge for most teachers and parents. We then outline and detail a selection of essential mathematical concepts for parents and students to consider. We argue that these concepts serve as necessary keys to understanding more complex mathematical topics. Some aspects of mathematics may not necessarily be easy, but it is surely a subject that nearly all students can understand, find useful, and learn to enjoy.

EMERGENT MATHEMATICS IN PRESCHOOL

A child might say to his mother on the subway platform: "Mommy, Mommy, the number seven train is coming!" Another child might say to her older sister at a bus stop: "Look, the one-O-four bus is turning the corner." Based on these statements, what does "7" mean to the child on the subway platform, or the number "104" to the girl waiting with her sister for a bus? Does the "number seven" train refer to seven trains? Or perhaps the seventh train that passes by? It means none of these; rather, "seven" refers to a name, a label of something, not the total number of objects. In other words, it does not refer to the cardinal number. The same is true with 104. This number does not refer to 104 buses or the 104th bus that passes by, but rather the name of a particular bus route. In yet another example, we might remember that your friend's phone number is 555-1234. This number does not mean that there are 5,551,233 phone numbers that come before it. Again, a phone number is like the ID of a home, or in the case of a cell phone number, it's a label that identifies the way in which contact can be made with the person who owns a particular phone.

To be sure, during early childhood and primary school, children begin to make sense of their world and learn how to interpret numbers and other mathematical symbols in their environment. It is now clear to mathematics education researchers and practitioners as well as developmental and cognitive psychologists that young children have a profound sense of mathematical ideas before they enter formal schooling (Brush, 1978; Ginsburg, Pappas, & Seo, 2001; Ness, 2002; Ness & Farenga, 2007). Children as young as two and a half develop informal strategies for counting various objects in their environment. Although young children demonstrate a great deal of informal mathematical knowledge that parents are not commonly aware of, evidence of young children's cognitive propensities in mathematical ideas has been documented as early as the nineteenth century. We can see this in the writings of the well-known poet Samuel Griswold Goodrich, who in 1818 realized the ease with which children discover basic arithmetic concepts (Balfanz, 1999). We can also see this nearly fifteen years later in the writings of Warren Colburn, who expanded on Goodrich's observations and argued that young children learn mathematical ideas through inductive (and not deductive) reasoning—unlike formal mathematics instruction—and through everyday experiences. The constructivist-like observations and conclusions of Goodrich and Colburn seemed quite revolutionary for their day.

It is important to realize that children's mathematical abilities are not solely a product of what they learn in formal schooling. Rather, a big part of their mathematical knowledge stems from their everyday knowledge at home and in the world outside of school. In addition, children find ways to become more efficient in their mathematics strategies, with or without the purported benefits of formal schooling. For example, when counting two groups of gummy bears, five in one group and four in the other, children of three or four years might count each and every member—"one, two, three, four, five, six, seven, eight, nine." A child of five or six will find this task taxing and will eventually find a more efficient strategy, such as "counting on," rather than the earlier, more inefficient method of counting all. The process of counting on requires the child to use the larger number of the larger set (five) as the starting point and continue counting from there—"six, seven, eight, nine."

There is a growing body of evidence today that young children spend a great deal of time engaging in activities that promote mathematical thinking. Contrary to general opinion and beliefs about young children, Ginsburg and his colleagues (1999) found that preschoolers engage in mathematical thinking activities nearly 50 percent of the time during everyday free play. Three of these activities—enumeration, magnitude, and patterns and shapes—were shown to be quite prevalent. Moreover, in terms of social class, no significant differences were found among low-, middle-, and upper-class children, nor any significant differences in terms of gender.

Given the great extent of their informal mathematical ability, young children also make calculation errors that often have sensible origins. For example, when counting a group of objects, they might miscount the total number. Another illustrative example is when children approach formal, written subtraction for the first time, possibly in first or second grade. When attempting the problem $23 - 4$, they will often get the incorrect answer of

21. Although the answer is incorrect, the outcome is sensible—clearly, 4 − 3 = 1; in other words, children are taught to take the smaller number away from the larger one. They will then simply drop the 2 down to get 21 as an answer.

Children use a variety of strategies for counting objects, and these strategies generally increase in complexity over time. One of the first things they do when trying to figure out the number of objects in a given set is "push aside." The strategy of pushing aside involves literally pushing or moving each object off to the side as soon as it has been counted. So the child in this case will assign a number word to each object in a set, starting with one and ending with the total number of objects. Although this strategy is the most basic of the counting strategies, its strength is that one does not have to rely on memory during the counting process.

Although informal mathematical thinking is prevalent among young children who do not yet attend formal schooling, it is incorrect to conclude that children's informal mathematical thinking is easy or trivial. This is far from reality. To illustrate, try engaging a group of people during a party or get-together in the following activity. Ask your friends or acquaintances to count to around 22 in different languages—especially if they are fluent in those languages. While someone is counting in a certain language (English is fine, too), have the others listen for any irregularities with sounds and pronunciations of the numbers. For example, if we count to 22 in English we get: "one, two, three, four, five, six, seven, eight, nine, ten, eleven, twelve, thirteen, fourteen, fifteen, sixteen, seventeen, eighteen, nineteen, twenty, twenty-one, twenty-two." One particular inconsistency is related to base-10 structure. The word for "10 + 1" is eleven, not ten-one or one-teen; eleven is a word whose derivation is Old English and literally means "one left [over] after ten" (*ein lib*). Twelve also derives from Old English and literally means ten and two leave—that is, "two left [over]." The phrase "two leave" sounds a bit like the pronunciation of "twelve." In other words, we don't say "ten-two" or "two-teen." But the pattern stops here. Instead, a new pattern emerges from thirteen through nineteen. These numbers are literally associated with the base-10 structure—3 + 10, 4 + 10 . . . 9 + 10. After nineteen, we get twenty, then twenty-one, twenty-two, twenty-three, and so forth. The pattern changes once again. With the numbers 13 through 19, we say the "ones" number first, followed by the "tens" number. After 20, and all the way to 99, the "tens" number is uttered first, then the "ones" number.

As children develop their mathematical thinking, they begin to economize their counting strategies. The disadvantage of pushing aside is that it takes too long to count the total. A more sophisticated method is tagging. The strategy of tagging involves touching (not moving) or pointing to each object as it is being counted. Again, when compared to pushing aside, this strategy is an improvement in terms of counting efficiency. But tagging, too, can get cumbersome and inefficient; it still requires the tallying of each member of a set. As a means of developing counting efficiency, children creatively employ a method known as subitizing, in which they develop immediate recognition of a set's cardinality. Subitizing, a word borrowed from Italian (*subito*), which means "immediately" or "spontaneously," involves a child's eventual ability to recognize the total number of objects in a group fairly quickly. The child's ability to subitize marks the starting point to the more advanced forms of counting members of both sets mentioned earlier—namely, the child's ability to count on, rather than count all. This landmark ability defines the emergence of the addition concept.

We have now identified the general factors that characterize young children's emergent mathematical ideas. Accordingly, we are at the point where we can discuss formal—written, school-based—mathematics, and what parents and teachers can do for children in order to promote and foster a happy, healthy, and successful outlook on the subject of mathematics. We begin this discussion with mathematics habits that are necessary to instill in your child's developing mathematical outlook.

MATH HABITS

Your child's success in math is equally as important as his or her success in reading and writing. In fact, many of the habits that lead to success in language skills are simply variations of those that lead to success in mathematics. Moreover, a number of these habits are more process-related than content-related. We highly recommend that your child learn the following best-practice math habits: saving and organizing math schoolwork; writing neatly and legibly; reading the examples of a topic before jumping into the exercises; using math technology appropriately; making mathematical connections to everyday life; using answers in the back of a textbook correctly; exploring what topic is being covered during the math period; and writing the entire step-by-step procedure to a math problem and not just the answer itself.

Saving and Organizing Math Schoolwork

One of the most important habits that your child needs to acquire is the routine of saving math homework and tests. That's the beginning—and the easy part. The slightly more difficult part is ensuring that the work is organized. To do this, make sure your child dates all work that is assigned for any given day. Moreover, be certain that notes and exams are not crinkled, torn, or in disarray. A messy collection of homework assignments and tests is useless since the whole purpose of having that collection is being able to go back and review the material.

Writing Neatly and Legibly

It is true that famous poets, novelists, composers, mathematicians, and scientists were often sloppy when they put their work on paper, but that was the case for their initial drafts. For most of them, however, the final drafts of their work were scrupulously clear and legible when submitted for publication or used for teaching. In short, your child needs to get into the habit of good penmanship—whether it's for writing an essay or writing a formula in a math problem. Writing math problems neatly is important for a number of reasons. First, sloppy writing contributes to the reader's inability to make sense of what is written. Most teachers who are in the middle of grading a test or homework assignment will not waste another moment on a student whose writing is sloppy—especially if the answer to the math problem is illegible. Second, a student who writes sloppily is more likely to make a careless error in a calculation or an extended problem. And when a student writes too quickly and sloppily, the number of errors or miscalculations increases exponentially. Third, writing legibly from the start serves as a good precedent for success in future grade levels and prepares students for college and the workforce.

Don't Jump into the Exercises

Time and time again, when we ask students what they do when they attempt to complete their math homework, nearly all of them say that they only try to solve the problems assigned for homework. In other words, they don't even consider reading the lesson, examples, or chapter topic in the textbook. As a parent, you must encourage your child to read through the section that is being covered for each homework assignment. Diving into the homework problems is a mistake, especially if your child is rusty with the topic. Some students might find this habit particularly difficult if attempted during the middle or end of a school year. This is due to the sequential nature of teaching and learning mathematical topics; a student who is performing poorly in the middle of the school year may not understand the examples discussed in the textbook section before the homework exercises.

Use Math Technology Appropriately

Calculators and computer software for mathematics can be quite useful but only to a point. Children of any age should begin to use a calculator whenever they are interested in using it or exploring with it. They should not, however, use calculators to complete homework assignments that involve the following mathematics subtopics:

- Number facts: finding the answers to simple operations involving single digits. For example, $1 + 2 =$ ___, $9 - 5 =$ ___, $3 \times 5 =$ ___, and $12 \div 6 =$ ___ are typical number facts. Children must master these facts without the use of technology for a number of reasons. First, a second- or third-grade student who finds these calculations difficult to solve without a calculator will find it all the more difficult to solve related double- or triple-digit problems like $110 + 120 =$ ___, $90 - 50 =$ ___, $300 \times 500 =$ ___, or $120 \div 60 =$ ___—questions they will encounter in later grades. Second, it is important for students to understand why 1 plus 2 is 3, or 9 minus 5 is 4. It's not simply something "to do" or a task to complete. These problems have very practical connections to everyday life. Children must identify the conceptual underpinnings of a math topic before engaging in the more repetitious activity of working out a procedure or formula.
- Multidigit calculations involving the four operations: the purpose of adding 227 to 179 is to learn how to add two numbers whose numerals in the ones (or tens) column exceeds 9. So in this case, $7 + 9 = 18$. What to do next? This very assignment begs the student to learn how to add by carrying additions from the ones to tens place or the tens place to hundreds place. By its very nature, the children's use of a calculator to complete these problems simply defeats the purpose of doing them in the first place.

Make Math Connections to Everyday Life

As parents, it is essential to make connections between what your child is learning in math along with the everyday situations that require skills in math. These everyday situations include but are by no means limited to the following:

- Making sure that the grocery bill is accurate. This implies that you will also help your child calculate sales tax. Below is an example.

  Mr. D. purchases a half-gallon of milk for $4.19, a carton of eggs for $2.25, a loaf of bread for $2.99, six apples for a total of $3.89, and one pound of walnuts for $7.99. He also redeemed a 50-cent coupon for the milk and a 75-cent coupon for the walnuts. The local sales tax is 8.5 percent. If the total bill came out to $23.12, determine whether Mr. D's bill is correct or if the checkout system made an error.

The first thing to do is to find the correct subtotal. This is when you ask your child, most likely an 8 to 13 year old, to use addition and decimal skills to calculate the subtotal—$4.19 + $2.25 + $2.99 + $3.89 + $7.99 = $21.31. In addition, the supermarket charged Mr. D. an extra $1.81 in sales tax. One can determine the sales tax by either multiplying $21.31 by 0.085 (8.5 percent is equal to 0.085) and adding the result to $21.31 or by multiplying the subtotal of $21.31 by 1.085, thereby avoiding the additional step of adding the tax to the subtotal. The grand total, then, is $23.12. But the supermarket overcharged Mr. D. because the coupons weren't deducted. The correct grand total, then, should be: $21.31 (sub-total) − $1.25 (coupons redeemed, leaving a new subtotal of $20.06) + $1.71 (sales tax on $20.06), for a grand total of $21.77. (Teachers in states where coupon deductions are taken after tax has been incurred will have different outcomes. In these states, consumers would multiply $23.13—the subtotal—by the tax rate—1.085, if the state's tax rate is also 8.5 percent—and then subtract the coupon amounts totaling $1.25. The result will be different, namely, $23.85.)

- Measuring the dimensions of your house or apartment. This activity builds measurement skills in which your child learns about two-dimensional measure (i.e., rectangular measure).
- Determining the appropriate height for a shed so that nearby plants will receive adequate sunlight. In this activity, students learn the important everyday uses of trigonometry.
- Helping to budget for an addition to the house.

Use Textbook Answers Carefully

In most math textbooks, answers to exercises are provided in one of the appendices—usually the odd numbered problems. Ensure that your child uses the answer key carefully. The proper way to use the answer key is to first finish the homework assignment, showing all work. As soon as your daughter or son has completed the assignment, she or he may check the answer to verify its accuracy. In other words, don't simply go to the back of the book and copy the answers in order to manipulate the problem to fit the correct answer.

Ask What Is Being Taught in Math

One of the best ways to promote a conducive atmosphere and contextual backdrop for successful experiences with math is to ask your son or daughter to explain what has been discussed in the math classroom. Despite the somewhat cerebral nature of Piaget's theory of intellectual development, we can learn a great deal from his methods of inquiry to help children learn math as well as other subjects. More specifically, we can borrow from his well-known clinical method as a means of helping our children do well in math. In his clinical method, Piaget developed a protocol, which listed a variety of tasks he would use to determine the cognitive abilities of a particular child. Eventually, Piaget would use these outcomes to advance his general theory of intellectual development. Now, we are not asking parents, teachers, and other adults to run clinical interviews with their children. Rather, we are asking parents and others to ask the child questions about his or her math homework that allow him or her to think about how to answer the question correctly—don't simply ask "What's the answer?" or respond with "Yes, that's right," or "No, your answer is wrong."

Write the Procedure—Not Just the Answer

When completing math problems, it is important to avoid "answer-only" completions for several reasons. First, simply writing the answer to a problem without the procedure that precedes it negatively encourages students to produce careless errors. In other words, the written-out procedure supports the answer; if the procedure is not shown, it is much easier to make a computation error. Second, lack of a written-out procedure does not allow students to identify the origin of an answer or how an answer to a problem is derived. Third, lack of procedure contributes to poor study habits in note-taking and sloppiness, which may have negative repercussions when taking tests. In short, homework and in-class math assignments should always include both procedures and answers when answering questions.

FINDING PATTERNS: THE OPTIMAL WAY TOWARD MATH MOTIVATION

Here's an example of how to stimulate students in this notoriously intimidating subject. Examine figure 6.1.

How many squares do you see? One very common answer to this question is 4. Although that's a correct answer, it is not necessarily the only

Figure 6.1.

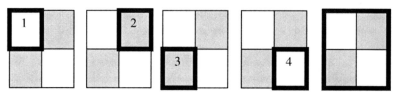

Figure 6.2.

answer. Here's why. Suppose the question was: what is the total number of squares in the diagram? Then one can argue that the figure consists of four small squares, which make up one bigger square—thus, a total of five squares (see figure 6.2).

Let's continue this train of thought with the next example. Suppose our diagram now consisted of the 3 × 3 square shown in figure 6.3. Now how many squares are there? In other words, what is the total number of squares in this diagram? Again, the simple answer is 9. Reason? Because one can simply count the number of small squares. Suppose we told you that the answer to this question is 14. Can you show that we're right? Surely we can include the nine small, 1 × 1 squares, but there are also four 2 × 2 squares. Finally, there is the original 3 × 3 square, for a total of 14 squares altogether (see figure 6.4).

The number of squares can also be determined by adding the number of perfect squares and finding the sum (because the area of a geometric square can be determined by multiplying adjacent sides, it is possible to create perfect squares, such as 1 × 1 = 1, 2 × 2 = 4, 3 × 3 = 9, etc.). For example, the number of squares on a checkerboard can be shown to be 204 by adding 1 + 4 + 9 + 16 + 25 + 36 + 49 + 64.

Solving this type of problem demonstrates the importance of one's exposure to multiple ways of problem solving. A student who is taught in an environment where this kind of problem is commonplace and has the opportunity to practice problem solving in this manner will appear intelligent to an outside observer. One reason why such students appear intelligent is

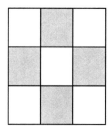

Figure 6.3.

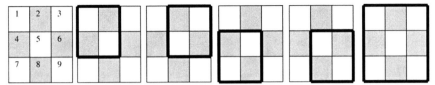

Figure 6.4.

because they have the ability to look at the problem in a more advanced way than students who have not had the advantage or the awareness to go about problem solving in this way. Over a period of time, with continued teaching, the student develops a more advanced understanding of not only the patterns that are intrinsic to mathematics, but the interrelationships of mathematics to other subjects. Simply teaching skills for high-stakes tests usually involves the lowest-level denominators for accomplishment. Contrary to the intent of most teachers, who attempt to teach mathematics in preparation for high-stakes tests, most students are not taught to detect and search for patterns and to think flexibly when attempting a problem. Consequently, they are context-bound and lost when slight variations are made to the same basic problem that they previously may have been able to solve successfully. This explains why the "outstanding" student in mathematics may score below average on these exams. The popular excuse for the outstanding student's low performance is test anxiety. However, our experience suggests that many of these students were not taught early on how to recognize important variations of patterns and how they affect answering the question.

A student quickly learns that there are a variety of ways to solve a problem. This also emphasizes the importance of quality teachers and challenging curriculum. An observation that we have made when instructing students on taking high-stakes tests such as the SATs, GREs, and LSATs is that intelligent students often have difficulties because they have not been taught to examine the problems flexibly and from multiple perspectives. This is most evident when dealing with the analytical sections of these exams. Students generally have greater success in the verbal and quantitative sections. Traditionally, students have been acculturated in an environment of education, which teaches the subskills needed for success in the verbal and quantitative sections of these exams.

Here's a second example using a classroom scenario: suppose a teacher penalizes a naughty student by asking her to find the sum of all the numbers from 1 to 100—in other words, $1 + 2 + 3 + 4 + 5 \ldots 99 + 100 = $ ___ —while the rest of the class does something "fun." This seems quite tedious, and for most people, it would undoubtedly be a grueling, monotonous enterprise. Well, finding the sum of the positive integers from 1 to 100 can be fun, too. How can this be possible? This scenario was allegedly a situation that occurred during the childhood of the famous eighteenth- and nineteenth-century German mathematician Johann Carl Friedrich Gauss. As the story goes, Gauss's teacher asked his students to find the sum of the positive integers from 1 to 100, most likely expecting them to start with 1, add 2 to 1, add 3 to the previous sum of 3, add 4 to the previous sum of 6, and so forth. As expected, Gauss's classmates completed the task in approximately an hour's time. But Gauss did something astonishing: he completed the assignment in approximately one minute! In examining what Gauss did to achieve this amazing feat, let's start off by examining what most of us would do. The typical student would complete this assignment as follows:

Add the first two integers of the series (1 and 2) together: $1 + 2 = 3$

Add the resulting sum (3) to the next next number in the series (3): $3 + 3 = 6$

Add the resulting sum (6) to the next number in the series (4): $6 + 4 = 10$

Add the resulting sum (10) to the next number in the series (5): $10 + 5 = 15$

Add the resulting sum (15) to the next number in the series (6): $15 + 6 = 21$

Add the resulting sum (21) to the next number in the series (7): $21 + 7 = 28$

Repeat this process *93 more times* until you finally add the number 100 to the previous sum: $4,950 + 100 = 5,050$

This method of completing the assignment is problematic for a number of reasons. We'll mention three of them. First, although it seems like good practice for learning the addition algorithm, it's a really boring, monotonous process. It will certainly turn most people off mathematics. Second, it's tedious and time consuming. It will take most students about an hour to accomplish. And third, given that it's quite tedious, it is increasingly possible that a student will make an error in the calculation process. Given the utter monotony of using this method, the likelihood of making a mistake is simply fueling the fire and perhaps increasing most students' feelings of mathematical incompetence. Gauss's method in solving this problem goes like this:

Add the first number in the series to the last number: $1 + 100 = 101$

Add the second number in the series to the penultimate number: $2 + 99 = 101$

Add the third number in the series to the third-to-last number: $3 + 98 = 101$

Add the fourth number in the series to the fourth-to-last number: 4 + 97 = 101

Add the fifth number in the series to the fifth-to-last number: 5 + 96 = 101

As soon as you see the pattern—namely, that all these pairings add to 101, all you need to do is to figure out how many pairings there are. Since half of 100 is 50, then there are 50 pairings! So, 101 × 50 = 5,050, the answer to this seemingly tedious problem. In short, as soon as you understand the pattern, you can solve any type of problem involving series. So, for example, if you were asked to add the positive consecutive integers from 1 to 200, the answer is simply 201 × 100 = 20,100.

This method of solving the problem is fun primarily because students are engaged in detecting mathematical patterns and relationships. It's always more motivating—in whatever you do—when there are patterns to detect or puzzles to solve. Without them, the activity of problem solving gets very monotonous, uninspiring, and simply boring.

IMPORTANT MATHEMATICAL TOPICS TO MASTER

Patterns or not, there are certain topics in which all students should be proficient in mathematics. If they fail to learn them, students run the risk of performing poorly in mathematics not only in middle school and high school, but also in college and, perhaps more important, in everyday experiences and ventures, like ensuring that you weren't overcharged on groceries, understanding the added fees when purchasing a house or car, knowing how much tax to pay on a particular item, or simply figuring out how much an item listed as 30 percent off will cost. The topics that we consider below include place value, percent, and problems concerning triangles.

Place Value

Place value is a topic that is introduced as early as first grade and should be mastered by third or fourth grade. The problem, however, is that it is often not mastered at all. What does it mean to understand the concept of place value? To answer this question, we examine the case of Penelope, a seven-year-old in second grade who is a subject in a clinical interview. The interviewer is both an elementary school teacher and cognitive psychologist.

Teacher: Penelope, I'd like you to find the answer to the problem 14 + 9 and show me your work on this sheet of paper, okay?

Penelope: All right. [*Approximately 2 minutes go by.*] I'm done.

Teacher: Okay, explain to me what you did, Penelope.

Penelope: Well, I added the 4 and the 9 in the ones column, and I got 13, then I added the 1 and the 1 together in the tens column to get 2. So my answer is 23.

At this point, we always ask student teachers-in-training whether Penelope's knowledge of the concept of place value is proficient. More often than not, these soon-to-be teachers will say affirmatively that Penelope "understands" the place value concept. The follow-up question that students are asked to consider is, what is the meaning of "understand." Teacher-education students then begin to consider Penelope's procedural knowledge of place value in comparison to her conceptual knowledge of the subject. The students then realize that although Penelope's procedural knowledge is strong, it is unclear as to whether she has a conceptual knowledge of the subject. To determine her conceptual abilities, the teacher asks Penelope if she can explain the differences between the ones place and the tens place.

Teacher: What does the ones column mean, and what does the tens column mean?

[*Approximately 20 seconds of silence as Penelope attempts to answer this question.*]

Penelope: Well . . . this is the ones column [*correctly points to the ones column*] and this is the tens column [*correctly points to the tens column*].

Teacher: That's fine, Penelope, but I asked you what it means when someone says "ones column" or "tens column." So I'm going to write down the number 13 and you tell me what represents the ones column and what represents the tens column.

Penelope: This is the ones column [*correctly points to the 3*], and this is the tens column [*correctly points to the 1*].

Teacher: Okay, so using these chips [*takes out several black circular chips*], take the number of chips that represents the number in the ones column, then take the number of chips that represents the number in the tens column.

Penelope: Okay. [*correctly takes three chips representing the 3 in the ones column, but mistakenly takes one chip for the 1 in the tens column*].

Teacher: So which set of chips represents 3?

Penelope: This one [*points to the set of three chips*].

Teacher: And which represents the 1?

Penelope: This one [*points to the "set" with only one chip*].

Teacher: Okay. So you're saying that those four chips equals 13.

Penelope: Yeah.

Teacher: But how could 4 be the same as 13?

[*Another 20 seconds pass, indicating that Penelope does not understand the concept of place value.*]

Penelope: Well . . . 1 and 3 make 4. . . .

Teacher: All right, let's do it another way. Take all these chips [*a container with approximately 100 chips*], and take out 13 chips for me.

Penelope: Okay [*correctly takes out 13 chips and lines them up in a row*].

Teacher: Good. So how many chips did you take out?

Penelope: Thirteen.

Teacher: Okay, now I'd like you to separate the number of chips among these 13 chips that represents the number in the ones column, and then separate the number of chips among the chips that represents the number in the tens column.

Penelope: Well, these are the number of chips in the ones column [*correctly takes 3 of the 13 chips*]. And this chip is the number in the tens column [*mistakenly takes 1 of the 10 remaining chips; there are now 9 remaining chips that are unaccounted for among the 13 chips*].

Teacher: All right then. But what are all of those [*points to the nine remaining chips*]?

Penelope: Oh, those are extras. . . .

Teacher: Oh. . . . Okay, those are extra.

In short, Penelope lacks conceptual knowledge of place value. Clearly, her answers reveal a lack of skill and ability in demonstrating a conceptual explanation of the subject. For instance, she was unclear how to connect the number of units represented by the ones place with the number of units represented by the tens place (see figure 6.5). If the tens place represents a single unit in Penelope's mind, then any attempt to teach her to recognize the distinction between "1 + 3" and the number "13" will be futile.

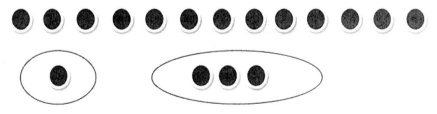

Figure 6.5.

There are a number of ways that teachers can help students overcome obstacles in understanding the place-value concept. One way is through the use of base-10 blocks—one of many manipulatives[1] used for the purpose of teaching mathematical concepts and linking those concepts with the appropriate procedures. Another is through 10-frame tiles (Losq, 2005), another base-10 manipulative.

Two overarching perspectives dominated early education in terms of young children's encounters with mathematical ideas. The first is the belief that children enter formal schooling as blank slates. Those who embrace this outlook on mathematics learning have argued that young children learn passively—and only when they encounter mathematics in the context of school. In some respects, Piaget, too, believed that children fail to reason until a certain point in their development, a point at which they begin to understand mathematical ideas (Baroody & Wilkins, 1999). The second is the perspective that children engage in the learning process actively, be it in mathematics, the sciences, language, or the arts. Those who embrace this perspective believe that young children engage in mathematical activities long before formal schooling and that they spend surprisingly long amounts of time during free play activities in mathematically related activities. Adults who embrace this perspective will have more opportunities to aid children in identifying patterns in arithmetic relationships. Additionally, parents (and teachers) who tap into children's out-of-school informal ideas will often find it easier to motivate these children, because they will be able to make connections between what they know informally and what they are learning in the formal school context. Some of these connections include children's realization that addition and subtraction are inverse operations and their emergent knowledge of addition as a commutative operation. Although children's informal mathematical ideas often contain errors, the basis of these errors often have sensible origins, but they can become aggravated, as seen in the earlier dialogue with Penelope.

How do the concept and the understanding of place value develop? After children master the concepts of addition and subtraction with single-digit numbers, they should then be ready to learn addition and subtraction with small double-digit numbers (i.e., 10 to 20). Questions will often involve part-whole relationships and missing addend problems in which one of the addends is unknown.

Again, one of the best ways to secure knowledge of number facts from 1 to 20 is to be familiar with addition and subtraction concepts. Once again, this can be facilitated through the use of manipulatives. For example, teachers can take color counters and present them on an overhead using a 2 × 5 array also known as a 10-frame tile. Whitenack and her colleagues (2002) demonstrate this activity using seven chips in which one child sees one group of four and a second group of three, while another child sees one group of six along with an additional single chip (see figure 6.6).

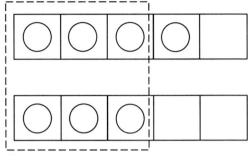

Figure 6.6.

There are many ways that students who have difficulty understanding mathematical concepts can learn about the addition and subtraction of numbers, particularly from 1 to 100. Oftentimes, students need more than just visual aids like overhead slides or book diagrams and pictures to help them learn. Children may also need to use their sense of touch to help them gain understanding of these concepts. To do so, Unifix cubes can be very helpful. Unifix cubes come as unit pieces that can be easily affixed or attached to other unit pieces. Moreover, they come in 10 different colors. So, for example, a student can connect 7 white unit pieces with 6 gray unit pieces and think of the attachment in terms of both addition and subtraction. It is seen as addition because the 6 connected gray Unifix cubes are attached to the 7 connected white Unifix cubes for a total of 13 Unifix cubes. As a subtraction problem, we can learn that the difference between 13 (white and gray cubes combined) and 7 (white cubes) is 6 (gray cubes). Similarly, the difference between 13 and 6 is 7 (see figure 6.7).

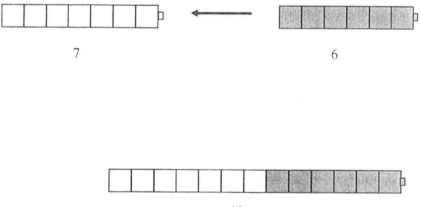

Figure 6.7.

Calculators can also serve to enrich young children's knowledge concepts and number facts regarding addition and subtraction of numbers from 1 to 100. Children can use calculators as a tool to explore of patterns and relationships related to iterations of adding and subtracting the same number from subsequent sums and differences (Huinker, 2002). For example, many calculators have a function that allows users to find repeated sums by repetitively pressing the = button. So, 0 + 6 = = = would yield 6, 12, and 18, respectively. Likewise, 100 − 4 = = = would yield 96, 92, and 88, respectively. It should be emphasized, however, that calculators should not be used at this level merely to find answers to problems for homework or in-class discussion.

For mathematically challenged students, base-10 blocks may not necessarily be the ideal manipulative to foster children's constructions of place value or computations of addition and subtraction problems from 1 to 20. Losq (2005) suggests that 10-frame tiles may be more suitable, especially for special needs students, for a number of reasons. First, this manipulative allows students to become familiar with patterns based on the orientation of dots within each set of 10-frame tiles. This helps with instant recognition of a given number of objects in a set, that is, their ability to subitize (Ginsburg, 1989). The dots in a 10-frame tile are also easier to count than the "longs" or tens piece from a set of base-10 blocks. Ten-frame tiles also demonstrate configurations of dots that are unique to each number. As in the example above, one child might see the number 7 as one group of 4 dots and another group of 3, while another child might see it as one group of 6 dots with an additional dot. Another might see it as 3 less than 10. Ten-frame tiles may also help students learn addition and subtraction concepts and facts. For example, figure 6.8, which was adapted from Losq (2005), shows how students can add 7 and 8 by moving two dots from the set of 7 to the two empty cells in the set of 8.

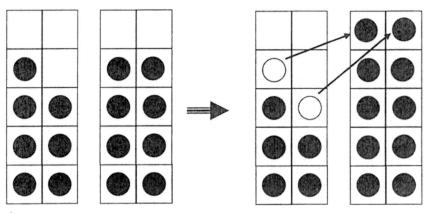

Figure 6.8.

The problem now is presented as 10 + 5, rather than 7 + 8, which may be easier for children to comprehend, given the closer connection with base ten. Ten-frame tiles provide numerous methods of learning subtraction. One method is to subtract 15 dots from 20 cells (20 − 15), eight dots minus seven dots (8 − 7), or ten dots minus five dots (10 − 5). Using this manipulative will also help young children develop an understanding of part-whole relationships, given that they generally have difficulty in solving missing addend problems (e.g., 11 + ___ = 19) (see Baroody, 2003, 2004).

It is also important for parents and teachers to realize that children who have difficulty in emergent calculation problems often have a great deal of difficulty with various mathematical symbols. For example, many children's inability to respond quickly with an answer to the problem 17 − 9 reflects their inability to use arithmetic symbols correctly. In addition to manipulatives, the inclusion of surrogate representations of numerals (e.g., tally marks, dots, words, and the like), along with terms with which young children are familiar, often help students bridge the gap between conceptual knowledge and procedural knowledge (Baroody, 2004). So before children master number facts, they need to first learn the concepts of addition and subtraction—followed by the procedures of addition and subtraction—as well as the concept of place value (Fuson, 1992; Lin, 2005). During the process of learning these topics, children will almost definitely make errors. Perhaps the most frequent error involves regrouping. This type of error demonstrates that a child has little knowledge of both place-value concept and arithmetic procedural knowledge. For example, when asked to find the difference between 23 and 7, the child may conclude that the answer is 24 because 7 − 3 is 4, and the "2" is just "brought down," as shown in figure 6.9.

Among other problems, this error demonstrates that the child does not know the meaning of the 2 in the number 21, hence, a lack of knowledge of place value. This example reflects the scenario presented earlier with Penelope and her teacher.

Percent Problems

If your child often has difficulty with percent problems, you are far from alone. Most people undoubtedly encounter a real-life or in-school situation

$$
\begin{array}{r}
2\ \ 3 \\
-\quad\ 7 \\
\hline
2\ \ 4 \\
\end{array}
$$

Figure 6.9.

that requires solving a percent problem. This type of problem is notorious for being unusually difficult for most individuals struggling with math concepts, but it need not be. In fact, you can have fun with problems involving percentages. The first thing to remember is that a percent is simply the answer (i.e., quotient) to a division problem involving a number divided by 100. For example, 23 percent is simply equal to 23/100. The second thing to keep in mind is that when a percent is placed within the context of "the dreaded word problem," you should convert it into a decimal, such as 0.23, or a fraction, like 23/100. Initially, we will start off easy and work our way up to more complex word problems.

Suppose you are asked to find 23 percent of 200. How do you start it off? Simply convert the percent into a decimal or fraction (as shown above), and multiply the newly converted decimal by 200. So we have $0.23 \times 200 = 46$, the final answer. Another way that you can write it is: $0.23(200) = 46$ (notice the parentheses around the 200 indicate that the numbers are to be multiplied). How do you know you are right? One way is to estimate by thinking of another problem, namely, 25 percent of 200. You might know that 25 percent of 200 is simply one-quarter of 200, or 50. Therefore, 23 percent of 200 will be a bit less than 50, so 46 is an excellent option for an answer. Now, suppose you were shown that 23 percent of a number is equal to 46. In this case, we make "a number" into a variable, say n, and multiply n by 0.23 to equal 46. So, we have: $0.23n = 46$. By doing it this way, we have turned an arithmetic problem into an algebra problem. The key here is to isolate the n—that is, get n alone, all by itself. To do this, we divide both sides of the equation by 0.23 to get the answer. Keep in mind that when we say "both sides of the equation," we should understand that the equal sign ($=$) separates one side of any equation from another. Further, when we say "divide both sides by the same number," we are balancing the equation—that is, making both sides of the equal sign *equal* to one another. If we only divided one side by a number and not the other side, then our math sentence would not show equality, and hence, not be an equation. Back to $0.23n = 46$. When we divide the left side of the equation by 0.23, we are simply left with n, because 0.23/0.23 equals 1, and 1 multiplied by any number is that number, hence we are left with n on the left side. On the right side of the equal sign, we have 46/0.23, which is 200. Therefore, $n = 200$.

Now we can tackle a word problem involving percents: "The Johnsons saved 7 percent of the family income. What was their income last month if they were able to save $539?" To answer this question, we need to do the following:

- Represent the Johnsons's income last month with a variable, n, since that is what we are trying to find. So, $n =$ last month's income for the Johnson family.

- Next, we use last month's income, n, to represent last month's savings, $0.07n$, since the percent savings (0.07) multiplied by income (n) equals last month's savings ($539).
- Next we put it all together into an equation. We write this equation as: $0.07n = 539$.
- We then solve the equation: $n = 7,700$.
- Finally, we need to check whether 7 percent of 7,700 equals 539. It is: $0.07(7,700) = 539$.
- We can conclude that the Johnson's income last month was $7,700

Interpreting Graphs

Another important mathematical skill that all students need to learn in order to succeed on standardized tests as well as in everyday life situations is the ability to analyze data. To do well in data analysis, students must learn how to make sense out of information (i.e., data) that is given to them. This is often accomplished in the form of graphs. The problem with students' encounters with graphs, however, is their frequent inability to interpret them correctly. The following problem is a case in point.

Figure 6.10 indicates the number of puppies that were born from a single dog, Millie, from the years 2002 through 2007. It shows the total number

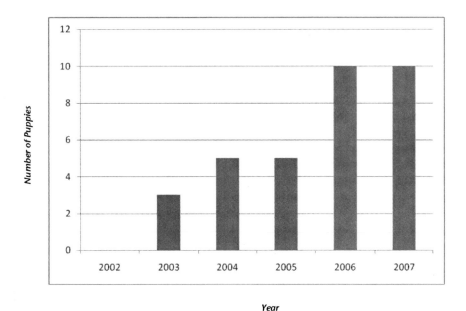

Year

Figure 6.10.

of puppies that Millie has given birth to since 2002. During one particular year in June, Millie gave birth to a litter of quintuplets. In which year were the quintuplets born?

To answer this question, students need to know the meaning of quintuplets. In addition, the inclusion of the month—June—in the problem is important; it places the time of the birth of the five-puppy litter squarely within the year in question. Students often answer this question incorrectly, because those who do know that "quintuplets" refers to five puppies will recognize that five puppies were in fact born by the year 2004—three puppies in 2003 and two in 2004, for a total of five. But these five are not part of a single litter of quintuplets. The year 2005 is also incorrect; during this year, Millie did not give birth to any puppies. The data in 2005 indicate that Millie had a total of five offspring *up to that point in time*, but no puppies were born in that year. The correct answer is that the quintuplets were born in 2006, by which time Millie had a total of 10 offspring.

Knowing and Understanding Key Math Algorithms

This section provides a selection of mathematical algorithms that your child—especially older children—should understand and eventually memorize. Below the name of each theorem or the definition with which each algorithm is associated, we have included everyday applications to these seemingly esoteric symbols. Again, memorize these formulas! It pays off in the long run.

Formula for the Area of a Rectangle

area of rectangle = length × width

It should be effortless to determine the area of a rectangular figure. We do it all the time—finding the area of a room for wall-to-wall carpeting, determining the size of a frame for a painting or photograph, examining the size of one's land property, the list goes on—but many of us don't even know the formal algorithm for figuring it out. Despite the apparent ease with which people determine the area of rectangular regions, it is important that students know how to transfer this everyday knowledge to the standard algorithm for measuring rectangular area.

The Pythagorean Theorem

$a^2 + b^2 = c^2$

In a right angle triangle, a and b are the legs, and c is the hypotenuse (longest side). How does one derive the Pythagorean theorem? The answer is actually simple: Build a square upon each side of the triangle. Next, divide each square into smaller single-unit squares. The number of unit squares for each side of the triangle should be based on the length of each side. So, for example, a right triangle whose sides are 3 units, 4 units, and 5 units will have 3 unit squares, 4 unit squares, and 5 unit squares, respectively. You will notice that the dimension of the small square is 3 × 3 (a total of 9 squares), the mid-sized square is 4 × 4 (16 squares), and the largest square is 5 × 5 (25 squares). If we use the Pythagorean theorem, we have $3^2 + 4^2 = 5^2$ or $9 + 16 = 25$ (see figure 6.11).

Formula for the Area of a Circle

$A = \pi r^2$

It is important to understand the basis for obtaining the area of a circle. The circle and each shape made from sectors of the same circle all have the same area. Students can cut a circle into eight sectors or perhaps even more and rearrange them to form a near-rectangle with dimensions of

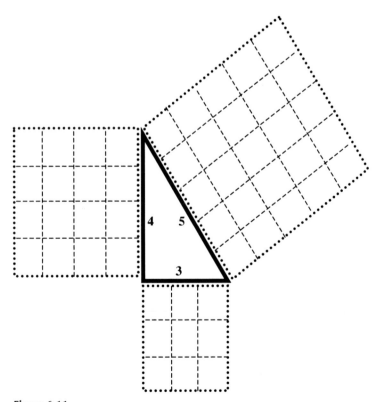

Figure 6.11.

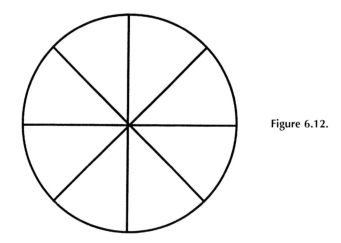

Figure 6.12.

half the circumference by the radius (figure 6.12). Eight sectors can be arranged to form a near-parallelogram (figure 6.13); 24 sectors is a closer approximation to a parallelogram (figure 6.14). As the number of sectors increases, the figure becomes closer to a rectangle—a special parallelogram (figure 6.15).

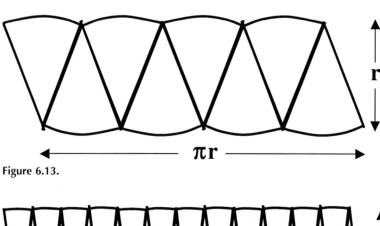

r

πr

Figure 6.13.

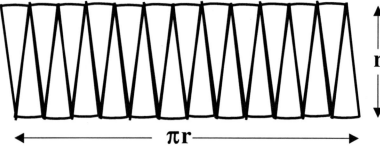

r

πr

Figure 6.14.

$$A = (\pi r \times r) = \pi r^2$$

r

πr

Figure 6.15.

Lengths of the Sides of "Special" Right Triangles

The 45-45-90 triangle and the 30-60-90 triangle are important, because the measurements of the angles are either divisions of 2 or divisions of 3 (see figure 6.16).

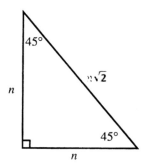

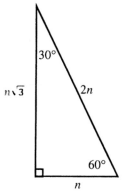

Figure 6.16.

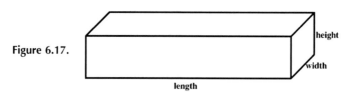

Figure 6.17.

Lengths of the Sides of Triangles

In a triangle, the sum of the lengths of the two shorter sides is greater than the length of the longest side. If the lengths of the two shorter sides are equal, their sum is still greater than the length of the longest side.

Volume of a Cube

length × width × height

The volume of a solid is the amount of space within the solid. One question a student might ask is: "How much can that cube fit?" or "How much can that cylinder (i.e., a can) hold?" Finding the volume of a cube is really the same as finding the volume of any rectangular solid (i.e., a brick-shaped figure) (figure 6.17). Simply multiply the figure's length by its width, and then multiply the resulting product by the figure's height.

Volume of a Cylinder

$\pi r^2 h$

With cylinders, it is important to understand that the key two-dimensional shape associated with a cylinder is the circle. The circle serves as the cylinder's base. So, in order to find the volume of a cylinder, simply find the area of one of the bases—the circle of the cylinder—and then multiply this area by the height of the cylinder. The formula for the area of a cylinder is $\pi r^2 h$, where r is the radius of the circle, h is the height of the cylinder, and π is the irrational number that approximates 3.1415926 (see figure 6.18).

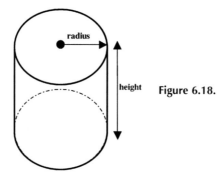

Figure 6.18.

AN "AVERAGE" SUCCESS STORY IN MATHEMATICS: THE CASE OF GEORGE PÓLYA, A LATE-BLOOMING MATHEMATICAL GENIUS

The importance of average in the case of mathematics and mathematical inquiry cannot be underestimated. It is often the case that high-ability stature can be reached with a little ingenuity and willingness to consider the subject as one based on open-ended inquiry and not solely a factually based enterprise. Like music, the subject of mathematics has been notorious in serving as an important area of intellectual inquiry for child prodigies to trumpet their facility. However, there are a great number of people who did not initially perform well in mathematics or who were mediocre at best but overcame their earlier mediocrity and blossomed into successful people—some of whom were good at mathematics, others great. One such person was George Pólya, considered by many historians as one of the greatest mathematicians of the twentieth century.

George Pólya was born in 1887 in Budapest, Hungary, the son of Jakab Pólya and Anna Deutsch. George, the fourth of 5 children, was 10 years old when his father died (incidentally, George Pólya lived until the age of 97).

George Pólya, an internationally renowned mathematician, was a poor to mediocre student in mathematics as a child and adolescent. In Albers and Alexanderson's (1985) interview, Pólya describes his childhood education as uneventful. He received a certificate from elementary school at the age of six. The following year, Pólya entered the Dániel Berzsenyi Gymnasium, where he studied Greek, Latin, German, and Magyar. He regarded biology and literature as his favorite school subjects. In fact, his highest grades were in these subjects, as well as geography and foreign language. Ironically, Pólya scored poorly in mathematics at the Gymnasium. He attributed a good deal of this failure in the subject to the lackluster teaching abilities of his mathematics teachers. In geometry, the very subject that would be the focus of his doctoral dissertation, Pólya received only satisfactory marks at the Gymnasium.

One would think, at this point in the life of a famous mathematician—adolescence—that mathematics would not only be an interesting subject, but a subject in which the individual excelled. Not so, in Pólya's case. In fact, his propensity in mathematics would not even appear during his years in college, prior to graduate, doctoral-level education. After his schooling at the Gymnasium, Pólya entered the University of Budapest in 1905, and at the behest of his mother, he entered law—a field that he disliked. He then decided to major in literature, a subject that he enjoyed. Two years later, he earned a degree that allowed him to teach literature at the Gymnasium level. Pólya wanted to continue his studies in philosophy but was advised by one of his professors to enroll in mathematics and physics courses as a prerequisite. So it was not until he was in his early 20s that Pólya excelled in mathematics and found it to be not only useful, but an essential subject to master in order to excel in other areas and disciplines. During this time, Pólya was most influenced by Lipót Fejér, a professor at the University of Budapest who inspired numerous twentieth-century mathematicians, including Paul Erdös and John von Neumann. After a year at the University of Vienna, Pólya completed his doctorate at the University of Budapest on the theory of geometric probability, a dissertation that he completed with little if any supervision from his advisors.

With much vacillation among academic interests—from literature to philosophy and eventually to physics and finally mathematics, it took Pólya nearly two decades—more than 15 years beyond elementary school—to show his interest and subsequent genius in mathematics. In other words, Pólya was not recognized, as nor considered to be, a mathematics wunderkind, as we often romanticize famous mathematicians and scientists from Sir Isaac Newton to Carl Friedrich Gauss and Évariste Galois, all the way to Albert Einstein and even to the present, with people like Andrew Wiles and Stephen Hawking. Pólya was a late bloomer in mathematics, but he was extremely successful in the subject. His outstanding achievements in mathematics as a young professional led him to become a professor at Stanford University in 1940.

So why was Pólya such an anomaly from the putative norm? For one thing, Pólya was a persistent student. His writings and interviews demonstrate a student with a great deal of initiative, not only in terms of subject content but also in the process of studying and learning. In fact, it was Fejér, his mathematics professor at the University of Budapest, who encouraged him to think of mathematical problems in a variety of ways—indeed, an influence that contributed to his grand project of mathematical problem solving, not to mention his important contributions to the field of mathematical analysis. Second, although he was influenced by his mother to study law, Pólya seemed to have the liberty to study what had interested him at any given time during his schooling. It seems evident from anecdotal records that Pólya's parents did not pressure him in any one academic direction. Third, there is no evidence to suggest that Pólya lacked self-confidence in math. Given this, we argue that positive attitudes toward math, as in other subjects, contribute to a healthy outlook on learning math and even to success in the subject. Fourth, based on evidence from his writings and interviews with Pólya and those who knew him, organization was without question one of the mathematician's strengths. You may recall our discussion earlier on math study habits about the great importance of organization as a general study habit. Pólya was a fastidious organizer of his work and made certain that he knew exactly where to search if he needed to review a particular topic for his research. Again, one can argue that this important habit may have contributed to his pragmatic approach to the subject of mathematical problem solving. Pólya illustrates the importance of the math habits described earlier in this chapter.

FINAL THOUGHTS

In this chapter, we have outlined a trajectory for both parents and teachers to follow in order to help children not only learn mathematics and develop their cognitive skills in the subject, but also support positive attitudes and outlooks on the subject as well. To do this, we provided a general overview of the development of mathematical thinking in early childhood. We then provided specific mathematics habits, based on years of research, which we strongly believe help children develop their conceptual and procedural skills in mathematics and at the same time improves their methods of study for optimal success. Our discussion continued on the issue of math topics that we found to be essential in forming the foundations of the subject for each and every child. We then homed in on some of those topics to discuss very common—and useful—algorithms that will not only help students tremendously in school, but also in daily life. We concluded the chapter with a miniature biographical account of George Pólya, an exemplary case of a world-class mathematician who was neither identified by his teachers or peers as a mathematical prodigy nor considered an expert in the subject during his early and formative years. Pólya's story should offer readers who don't think of themselves as "math people" a modicum of inspiration to change the negative "I can't do math" attitude to one in which mathematical knowledge is possible for those who pursue it.

7

The Right Start in Science: The Development of Scientific Thinking

Experiments are questions that one asks of nature.

—Mary Budd Rowe (1978)

Science education has been inundated with reform movements and standards development over the last few decades as an attempt to increase science literacy (NRC, 1995; NSF, 2005). In 1989, the landmark report *Science for All Americans* grimly assessed the mood of policymakers, educators, and the general public regarding the condition of science education. As stated in the report, "A cascade of recent studies has made it abundantly clear that both by national standards and international norms, U.S. education is failing to adequately educate too many students—and hence failing the nation" (AAAS, 1989). These types of reports and commentaries are not new and seem to continually flood the educational landscape. Similar statements were made after the launching of Sputnik, with the publication of *A Nation at Risk* (1983), and even today after comparing test results from the Trends in International Mathematics and Science Study (TIMSS) and the Programme for International Student Assessment (PISA) study (PISA, 2009; TIMSS, 2009). Although there is always room for improvement in the teaching of any subject, the doom-and-gloom crises in education may be more a creation of the interpretation of test scores than an outright failure of the educational system (Berliner & Biddle, 1995; Johnson, Johnson, Farenga, & Ness, 2005).

In response to these national "crises," attempts have been made to overhaul curriculum, retrain teachers, increase graduation requirements, develop scope and sequence programs, create new standards, and test, test,

test—until no child is left untested (Johnson, Johnson, Farenga, & Ness, 2005, 2008). The present movement to increase science achievement has only exacerbated the widely held view that the subject of science is primarily the memorization of facts that are removed from reality, the performance of cookbook experiments, the taking of tests, and the belief that it is not for "average" students. Unfortunately, this is not a crisis that the government and poorly administered schools will be able to test their way out of. The problem of learning and teaching science in our estimation is not quantitative but qualitative. Scientific reasoning requires one to be able to conduct inquiry and develop qualitatively based skills. Engaging in higher levels of scientific inquiry involves the application of qualitatively related process skills to identify problems, plan strategies, solve problems, conduct investigations, and evaluate outcomes.

Recent work in the area of cognition suggests that scientists and mathematicians spend a vast amount of time solving problems using qualitative reasoning. These works demonstrate how highly skilled individuals or experts solve problems in a variety of domains (Bransford, Brown, & Cocking, 2000; Carey, 1986; Chi, Feltovich, & Glaser, 1981; Clement, 1982, 1987; Chi & Glaser, 1981; Halloun & Hestenes, 1987). A new look at what is most important in an expert's conceptual understanding and how they solve problems is discussed in the book *How People Learn* (Bransford, Brown, & Cocking, 2000), and demonstrated in the video documentary *Minds of Our Own* by the Annenberg Foundation (2008). What stands out in each of these works is the importance and reliance that experts place on qualitative thinking skills to propose explanations, demonstrate understanding, and solve problems. The qualitative aspects in learning science are what many early childhood researchers refer to when making the Piagetian comparison of the young child as scientist or mathematician and the Vygotskyan comparison of the young child as apprentice who uses language and culture to mediate cognitive development through adult-peer interactions (Driver, 1983; Ness & Farenga, 2007; Vygotsky, 1962). Yet it is the qualitative component of teaching and learning science that is often ignored after the early years for a greater emphasis on quantitative skills. The sole emphasis in too many science classes has shifted from the qualitative component to the easier-to-assess, rote, quantitative component of a subject that is driven by high-stakes examinations. What many students experience is that the one-time appealing qualitative components of creativity and divergent possibilities are devalued and replaced in the later years by algorithms and the search for singularly correct solutions.

Roe's (1951a, 1951b, 1952, 1981) psychological studies of eminent scientists clearly identify the salient traits of childhood associated with selecting a science-related career. The aspect of science that many experts vividly recall from their own childhood, the so-called playing of science—experimenting, tinkering, and wondering—is eliminated from the curriculum (Roe, 1952; Rowe, 1978). This is troublesome, since it is the qualitative aspect that science shares with all other creative processes and precisely what children find most appealing and engaging. The outcome of this qualitatively related behavior is often manifested in advanced knowledge of a particular subject in which the child has developed interest. Science, like play, requires the creation of a script to plan strategies, solve problems, and resolve conflicts. In other words, the qualitative component used in scientific thought parallels scenario development in play.

Interwoven in this chapter are five objectives that are necessary to help teachers and parents foster science learning in young children. The first objective is to recognize the child's natural propensities to learn science. The second objective is to bridge the conceptual learning of science with inquiry-related skills. Third, parents and teachers need to recognize the importance of the creative process that is not measured by standardized assessment. Fourth, it is necessary to provide students with ample time and repeated opportunities to plan and conduct investigations that are directly related to their immediate interests whenever possible. And finally, it is critical to teach students the importance of cause-and-effect relationships that reinforce a level of internal control, allowing children to affect and predict events.

THE IMPORTANCE OF RECOGNIZING
A CHILD'S NATURAL PROPENSITIES

We have all witnessed children who demonstrate advanced proficiencies in subjects that are far beyond their years: the young child who speaks as if he or she is a paleontologist providing a treatise on dinosaurs, the child whose Lego or block constructions cause architects to marvel, or the child who displays a type of spatial ability to guide an adult through a zoological park like an orienteer. Each of these examples exhibits a child with intrinsic motivation and seemingly advanced abilities. Clearly, we all have similar stories of such behaviors that demonstrate vast learning potentials. Many in the fields of psychology, education, and child development are in pursuit of ways to identify the origins of similar behaviors in order to prescribe ways to foster their continuance. Preliminary explanations for these behaviors suggest that a confluence of interest, self-regulation, and environmental conditions may create an opportunity to change average ability into extraordinary performance.

Children are natural problem solvers. When given the opportunity, young children can be observed playing with ordinary materials in creative and innovative ways. Have you ever been surprised by the short amount of interest a young child might display in that special birthday present? The present is often put aside as the child becomes more engaged by the packaging the gift came in. Without any special directions, many children can take discarded materials and weave them into a medical bag for playing doctor, a garage for housing cars, or a doll's house for replicating daily household activities. Simply, the packing material serves as the concrete prop that fosters the development of abstract thinking through the creation of play scenarios. The packing material with its numerous roles provides the child with a bridge between reality and fantasy, allowing the child to create and explore numerous possibilities. Although sometimes puzzling to the adult, the child has a purpose and reason for the activity at hand. These observations support Piaget's beliefs that children's thinking is qualitatively and quantitatively different from that of adults. This is evidenced when we ask the child, "Why did you make such a thing?" The child gives the usual incredulous stare, along with the common answer, "Why can't I do it?"

Here is the importance of recognizing and fostering creative abilities for young children—the awareness of the importance of imagination. We define imagination as the ability to take the lifeless and give it life, provide purpose for the purposeless, and supply possibility where things seem impossible. Imagination provides the opportunity for the child to take more responsibility for the activity and to move beyond one's level of competence (Bodrova & Leong, 1996). We are not suggesting that imagination is a substitute for knowledge but rather that active imagination can enrich knowledge acquisition. Clearly, imagination occurs in a social and cultural context that helps to shape the development of thinking skills (Berk & Winsler, 1995). Vygotsky (1978) suggests that children function at their highest intellectual level when engaged in sociodramatic play. He discusses the role of play in a child's development and the link between private speech and self-regulation. Research has demonstrated that what we may perceive as nonsense utterances by a child are mechanisms to guide one's behavior throughout a task. Krafft and Berk (1998) provide support that sociodramatic play serves as a context for developing self-regulation, which is the ability to control, monitor, and assess one's actions. Self-regulation is considered a higher-order executive function of metacognition, the process of self-awareness of one's own thinking and actions.

SELF-REGULATORY BEHAVIORS, CREATIVITY, AND PLAY

The creativity that children possess needs to be fostered throughout their development. Research suggests that the overstructuring the child's environment may actually limit creative and academic development (Elias & Berk, 2002; Krafft & Berk, 1998; Rowe, 1978). In our view, this is a central problem with much of science instruction. The exercises or activities are devised to eliminate divergent options and to focus on predetermined results. The answers are structured to fit the course assessments, and the wonder of science is lost along with cognitive intrigue. We define cognitive intrigue as the wonder that stimulates and intrinsically motivates an individual to voluntarily engage in an activity. The loss of cognitive intrigue may be initiated by the sole use of play items with predetermined conclusions and reinforced by rote instruction in school. This is exemplified by toys, games, and lessons that are an end in and of themselves and require little of the individual other than to master the planned objective.

Contrary to closed-ended activities, the act of taking a tree branch and turning it into a magic wand may actually have more influence on promoting cognitive intrigue than a plastic, manufactured version of Darth Vader's light saber. The five-year-old son of one of the authors of this book was invited to his friend's birthday party, where approximately 20 boys played in the backyard, imagining they were *Star Wars* characters. His friend is an avid fan of superheroes and *Star Wars* figures. So *Star Wars* paraphernalia, mostly light sabers, were strewn throughout the backyard. The "problem" was that although there were about 20 boys, there were only 12 or 13 manufactured light sabers. What is a young boy to do without a light saber, especially one of the seven or eight who weren't lucky enough to get one? A couple of the boys at the party picked up small hockey sticks and used these instead of the plastic light sabers. Some of the other boys went with this idea and picked up generic, surrogate objects—such as a piece of wood or stick—that they pretended were light sabers. The remaining two or three boys were not interested at all in the surrogate objects and thus tried to negotiate with one of the boys who had plastic light sabers. Over time, the boys using the surrogate objects in lieu of the plastic sabers became more spirited, committed, and imaginative in their play than did the other boys. This was evidenced by a longer play period with fewer interruptions and a play activity that went beyond Darth Vader, Storm Troopers, and the magical wonder of the Force. The novelty of the manufactured plastic light saber eventually wore off, but the use of the surrogate objects did not.

The key point is that children's play using products manufactured with a specific design or function may limit or even stifle self-regulatory behaviors during both social and cognitive development. This form of play, which we refer to as high-stakes play, has a specifically defined outcome as prescribed by a set of instructions that must be followed in order to obtain a correct result. Central to this form of play are repetitive actions with no latitude for variation in the activity or freedom for the child's imaginative expression. High-stakes play is analogous to high-stakes test questions designed to elicit specific responses from students. In other words, there is little creativity required of the students in designing their responses. Many products come with a whole host of explicit and implicit scenarios for their use. Therefore, the development of scenarios required for play activities are no longer the child's responsibility but that of the product's manufacturer (i.e., adults). The creativity exhibited by the child to transform the tree branch into a magic wand, light saber, or conductor's baton is lost and what we see as the spark that ignites inquiry is ultimately extinguished. The ability to transform the stick into its new form parallels the important inquiry skills of devising a procedure to conduct an experiment. In each case, the participant is required to think ahead to continue the activity, which may have multiple possibilities depending on the variables encountered. It is a form of work, and each activity requires the participant to create a script with possibilities to solve a problem. In some cases, the cognitive complexity involved in play-related behaviors may exceed that in devising protocols for a science-related investigation. Clearly, many human activities come complete with a variety of props. In fact, the creation of such materials is considered by many to be a unique human quality (Kinget, 1975). Our concern is when the props come fully scripted, and no room exists for seeing things any other way than that of their original purpose.

The songwriter and vocalist Harry Chapin probably best summarized this idea in the song "Flowers Are Red" (1979). Chapin describes a teacher best characterized as rigid or inflexible, who explains to her young student why his painting is "wrong," as if only red flowers are found in nature. The boy insists that flowers can be of any color, but the teacher ignores his pleas, instructing him that flowers must be red—as if this were a scientific law. The boy's insistence that the flowers can be any color causes him to be removed from the group of children and placed alone in a corner of the classroom. Alone and isolated, he is coerced into accepting the teacher's point of view and repeats the refrain, "Flowers are red." The lyrics of the song demonstrate an autocratic classroom where inquiry and personal expression are held to an absolute minimum. The child is not only taught to color within the lines, following all the predetermined guidelines, but that this is the only way to complete the lesson. Those of us who have had experience teaching young children realize the importance of teaching children how to listen and follow directions. However, consistently decreasing free play and increasing structured activities to promote self-regulatory behaviors create concern and may produce the opposite effect. Children who are constantly placed in adult-structured settings may not learn what to do without adult input. One example in our society is when young college students have their parents intervene to negotiate assignments and grades. These children require a completed script or program to function. Parallel in form to the pedantic, scripted lessons are many science laboratory-based activities that are taught in a manner that promotes a single problem-solving methodology known as the scientific method. While examining most science textbooks, one finds this holy grail of problem solving with slight variations, which extend the procedures of the methodology from five to nine steps. The scripted lessons for "one size fits all" are firmly established as if to meet factory output quotas. However, this is the antithesis of open-ended inquiry and freedom of expression that is needed for a conducive environment in which questioning is a key component for furthering conceptual understanding and healthy scientific skepticism.

CONCEPTUAL LEARNING AND INQUIRY-RELATED SKILLS

Our collective classroom experiences have demonstrated the parallel nature of the development of inquiry-related behaviors that are evident in play activities and science investigations. The same process skills that allow young children to conduct inquiry—observing, questioning, manipulating materials, creating, and exploring—are required in play and science. At a young age, the world of play and science converge as children begin to explore their surroundings. Research suggests a strong link between play and the development of emergent science concepts (Ness & Farenga, 2007). Roeper argues that "through playful interaction children develop many concepts of science" (1988, p. 123). She brings this connection to the forefront when she argues that:

> Play and exploration remain the best learning tools for the young child. Children develop a sense of inner freedom and permission to reach out if they (and their goals and idiosyncratic ways of learning) are supported by the adults at the school. This security and freedom requires a flexible atmosphere with much opportunity for discovery, individualized and group learning, play, and stimulating enthusiastic adults who are learners themselves. (p. 133)

The world of physical science is extremely important to young children in that it can provide the context for play and exploration. Ness and Farenga (2007) suggest that numerous science and mathematics concepts can be learned through block play. The recognition of emergent mathematics and science concepts such as mass, matter, interaction of forces, symmetry, area, volume, and shape can be experienced through free play (see figures 7.1 and 7.2). The concept of pattern recognition in the natural world can be thought of as an emergent behavior required for the development of more complex process skills. This is supported by the comments of the Nobel Prize winner in physics, Richard P. Feynman, the former professor of physics from the California Institute of Technology. Feynman's poignant article entitled "What Is Science" describes how he was introduced to the field of science as a young boy by his father, a businessman. He explains how all of his early science-related experiences were embedded in games. Through

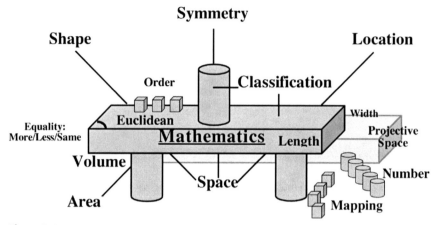

Figure 7.1.

games, Feynman's father taught his son to look for patterns. Feynman later described his father's method as "insidious cleverness: first delight him in play and then slowly inject material of educational value!" (Feynman, 2000, p. 174). A second lesson from Feynman's recollection is of how little importance knowing the name of an object is to understanding and concept development. Feynman relates an incident when a friend asked him to name a bird that was seen in the distance. After recalling that he did not know the name of the bird, his friend replied, "Your father doesn't teach you much about science" (Feynman, 2000, p. 177). Feynman's story con-

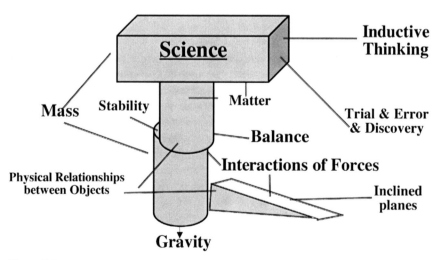

Figure 7.2.

tinues, illustrating what we argue is the most critical lesson for teaching and learning science. In explaining the essence of the bird—a brown-throated thrush—Feynman argues, "In Germany it's called a *halzenflugel,* and in Chinese they call it a *chung ling* [italics added] and even if you know all those names for it, you still know little about the bird" (2000, p. 177). In other words, the ability to identify something by name tells little about it.

Unfortunately, the names of things and their definitions take up a large part of the science curriculum. The memorizing of superficial information is what too many people still consider the purpose of studying science. All too often, it is this superficial kind of knowledge that is measured by high-stakes tests. The salient information that leads to broad concept attainment is often ignored. Rather than studying and learning the names of objects, students might be better served by observing "what goes on" (p. 177) and developing an understanding from related exploration.

Feynman's point about injecting educational value through play and exploration is demonstrated by both Rowe 1978 and the National Aeronautic and Space Administration (NASA) 1978. Both Rowe and NASA authors use kites to provide real-world experiences to demonstrate scientific and mathematical concepts. Through the activity of kite building, design, and flying, students have the opportunity to gain an understanding of concepts and process skills integrated with subjects such as physics, engineering, history, meteorology, mathematics, and the arts. The science and mathematics fundamentals listed in table 7.1 provide the opportunity for students to develop conceptual understanding through application. Salomon and Perkins (1996) aptly describe the demonstration of the attainment of knowledge as a "performance of understanding" (p. 116). Upon further examination of the topic, one realizes that kites are not simply toys; they provide a venue for the development of advanced concepts and process skills.

Free play activities can provide the opportunity for experimentation on the natural world and help to reinforce control over the environment and increase the child's locus of internal control (Rowe, 1978). Internal locus of control, self-regulation, and a realization of cause-and-effect relationships may be at the core of educational achievement and, more specifically, science achievement. Further, close observation of children engaged in spontaneous science-related activities provides support for the need to link the understanding of cause-and-effect relationships to one's internal locus of control and self-regulation skills. It is informative to observe which young children can take an interest in a pile of unrelated materials and create their own investigation. What can be created from a pile of interlocking triangles or a pile of straws with some masking tape? The manner in which the tasks are approached may suggest certain attributes of an individual. As you may recall from our discussion on attribute theory in chapter 4, children

Table 7.1 Concepts and Process Skills Learned through Kite Building

Science Fundamentals
Three States of Matter
Newton's Laws of Motion
Newton's First Law
Newton's Second Law
Newton's Third Law
Torque

Math Fundamentals
Function
Area
Volume
Scalars and Vectors
Comparing Two Scalars
Comparing Two Vectors
Vector Addition
Vector Components
Trigonometry
Sine/Cosine/Tangent
Ratios in Triangles
Pythagorean Theorem

Kites
Kite Construction
Kite Geometry
Control Line
Bridle Point Geometry
Forces on a Kite
Balance and Stability
Launch and Flight
Control Line Equations
Determine Flight Altitude
Altitude Equation Derivation
Flight Altitude
Kite Safety

The Atmosphere
Air Properties Definitions
Air Pressure
Air Temperature
Air Density

Aerodynamics
Aerodynamics of Kites
Dynamic Pressure
Kite Center of Pressure
Kite Torque Equation
Kite Lift Equations
Inclination Effects
Downwash Effects
Density Effects
Velocity Effects

Height
Determining Kite Weight
Weight Equation
Center of Gravity
Kite Center of Gravity

Aircraft Forces
Four Forces on an Airplane
Wing Geometry
Aerodynamic Forces
Center of Pressure
Aerodynamic Center
Lift Equation
Lift Coefficient
Drag Equation
Drag Coefficient

Miscellaneous
Relative Velocity
Bernoulli's Equation

Source: This table is borrowed from the NASA Glenn Research Center *Kite Index* (NASA, 2008).

who have been encouraged to self-regulate will often take on a challenge and spend more time searching for an answer. These simple challenges are usually what separate those children who have positive experiences with self-regulatory behaviors and express persistence from those children who do not. Children who create challenges—for themselves such as building the tallest, sturdiest, or most aesthetic structure with the supplied materials—demonstrate persistence, creativity, and the ability to self-challenge. At the very least, design-related questions need to be addressed for each of their attempted structures. Questions as to how the straws can be connected to build the most stable structure or how to lay out the triangular piece to obtain the greatest height must be explored, tested, and evaluated.

LANGUAGE, SCIENCE, AND MEANING

Other than perhaps physical education, there is the possibility for more active learning and excitement when teaching science than when teaching other subjects. Science educators who provide an opportunity for children to observe and explore the behaviors of any number of live arthropods—such as crayfish, mealworms, or grasshoppers—know the high level of excitement and interest that can be exhibited by a classroom full of children. Although not common, intense silent periods may occur when children are engrossed in observing a discrepant event. Some students who have little concern for school will often become immersed in a scientific topic that interests them. When taught in a cognitively appealing manner, the subject of science has the ability to hook students into further study. These seemingly average students who were initially unenthusiastic about their studies are now motivated to read, write, or complete assignments and do what is necessary to learn more about the topic. This is where a science teacher who is aware of potential shifts in students' abilities can recognize that a seemingly average child is capable of extraordinary performance. If documented, catalogued, and assessed appropriately, the samples of behavior of the average child would instead demonstrate above-average or advanced ability. An easy way to recognize average ability is to stop and listen to what is being said.

It is instructive to observe and listen to the discourse of children solving problems without adult intervention to gather an overall awareness of attitude, aptitude, and knowledge. Language, in combination with an activity's outcome, can offer insight into what a child understands. The manner in which the child expresses similarities and differences in meaning provides clues to the depth of that understanding. It is necessary to listen to what is being said because ideas or concepts only have meaning when they are placed in context to other ideas or concepts (Lemke, 1990). In addition, certain ideas may be present without being expressed, and evidence of their existence needs to be made known. Through a questioning technique known as "tacit dialoguing," students uncover this evidence by explicitly stating what they think in their own words as they are completing the activity (Ness & Farenga, 2007). Since children's use of language is different from that of adults, it is critical to have some form of physical evidence when interpreting what is said. That is, the evidence or product serves as a proxy for meaning.

The use of techniques, such as observation and tacit dialoguing, are formative assessment processes to gather data from children's encounters with materials, language, social interactions and concepts. The structure of the discourse is often quite orderly, even though the processes that surround it appear somewhat unorganized as the children manipulate materials or draw graphic representations in order to create evidence of understanding. Some children simply jump into an investigation, as if preprogrammed, talking themselves through the activity while working. Others sit back and contemplate the possibilities at hand and have mini-discussions with themselves prior to beginning the activity. However, after a short time, it is difficult to notice any difference between the two groups. Each group is working with the materials and creating a dialogue to support the activity. At times, the speech or dialogue is relevant solely to one of the participants (as he or she is thinking aloud), and at other times, it is speech related to controlling the group activity. The language-related experience provides an opportunity for children to establish meaning through a product. One can think of a product as the concrete expression that supplies meaning to an abstraction by use of words, diagrams, or pictures.

Feynman's childhood experience resonates with Ludwig Wittgenstein's famous "beetle-in-the-box" analogy. Wittgenstein's analogy serves as the foundation for the problems associated with language and introspection. The beetle-in-the-box analogy goes something like this: You are sent to a room with many people. You may not even know anyone in the room. Everyone in this room is given a box, including you. The rule for opening the box and looking inside is simple—you may look at the contents of your box, but under no circumstances are you permitted to look at the contents of anyone else's box. It turns out that when you open your box and are asked what you see, you say, "Beetle!" (i.e., "there's a beetle in my box"). It also turns out that when your neighbor opens her box, she says, "Beetle!" In fact, everyone in the room opens his or her box and says, "Beetle!" All the observer knows is that the word that is associated with opening the box and looking inside is "beetle." In other words, the thing in your box might be a six-legged organism, walking from one corner of the box to another.

The thing in your neighbor's box might be something that represents a ping-pong ball. The thing in a third person's box might be something representing a matchstick. There might be nothing at all in a fourth person's box. The connection between Wittgenstein's "beetle-in-the-box" thought experiment and our argument is this: the use of language is culture-bound—not universal. When we use language in science, or even mathematics for that matter, we need to be wary of using language that obscures our ability to comprehend a phenomenon. Unfortunately, much of the time learning science is spent learning terms for abstract concepts. This often results in the common situation in which students can identify the term for a concept without being able to explain what the concept means (Linn, 1986; Resnick, 1983, 1987). For example, students study the process of photosynthesis in elementary school, middle school, and secondary school. And still at the college level, students have difficulty explaining the role of carbon dioxide (CO_2) and its relationship to the mass of the tree (Wandersee, 1983). As demonstrated by the authors of the Annenberg Project (2008), college students presented with a log from a tree were unable to explain the material responsible for the log's composition. This was most disconcerting, since photosynthesis is a universally taught and tested concept in science. The Annenberg Project authors state:

> Just about everyone will agree that trees are made from sunlight, water, and soil the trees suck up from their roots. But the surprising truth is that trees are made from air! Trees are solar-powered machines that convert air into wood. Why is it that, despite the fact that photosynthesis is one of the most widely taught subjects in science, so few people really understand the central idea underlying this system?" (Annenberg Project, 2008)

The authors attempt to uncover why such a ubiquitous topic as photosynthesis is not understood by large numbers of students.

WHY EXPLORE?

Our work suggests that the inquiry-related behaviors developed during the exploration phase of an activity are especially important to the successful study of science years later. Unfortunately, these science-related behaviors are extinguished in most traditional science classes that focus on learning facts for the purpose of circling the correct answer. Concepts are held at bay for lack of instructional time and for the sustained work required for their formation. The sought-after conceptual understanding does not occur from disconnected science-related tasks that superficially cover multiple topics. Feynman's story stresses two important points for conceptual development. The first is that it requires consistent lessons over time; the second is that simply knowing a name does not demonstrate understanding. As Feynman's example suggests, knowing the name of the bird tells one nothing about migration, flight, reproduction, or any other concepts related to the bird. Simply put, the "what is it called" is easy to answer, but the "why" and the "how" it does something provides the scientific challenge and remains unanswered. According to the National Research Council, "Teachers must teach some subject matter in depth, providing many examples in which the same concept is at work and providing a firm foundation of factual knowledge" (Bransford, Brown, & Cocking, 2000, p. 20). Adler (1982) discussed the results of an educational environment that does not require the students to be challenged and actively engaged nor given the opportunities to develop deep understanding of subject matter:

> There is little joy in most of the learning they [students] are now compelled to do. Too much of it is make-believe, in which neither teacher nor pupil can take a lively interest. Without some joy in learning—a joy that arises from hard work well done and from the participation of one's mind in a common task—basic schooling cannot initiate the young into the life of learning, let alone give them the skill and the incentive to engage in it further. (Adler, 1982, p. 32)

This position is further supported by John Goodlad (1984), who warned of the damaging aspects of rote memorization on students' motivation and their inability to meaningfully develop a deep understanding of subject matter. Goodlad further supported the position that children need to be engaged in authentic inquiry, as demonstrated by the study of kites, and to be taught from their strengths and that we start the teaching process from what students bring to the classroom.

In utilizing their prior knowledge, all children should be encouraged to create explanations and be provided with the opportunity to explain their reasoning. These everyday child-developed explanations are what Vygotsky (1978) refers to as spontaneous concepts—concepts that deal with the child's conceptions, understandings, and explanations of the workings of the everyday world. These explanations may be wrong, incomplete, partially correct, or correct in their composition. The explanations that young children acquire before formal science instruction are commonly known as naive theories and are stored as prior knowledge. It has been demonstrated that an individual's prior knowledge is a critical component that either fosters or hinders future learning. Children, like adults, are reluctant to give up their prior beliefs, even when confronted with contradictory evidence. The extensive research from the Annenberg Project on science education has provided numerous examples to support the tenacity of an individual's prior beliefs and how it hinders the acquisition of new information. The key point here for both teachers and parents is to uncover what a child knows prior to teaching new information.

The subject matter that should be taught in science class is debatable. However, many science educators feel that children need to recognize the big ideas or the unifying concepts of science in which to place their everyday experiences of the world. According to the National Research Council (Bransford, Brown, & Cocking, 2000), the unifying concepts for the teaching of science are: organization, cause and effect, systems, scales (relative and absolute), models, change, structure and function, variation, and diversity.

Organization is a basic component of science content. It requires students to recognize properties, characteristics, or attributes of things in their environment. Children need to first know basic descriptive terms such as color, size, shape, texture, and odor. These attributes are encountered through their interactions with objects within the everyday environment. Ness and Farenga (2007) suggest that these exploratory attribute-related interactions within the environment are the protobehaviors that contribute to basic and complex process skills (see figure 7.3). Protobehaviors are exploratory drives that cause one to come into contact with the everyday environment through at least one of the five senses, which is then interpreted by the brain. The mental representation or schemas that are formed from this experience serve as patterns of understanding that the child will use to evaluate further encounters. When we walk outside, do we notice the shapes of clouds in the sky, shadows at different times of the day, insects on plants, and the color of leaves on the trees? Do we teach children to couple these observations with additional observations, such as finding the conditions that are necessary to form long shadows or determining when we see red, yellow, and orange leaves on trees? Do we record our observations to help us remember what we saw? A simple exercise to help children remember their observations is to record them in an organized manner. An example of this is recording the moon's phases on a calendar so children can make predictions based on data that were collected or examining the sky to predict tomorrow's weather. Many of the examples of common environmental observations help children to recognize other big ideas that can be categorized as cycles.

In nature, many things occur in predictable patterns called cycles. Science content that can be taught relating to the cycle theme include day and night, moon phases, tides, seasons, animal migration, hibernations, water cycles, plant growth, metamorphosis (complete and incomplete), rock formation, and weather. As children observe these cycles, they may notice that some changes occur quickly and others are relatively slow. Children can compare the rate of change of a butterfly as it emerges from a chrysalis and to that of the moon's phases from new moon to full moon. Children who learn to experience and recognize the patterns that occur are introduced to the concept of rate of change. As children study cycles and recognize patterns

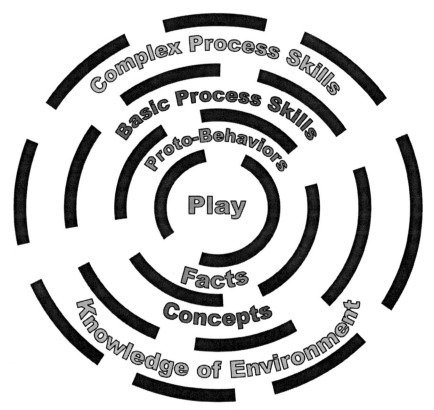

Figure 7.4.

of change, they can start to predict outcomes. Predicting outcomes success-fully introduces the powerful idea of cause and effect. Children who begin to understand cause-and-effect relationships recognize that things in nature behave in orderly and predictable ways. These children increasingly gain control over their environment and realize that effects or outcomes are not possible without causes. This is the powerful lesson behind all scientific thinking.

SEEING THE BIG PICTURE OF SCIENCE

Many parents and teachers feel ill-prepared to teach science. This is sup-ported to a certain extent by research that suggests that early childhood and childhood educators have little formal science training (Johnson, Johnson, Farenga, & Ness, 2005). One way to compensate for limited training is to develop a positive attitude about science. Science is a composite subject consisting of content, skills, attitudes, and products. Content is the subject matter, skills are applied behaviors used to find an answer, attitudes deal with values, feelings, and interests that guide one's behavior, and products are the tangible outcomes that are a result of an investigation. Although many people may find the teaching of science a daunting task, it can be an enjoyable experience. Science fosters intrinsic motivation by tapping into children's sensibilities to explore and interact with their environments (Farenga & Joyce, 1999b).

Similar to mathematical environments, children's science-related environments are filled with numerous opportunities to learn. One of the most important process skills is observation. Children need to observe the world around them and identify patterns that help them make sense of the environment. Past civilizations took this task to heart and could readily describe the motions of the moon, sun, and stars. Directionality was intricately tied to keen observations and the concepts of east, west, north, and south. Stop and ask an adult to write directions to his home and note the convoluted response. After all, one needs only a global positioning device or computer-mapping program to answer the question. Further, most individuals would be at a loss to describe where or at what time the morning sunlight will shine upon their home and how it changes as the year progresses. As a technologically advanced society, it is surprising to encounter the large numbers of children who are unfamiliar with natural environmental rhythms. Perhaps as we become engrossed in technology, we are less dependent on the rhythms of nature for telling time, predicting weather, recognizing seasonal changes, creating calendars, and responding to circadian rhythms. At the risk of sounding like a Luddite, we suggest that it may be necessary to question the wisdom of speeding up development by promoting a curriculum of the abstract and highly technical just because it is possible. The further a child is removed from direct observation and experience, the less meaningful the explanation is for developing a deep understanding. Much of what can be directly experienced is what is missing in the science curriculum. In many classes, teaching science is little more than storytelling. The opportunity to integrate visceral experiences with inquiry and explanation is lost. Although others may disagree, it is at this point that science education has taken a wrong turn. It is incredible to think that some fifth-grade curriculums include the topic of cell division, complete with the concepts of mitosis and meiosis. Even though students can recite the sequential transition a cell makes from interphase to telephase, do they truly understand mitosis? And is this subject matter that important to an 11- or 12-year-old child? Here we emphasize not only the need to reexamine what is taught, but how and when it is taught. It is apparent that we fail to notice that for many students, the glossy pages filled with colorful photographs and diagrams pale in comparison to a long-term, project-based investigation of life in a mud puddle.

BASIC LESSONS

The following activity offers parents and teachers an informal introduction to observational astronomy for children. At the start, children can be slowly introduced to the three most apparent celestial bodies—the sun, the moon, and the stars. Each can provide a variety of lessons that will not be time consuming but can and should be conducted during intervals over a long time period to help strengthen conceptual knowledge.

Activity: Where Is the Moon?

A simple activity that develops observational skills involves watching the moon as it appears in the sky and recording how change occurs over a period of time. To help children recognize patterns, it is important to conduct the activity in the same location and at the same time for a period of at least three months. Children can draw the moon's shape and follow its transition from full moon to new moon and back to full moon once again. The use of a calendar to record daily observations may make it easier to recognize patterns that are the basis for conceptual relationships. When children recognize a pattern, they may require a new vocabulary to explain their discoveries. While making their observations, children should be encouraged to question. The key point here is to encourage conversation in order to foster questioning skills and interest. The simple questioning exercise of calling children's attention to their surroundings lays the foundation for conceptual knowledge. The following questions may help as examples: Describe the objects that you see when you look at the evening sky. Does the moon appear in the same location each night? If not, in which direction does the moon appear to travel? In what section of the sky does the moon appear? Is the moon only visible at night? Does the moon appear in the evening sky at the same time and location? Although these questions may seem simple, they are some of the same questions that are posed to students in earth science classes. It should be evident that the answers are based on observational data. If additional questions arise, one can consult trade books, Internet resources, or, better still, plan a trip to a planetarium.

BASIC LESSONS NOT LEARNED

"You can fool all of the people some of the time and some of the people all of the time. But you can't fool all of the people all the time." This statement, which has been attributed to Abraham Lincoln, according to Alexander K. McClure (1901), could be applied to science curriculum, instruction, and assessment. No single subject area, assessment technique, or pedagogy is successful with all students all the time. It sounds logical, but in our constant search to increase test scores and produce temporary gains in achievement, policymakers, administrators, teachers, and parents are engaged in a never-ending search for the "next best thing." This rationale has led to the abandonment of many good science programs that could have proved useful to large numbers of students if they were appropriately valued, supported, and assessed. All too often, science programs are adopted, teachers are trained, initial materials purchased, and then everyone sits back and waits. The expectations of the stakeholders have been raised, and when not met, interest in the programs begins to wane. In addition to the vast amount of time and money that is wasted, the sought-after achievement remains in the distance for all but a select few.

Our work suggests that the best way to increase student achievement is to be flexible in one's approach toward teaching science. Learners vary in their abilities, aptitudes, and attitudes, and therefore one's pedagogical approach needs to change to meet the students' needs. Adaptive inquiry is a flexible approach that integrates students' prior knowledge, the curriculum to be taught, the pedagogical intent, and the method of assessment (Farenga, Joyce, & Ness, 2002, 2006). In order for adaptive inquiry to be successful, a knowledgeable teacher should possess a large repertoire of skills and knowledge, along with the freedom to modify the three areas of curriculum, instruction, and assessment in a way to maximize student learning and achievement. Assuming that the teacher has made modifications in any of the three areas for students, potential to work toward a zone of optimal learning has been established (Farenga, Joyce, & Ness, 2002, 2006) (see figure 7.4). The significance of the zone of optimal learning is to create the best environmental press in order to maximize students' potentials. Students who may be initially thought of as "average" can be offered the opportunity to excel and make achievement gains through the support of valid assessment methods. A valid measure would require students to be assessed in a manner in which they are taught, in addition to an assessment instrument that is aligned with instructional objectives. Students should not be penalized for instruction and curriculum that does not match the assessment instrument. This, however, is not always the case. For example, one of the goals of science education is to have students work in collaborative groups to develop experimental protocols, share information, and test ideas. Unfortunately, these learned behaviors are not measured on high-stakes science examinations.

All high-stakes tests in science require students to work independently on written and manipulative skills sections. These tests do not allow students to problem solve collaboratively, to participate on research teams, or to

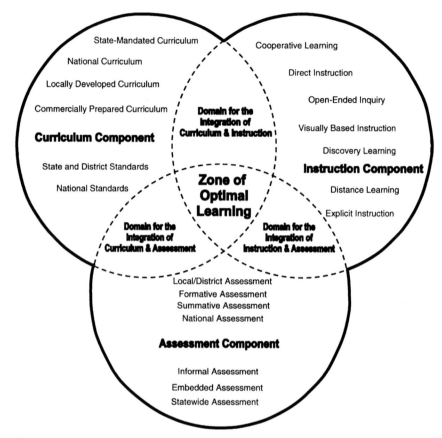

Figure 7.4.

review outcomes with their peers. Many students' experiences with these summative assessments are in opposition to classroom practices that they encountered throughout the year. This misalignment of instruction and assessment hinders students' achievement and calls to question the validity of the assessment. Farenga, Joyce, and Ness (2006) argue: "A basic premise of assessment validity is that the instrument mirrors the alignment of content, process, and product experienced in the classroom. If an element of the method of assessment is the antithesis of the method of instruction, then the validity of assessment results is questionable" (p. 46). This is where a student with advanced academic potential can be mistakenly identified as possessing average ability. The use of test results in this manner establishes a student profile that suggests lackluster achievement in science. As the quote from the American Association for the Advancement of Science at the beginning of this chapter implies, we may be losing the achievement race in science as reported by high-stakes test scores. To many of us who enjoy teaching science, it is evident that what we are testing does not correspond to what is important in the development of students' attitudes and abilities in science. More importantly, however, we are unquestionably losing the hearts and minds of average students who enjoy science at a young age and have the potential for extraordinary performance under the appropriate conditions. At stake is the vast loss of potential that goes unrecognized and underutilized.

8

The Right Start in Social Studies: Building a Foundation for an Informed Citizenry

> We are called the nation of inventors. And we are. We could still claim that title and wear its loftiest honors, if we had stopped with the first thing we ever invented—which was human liberty.
>
> —Mark Twain (in Fatout, 2006)

From Patrick Henry's stirring "give me liberty or give me death" speech to the Virginia Convention in 1775 to today's small-town and big-city July 4 celebrations, Americans have proudly and steadfastly declared, fought for, and celebrated their freedom.

Some groups were not politically included when our fledgling country was established. As Barbara Jordan (1936–1996), an African American congresswoman noted:

> "We, the people." It is a very eloquent beginning. But when that document was completed on the seventeenth of September in 1787 I was not included in that "We the people." I felt somehow for many years that George Washington and Alexander Hamilton just left me out by mistake. But through the process of amendment, interpretation, and court decision I have finally been included in "We the people." (Carruth & Ehrlich, 1988, p. 136)

Our nation's continuous efforts to right wrongs and to maintain our freedom depend on an informed, conscientious citizenry.

The principal goal in social studies is not to memorize dates or to determine a location's precise latitude and longitude, although both endeavors are a part of social studies content. Welton and Mallan (1996) pointed out:

The main purpose for teaching social studies is to produce thoughtful, competent, well-informed, and responsible citizens. In other words, the purpose for teaching social studies parallels the purposes for which schools exist—to produce good citizens. Not every child will become an engineer, a doctor, or a scientist, of course, but everyone will be a citizen; it's an office that every one of us occupies. (p. xxvii)

One might argue that no goal is more noble in a democratic society than to produce good citizens. After all, some of the most heinous crimes against humanity, such as those detailed at the post-Holocaust Nuremburg trials, have been perpetrated by people who could read, write, and work with numbers.

The essential mission of citizenship education has been thwarted by the emphasis on high-stakes testing in America's public schools (Johnson & Johnson 2006; Johnson, Johnson, Farenga, & Ness, 2008). Social studies instruction has become an afterthought—something to be squeezed in after "more important subjects" such as reading and math have been taught and tested. When social studies is a part of a school's curriculum, it often is a dumping ground for topics that don't fit into other subjects. Bicycle safety, drug awareness, littering—all have found their way into social studies because no one knows where to put them. The oft-heard adage, "everything is social studies," may in principle be true; however, adherents to this maxim can instigate a bloated, disjointed curriculum manipulated by special interest groups.

Social studies is an interdisciplinary subject composed of history, geography, economics, anthropology, sociology, political science, and psychology. At the core of each of the disciplines is human behavior. Although curriculum varies from state to state, the following foci for kindergarten through grade 8 are common.

Grade	*Focus*
Kindergarten	self, family, special days
Grade 1	self, family, school
Grade 2	school and neighborhood
Grade 3	local community and communities around the world
Grade 4	the state and regions of the country
Grade 5	multidisciplinary study of the United States
Grade 6	multidisciplinary study of the world
Grade 7	multidisciplinary study of the world
Grade 8	multidisciplinary study of the United States

For the purpose of discussion, each of the social studies disciplines will be examined separately. In real life, however, the disciplines overlap. One cannot study the history of slavery in the United States without being familiar with the geography of the slave trade, the economics of slave labor, the anthropological and sociological aspects of antebellum African American and Southern life, and the psychology that kept the slave trade in business.

Some historians devote their careers to the study of a particular historical event such as D-day or to the study of an individual such as Thomas Alva Edison. Books on ancient Greece and Rome could fill a good-sized library. Geographers might spend decades conducting research on a particular landform. How can parents and caregivers possibly hope to help children learn social studies with its overwhelmingly vast content?

The most effective strategy for parents or caregivers is to stimulate an interest in the disciplines of social studies at an early age. This chapter includes novel strategies not often found in classrooms due to time constraints, which we have found useful in sparking this interest and maintaining it throughout the grades. Each strategy lends itself to development in the home.

HISTORY

The discipline that immediately comes to most people's minds when thinking about social studies is history. History tells tales of past achievements and calamities, victories and tragedies that should inform the present and the future. Responsible citizens need grounding in what has come before so that present and future decisions have the perspectives and wisdom of the ages. History can be a difficult subject for young children, however, because they do not have a clear sense of time until around age 11 or 12. A year, from birthday to birthday, seems remarkably long to young children. Dates such as 1776, 1865, and 1945 are incomprehensible. The only way to address events that happened in the distant past is to tell young children that they happened "long ago." George Washington was our first president long ago. People moved in covered wagons to new places long ago. Not so long ago, Dr. Martin Luther King Jr. worked hard so that all people would be treated equally.

A parent's best resource for teaching history to young children is the public library. Children respond to narratives—stories—about the past, and children's books can relay historical information without getting bogged down in dates and cumbersome details not essential to the story. Styles of dress, conveyances, architecture, and perhaps manner of conversation serve as clues that the story did not take place recently. An example of enduring children's literature with long-ago settings is Laura Ingalls Wilder's *Little House* books. Each year the National Council for the Social Studies (www.ncss.org) selects and publishes a free, annotated list of "Notable Trade

Books for Young People" in grades K–8. Many of their selections have historical themes.

Point of view should be discussed when reading any historical information, because the accuracy of historical events depends on who is doing the telling or writing. Firsthand accounts of Civil War doctors serve as an example. One Confederate medical administrator was "satisfied that never before in the history of wars was there such a corps of medical men as served the Confederate soldiers" (Cunningham, 1958, p. 261). Complaints from the soldiers about their doctors, however, were not uncommon. A soldier from North Carolina wrote:

> I used to think that Dr. Strudwick was a splendid Dr., but if I was to get sick here I should hate to have him at attend on me. . . . Last Saturday night he was sent for to go to see a felow with pneumonia. He said that the felow was just as able to come to see him, so he never went atall. in the morning the felow was ded. Any thing that he goes at he don't half do it, he has set several bones here and they either growed crooked or they had to be set even again. (Cunningham, 1958, p. 256)

A war correspondent reported that he witnessed "surgeons so stupefied by liquor that they could not distinguish between a man's arm and the spoke of a wheel" (Cunningham, 1958, p. 259). Various Confederate generals, however, referred to Confederate physicians "untiring in their attention to the wounded," and "prompt and attentive" (p. 260). "History" always reflects the experiences and biases of the observer.

ACTIVITIES TO DEVELOP AN INTEREST IN HISTORY

Oral Histories

An oral history is a narrative based on the recollections of an individual. The history is gathered through an interview or series of interviews with the source. Oral histories probably have been listened to—if not recorded—since elders have had the language capabilities to tell tales of their lives to their descendants. They have become increasingly popular as technology has improved and become more commonplace. Over a decade ago, Ritchie (1995) wrote:

> It is impossible to pinpoint a place on the globe where people are not now doing oral history. Since the appearance of the first recording devices . . . interviewers have questioned politicians and protesters, indigenous peoples and immigrants, artists and artisans, soldiers and civilians. . . . Oral historians have recorded the reminiscences of survivors of the Nazi Holocaust, the Japanese-American internment, and the Soviet gulags. Interviews have also captured the

everyday experiences of families and communities, whether in inner cities, satellite suburbs, or remote villages. When historians came to realize that women and racial and ethnic minorities were missing from the pages of most history texts, oral historians recorded their voices to construct a more diverse and accurate portrait of the past. (p. xi)

Tracy, one of our undergraduate students, told us:

People, for the most part, like to talk about their life but don't always have the opportunity to do so. My grandmother would say, "You know, I haven't thought about that for a long time," or "I'd almost forgotten about that," and then she would smile at the memory. I was happy I could help bring those memories back. I learned that listening to other people talk about their lives helps give you a clearer picture of your own life.

Tracy had just recorded her grandmother's oral history. You may consider steering your child toward interviewing a special relative or family friend.

Johnson and Johnson (1996) offered several tips for gathering oral histories. Before conducting an oral history of a relative or friend, it is advisable to make some advance preparations. Locate a quiet room, free from distraction. Write questions for the interviewee in an open-ended format—that is, the questions should not require merely a yes-or-no answer. Do not give the questions to the interviewee before the interview; to do so would curtail spontaneity. Avoid insensitive questions such as those relating to failures or money problems. Oral histories are most beneficial when the interviewees are at least 20 years older than the majority of the intended audience.

During the interview, the interviewer should remain neutral. Comments such as "How terrible!" or "Wow!" or "That's great!" should be avoided. They add nothing and disrupt the flow of the interview. Any additional questions during the interview should develop from prior responses. Examples include, "Could you tell me more about that? What did that mean for your family? What made _____ such a memorable president?"

Oral histories give viewers and listeners personal accounts of good times and bad, of neighborhoods and national events, of the determination and resiliency of the American people. Possible oral history interview topics include prominent people in the news during an era, historical events witnessed, food, clothing, fads, prices, and wages during a specific time span, natural disasters, teachers and classrooms, transportation, housing, advice to today's youth, and predictions for the future.

In-depth Studies

Another engaging activity that usually is not found in schools is an in-depth study of an historical event or historical figure. Historical events can become distorted—even mythical—over time. An in-depth family study of an event can help to set the record straight—or as straight as available historical information will allow. The following examples show how one can pique interest in topics for in-depth studies.

Example 1: The Pony Express

Most people have heard tales about the Pony Express with its rapid ponies and their fearless riders crossing the expansive West to deliver the mail. The much-heralded Express has appeared in numerous books, movies, and paintings. It often comes as a surprise, however, that the Pony Express lasted only 18 months—a blip in American history. Buffalo Bill Cody and Wild Bill Hickok are just two people who were responsible for turning this enterprise into an American legend (see Corbett, 2003). An in-depth study of a topic such as the Pony Express would not be conducted to memorize minutiae about the Express but to learn about overcoming harsh conditions and how hungry people in the West were for news. The saga also shows how hype and tales of derring-do can capture the attention of a nation.

Example 2: England's Efforts to Settle in Australia

In 1787, ships carrying 787 convicts left England. The final destination of the ships was the continent of Australia. One might think that the crimes of those sent so far from home were of the most serious nature. Cobley (1970) painstakingly compiled a list of the convicts' names, ages, occupations (when available), places and dates of trials, the crimes, and the sentences for 733 of the convicts. The point of studying the extensive data is not to memorize the facts of each entry but to understand that little attention was paid to the ages of the convicts or their crimes. Several entries list "highway robbery" as the crime, but many appear to be petty thefts. For example,

> James Grace (a boy of eleven years old) was indicted for burglariously and feloniously breaking and entering the dwelling house of Samuel Burton, at the hour of six in the night, on the 22nd of December last, and feloniously stealing a pair of silk stockings value 7s, and ten yards of silk ribbon, value 2s. the property of said Samuel. (p. 106)

Ann Thornton, a 32-year-old servant, was "indicted for stealing, on the 16th of November last, one muslin apron, value 5s. one shirt, value 6 d., one pair of cotton stockings, value 2s. one one linen handkerchief, value 6d. the property of William Cooke" (p. 268). James Bradley (no age recorded) was "indicted for feloniously stealing on the 8th of June one white linen handkerchief, value 2s. the property of Robert Thornton, Esq." (p. 34).

When perusing the charges against the convicts, the question arises: why did the courts take drastic measures for petty infractions? Cobley (1970) pointed out that although the crimes might seem trivial to us today, "the State imposed harsh penalties in the eighteenth [century] in an attempt to protect property" (p. vii). Also, we can infer that English prisons must have been filled, the English wanted to further populate Australia, and juvenile courts did not exist.

To help with in-depth studies of events, eyewitness accounts can be found. Some accounts are surprisingly old. For example, there are eyewitness accounts of the eruption of Mt. Vesuvius, which buried Pompeii in 79 A.D., the Black Death that swept through Europe in the mid-1300s, the Boston Tea Party, the signing the Declaration of Independence, Napoleon's campaigns, the Irish potato famine, the gold strike at Sutter's Mill, the sinking of the Titanic, and many more. Books such as *Eyewitness to History* (Carey, 1987) and *Eyewitness to America: 500 Years of America in the Words of Those Who Saw It Happen* (Colbert, 1997) contain numerous firsthand accounts.

Example 3: Historical Figures

History is predominantly a story about people. Parents and caregivers can encourage research about historical figures so those who shaped history seem less distant to contemporary students. Even young children can benefit from historical biographies written in narrative form as long as they understand that the characters lived "long ago" or "not so long ago." Children's interest in Albert Einstein, for example, often is heightened when they learn that in his early years, Einstein was not a stellar student. Math was a particularly difficult subject for him, and he had to engage in remedial work for a year before he was allowed to enter the Federal Polytechnic Academy in Zurich (Morrow, 1995).

One of the best resources for more contemporary figures is the obituary section of the *New York Times* or any other widely circulated newspaper. Books, such as *The Last Word: The New York Times Book of Obituaries and Farewells: A Celebration of Unusual Lives* (Siegel, 1999), report on the lives of people who do not immediately come to mind as historical figures, such as popcorn magnate Orville Redenbacher, but who nonetheless contributed to the American way of life.

Another strategy to spark interest in historical figures is through the study of eponyms, words named after people. There are entire dictionaries consisting of nothing but eponyms. The medical profession alone has thousands of eponyms (e.g., Alzheimer's disease, Parkinson's disease). Here are just a few frequently used eponyms.

blanket: Thomas Blanket, who lived during the late 1300s, is credited with making these coverings.

boycott: Captain Charles Boycott (1832–1897) was a landlord who levied unreasonable rents. His tenants shunned or "boycotted" him.

diesel: Rudolf Diesel (1858–1913) was a German engineer whose name is associated with diesel fuel.

Fahrenheit: Gabriel Daniel Fahrenheit (1686–1736) was the inventor of the mercury thermometer.

Ferris wheel: George W. G. Ferris (1859–1896) was an American engineer who designed the first Ferris wheel in 1893.

leotard: This article of clothing is named after Jules Leotard (1842–1870), a circus performer.

melba: Nellie Melba (1861–1931), an internationally renowned opera singer from Melbourne, Australia, was the inspiration behind the dessert peach melba and melba toast.

tetrazzini: Chicken tetrazzini is named for Luisa Tetrazzin (1872–1941), a well-known Italian opera singer.

watt: Watt, used in reference to light bulbs among other things, is named after James Watt (1736–1819), a British inventor.

Example 4: The Bad Old Days

"The good old days," is a phrase commonly heard in casual conversation. Young people might wonder what was so good about these times. Humans, with the passage of time, have a tendency to forget or overlook challenging episodes and magnify more pleasant remembrances. Days gone by, however, often were not as carefree and delightful as some portray, and a parent or caregiver can pull back the dreamy curtain of nostalgia. For example, there were no national child labor laws until 1904, when the National Child Labor Committee was established. Prior to 1904, a factory manager said, "We take them as soon as they can stand up" (Bettmann, 1974, p. 77). Bettmann reported that cold water was splashed in children's faces to keep them awake late at night. Some children worked until the early hours of the morning when "In the utter weariness, after work, these children often forgot their hunger and fell asleep with food in their mouths" (p. 77). Most medical care in the good old days was appalling. Rats in hospitals were a vexing problem. Bettmann wrote of a hospital in New York where "Authorities admitted 'the building is swarming with rats, as many as forty having been killed in a bathroom in one evening'" (p. 146).

The Pessimist's Guide to History (Flexner & Flexner, 2008) is chock-full of bad news. Diseases, fires, revolts, famines—it's all here. The volume also serves as a reminder that natural occurrences, such as floods, hurricanes, earthquakes, tsunamis, blizzards, tornadoes, and droughts shape history.

Pundits and others outside the field of education persistently criticize social studies instruction by citing historical facts that public school students do not know. But which events should be studied? The barter for Manhattan in May 1626? Napoleon's escape from the island of Elba in February 1815? Andrew Jackson's victory in the Battle of New Orleans also in 1815? The Mississippi Valley floods of 1927? The Los Angeles riots in 1965? And who said, "Don't shoot until you see the whites of their eyes"? Which Mongol Emperor of China was born in 1215? Who was the woman who seized the Russian throne in 1741 and ruled for 20 years? No one could know all of the events and all of the prominent people of the past, but parents and caregivers can tap into children's fascination with stories about human behavior and curious happenings to nurture an interest in history.

GEOGRAPHY

The second discipline most often associated with social studies is geography, the study of places and human interaction within places. As with history, critics of public education often bemoan children's lack of geographic literacy, and as with history, high-stakes tests have not included geography, so it is ignored or pushed into the curricular background.

With history, children have a problem with time, but geography can be a difficult subject for young children because they have problems with the concept of distance and place. Even some third graders, for example, confuse cities, states, and countries. They may think that Chicago is a state and Illinois is a country. Maps and globes have evolved into sophisticated interactive tools, but technological bells and whistles cannot eclipse normal child development. Scale of miles, latitude, and longitude are introduced in the elementary curriculum, but the topics, because of their abstract nature, are too challenging for many pupils. There are, however, several engaging geography activities that parents or caregivers can do with young children. These activities go beyond those usually included in classrooms.

Colorful Town Names

The introduction of colorful or funny place-names is an enjoyable way to interest children in the locations of towns and cities. Each of the 50 states has unusual place-names. Here are just two from each state.

Alabama: Bug Tussle, Octagon
Alaska: Candle, Coldfoot
Arizona: Snowflake, Why
Arkansas: Figure Five, Nail

California: Happy Camp, Weed Patch
Colorado: Firstview, Last Chance
Connecticut: Hattertown, Long Society
Delaware: Pepperbox, Shortly
Florida: Frostproof, Two Egg
Georgia: Between, Experiment
Hawaii: Cod Fish Village, Crater Village
Idaho: Headquarters, Good Grief
Illinois: New Design, Oblong
Indiana: Easytown, Santa Claus
Iowa: Coin, What Cheer
Kansas: Buttermilk, Neutral
Kentucky: Eighty Eight, Oddville
Louisiana: Start, Waterproof
Maine: Bingo, Grindstone
Maryland: Accident, Rising Sun
Massachusetts: Loudville, Sandwich
Michigan: Bad Axe, Wooden Shoe
Minnesota: Sleepy Eye, Young America
Mississippi: Hot Coffee, Whynot
Missouri: Peculiar, Tightwad
Montana: Checkerboard, Twodot
Nebraska: Hazard, Magnet
Nevada: Dinner Station, Jackpot
New Hampshire: Breakfast Hill, Cowbell Corners
New Jersey: Double Trouble, Yellow Frame
New Mexico: Pep, Truth or Consequences
New York: Endwell, Painted Post
North Carolina: Tar Heel, Toast
North Dakota: Concrete, Zap
Ohio: Charm, Jumbo
Oklahoma: Cookietown, Okay
Oregon: Drain, Wagontire
Pennsylvania: Bird in Hand, Coupon
Rhode Island: Chopmist, Watch Hill
South Carolina: Lone Star, Nine Times
South Dakota: Plenty Bears, Tea
Tennessee: Frog Jump, Only
Texas: Cash, Uncertain
Utah: Hardup, Helper
Vermont: Bread Loaf, Birdport
Virginia: Big Fork, Lively
Washington: Kid Valley, Plain

West Virginia: Dent, Odd
Wisconsin: Cable, Siren
Wyoming: Goose Egg, Ten Sleep

Children, with the help of an adult, can locate these unusual place-names on a detailed map of the target state or the state map in a road atlas. The Internet also can be helpful. Children who do not have difficulty working with a scale of miles can determine the distance from one colorfully named town or city to another (e.g., the distance from What Cheer, Iowa, to Tight-wad, Missouri).

There is a story behind every town and city name. *A Place Called Peculiar: Stories about Unusual American Place-Names* (Gallant, 1998) is a valuable resource for learning about these tales. Several examples are given for each state: Snowflake, Arizona, was named for its founders, Mr. Snow and Mr. Flake. The name "Oddville" was chosen for a town in Kentucky when the original choice, Mt. Washington, was rejected by the federal government because of numerous Washingtons throughout the country. Prominent citizens decided on "Oddville"—a safe bet for being unique among names. In 1890, a citizen of Swedish descent was applying for a post office to be located in a tiny Wisconsin town. Many *syrens* were blooming. When the postal workers in Washington saw "Syren" on the town-name application, they "corrected" the name to "Siren." "Syren" should have stayed on the application; it is Swedish for "lilac." Your child can write letters or send e-mails to mayors or post offices in towns of interest to inquire about the origins of the towns and their names.

Odonyms

Odonyms, or street names, also can spark geographic interest. There is a "Road to Happiness" in Vermillion, Ohio, and an "Almosta Road" in Darby, Montana. "Stone's Throw Road" and "Goodgoin Road" are in Ruston, Louisiana (see Johnson, 1999). Street names provide not only opportunities for geographic research but also for some historical digging. Dickson (1996) categorized street names into three time periods. From 1682 to 1945, streets mainly were named for numbers (e.g., "First Street," "Ninth Avenue"), trees (e.g., "Maple Way," "Birch Boulevard"), well-known people (e.g., "Franklin Drive," "Jefferson Road"), prominent businesses on the street (e.g., "Bank Lane"), and for where the street eventually ended (e.g., "Green Bay Drive"). From 1945 to 1960, streets took on names that implied comfort and relaxation for veterans of World War II and work-weary suburbanites. Examples included streets with the words "Haven" or "Grove" in them. Street names from 1960 until the present have themes (e.g., "Agatha Christie Circle," "Sherlock Trail," and "Watson Way," or "Rose Road," "Tulip Drive," "Lily

Lane"). With your supervision, your child can take a walking tour of the immediate community and write down street names. With the help of town or city personnel, the origins of those names can be found.

Menus and Cookbooks

Restaurant menus can give children insights into geographic differences. Most major restaurants post their menus on their Web sites. For example, a menu from Prejean's, in Lafayette, Louisiana, the heart of Cajun country, features a variety of gumbos, dishes made with Acadian andouille (sausage), alligator, Tasso (dried meat), and sides of dirty rice (rice with chicken giblets and chicken liver), and corn macque choux (a Cajun dish of tomatoes and corn).

Regional cookbooks also reveal information about local ingredients that are used in dishes. These cookbooks are available through groups such as the Junior League. An example of regional recipes from the Junior League of Monroe, Louisiana (2000), includes butter bean casserole, crawfish étouffeé, okra gumbo, pickled black-eyed peas, pralines (a type of candy usually containing pecans), and yam pie. Butter beans, crawfish, okra, black-eyed peas, and pecans are all readily available in northeastern Louisiana.

ECONOMICS

Economics, "the study of the production, distribution, exchange, and consumption of goods and services that people need or want" (Parker & Jarolimek, 1997, p. 108) is usually addressed through consumer education in the lower grades. Your child can learn the difference between "needs" and "wants" by cutting out pictures from magazines and newspapers and pasting them on sheets of paper labeled "needs" or "wants." Children soon realize that their wants exceed their needs.

Everyday errands can turn into lessons in economics. The local supermarket is an ideal location for price comparison of various brands; local banks give children a notion of check cashing, ATM functions, coin-counting machines, and establishing a savings account. A mall can serve as an example of how some businesses are geared toward goods (e.g., clothing stores, sporting goods stores) or services (e.g., dry cleaners, hairdressers). Your child also can learn about various occupations at these locales.

Every meal eaten away from home can be a lesson in economics for learners of all ages. Petchesky (2007) recently exposed some tricks that are used to make salad bars more profitable. He wrote:

> In 1997, Sysco, the country's largest food-service distributor, published a profitability guide that advised salad bar operators that the most expensive

ingredients should be placed in smaller or high-sided containers so items are more difficult to see and remove. And to make your quest even harder, Sysco also recommended providing puny serving utensils for low-margin foods. "The intended goal," the guide reads, "should be to make expensive items relatively hard to get so that indiscriminate diners don't load up on crab instead of carrots." (p. 110)

Petchesky revealed many other salad bar tricks. For example, if the restaurant wants to get rid of a certain food on the salad bar, white containers should be avoided and the containers should be propped up higher. Also, inexpensive items should be placed near the beginning of the salad bar so that there is little room for more expensive items by the time customers get to the end.

Markups on salad bar items are staggering. Petchesky found that iceberg lettuce, on average, has a 3,579 percent markup, carrots a 2,396 percent markup, potatoes a 6,255 percent markup, and fruit a 1,897 percent markup. Seafood and meat and poultry have a 75 percent and 288 percent markup respectively. Petchesky quoted Jeffrey Summers from Restaurant Coaching Solutions: "It's a store owner's dream when you fill up with veggies. . . . And most people do" (pp. 110–11). Petchesky added, "If you want to be a savvy shopper, go easy on garden-variety choices like carrots, cukes, and tomatoes. Mushrooms and avocados, at $2 per pound wholesale, offer the best veggie value" (p. 111). And if customers are paying for items at a salad bar by the pound, they should avoid items with pits, bones, and shells.

No novel study of economics would be complete without examining the lives of some of America's most famous businesspeople. When we see or hear a brand name, we seldom think of who was behind the name. Here is just a brief list of some famous people behind the brand and what they are best known for.

Clarence Birdseye (frozen foods)
Joseph Campbell (soup)
Joseph Gerber (baby food)
Godfrey Keebler (baked goods)
William Keith Kellogg (cereal)
Harry Reese (peanut butter cups)
Esteé Lauder (cosmetics)
John Michael Kohler (bathroom fixtures)
Calvin Klein (clothing and more)
Liz Claiborne (clothing and more)
Rowland Macy (department store)
Charles Tiffany (jewelry store)
Warren Avis (rental cars)

William Boeing (airplanes)
Herman Guy Fisher and Irving Lanouette Price (toys)
William Harley and Arthur Davidson (motorcycles)

Books such as *So Who the Heck Was Oscar Meyer? The Real People behind Those Brand Names* (Gelbert, 1996) will help with your child's research on giants in the business world.

SOCIOLOGY

Sociology, the study of groups of people and their social relationships, usually is addressed through discussions about families and schools in the lower grades. Books such as *The Story of Ruby Bridges* (Coles, 2004), about the integration of the New Orleans public schools by a brave young girl, can introduce young children to sociological issues such as prejudice and racism in a narrative format.

Older children might look at citizens of this country and select one aspect of interest—bumper stickers, for example. Bumper stickers are American in origin. Dickson (1990) wrote:

> As best as can be determined, one of the first, if not the very first, true bumper stickers came out of the Gill Studios of Shawnee Mission, Kansas. The firm's founder, Forest Gill, had been working with fluorescent inks and with self-sticking labels. As World War II ended, he was getting orders for cardboard bumper signs, and he began experimenting with self-sticking signs with color-ful ink. (p. 9)

Common humorous bumper stickers have included: "Be alert: This country needs more lerts," "If you don't like the way I drive, get off the sidewalk," and "I'm in no hurry, I'm on my way to work" (Dickson, 1990, pp. 213, 269, 302). On a road trip or simply walking back to your car in a parking lot, your child could record and tabulate the different bumper-sticker state-ments he or she encounters. How many are political? Humorous?

Other sociology home-research projects could include examining com-mon topics among popular comedians (e.g., politics, celebrities, the econ-omy), researching American fads, television viewing habits, and best-seller book lists.

ANTHROPOLOGY

In the lower grades, anthropology, the study of the similarities and differ-ences of cultures, is best addressed through picture books about children in other lands. Free lists are available on the National Council for the Social Studies Web site (www.socialstudies.org). A novel way for older students to examine one aspect of various cultures is to examine their proverbs.

A proverb is a saying that makes an observation about life or offers advice. "Haste makes waste" is a proverb. Johnson (1999) stated that proverbs

1. are not wordy or syntactically complicated;
2. often rhyme or are alliterations;
3. are sometimes stated metaphorically;
4. often are very old and anonymous;
5. deal with tangible, unpretentious topics;
6. are a part of every culture; and
7. are timeless and universal in their application. (p. 98)

Johnson observed that proverbs can be found in every culture because "it is characteristic of cultures to pass wisdom on from one generation to the next" (p. 104). Entire dictionaries of proverbs from around the world are available in public libraries. Here are some proverbs from various countries.

France: A day is lost if one has not laughed.
United States: The best things in life are free.
Italy: Since my house must be burned, I may as well warm myself at it.
Argentina: A dog that barks all the time gets little attention.
China: Never eat in a restaurant where the chef is thin.
Denmark: Better to ask twice than to lose your way once.
West Africa: Not to know is bad, but not to wish to know is worse.

Books of American proverbs can be found in most public libraries.

PSYCHOLOGY

Psychology, the study of behaviors, usually is not addressed in the lower grades. This discipline, however, can be introduced at an early age through the topic of advertisements that are aimed at children. Television commercials, Internet ads, and print media ads are ubiquitous. Adults can help children dissect ads through guided questions: Why do you think the advertiser used such bright colors and loud music? Why do the kids in the ads look so happy? Do you think that the toy really makes someone happier? Does the toy in the ad look smaller in real life than in does in the commercial? Why do you think that those cereals use cartoon characters? Why is there a rhyming song with that commercial? Why are so many candy/toy/fast food/junk food ads shown during that program? Children also can be introduced to the psychology of words used in advertising. Terminology such as "new," "improved," "moister," "light," "all natural," "free offer," or "richer" can influence a purchasing decision.

Packages do more than protect items for sale. Packages help sell things. Shell (1996) wrote that packages

> make us hungry for things we don't need, even for things we don't want. In the eight seconds or so that it takes to choose a laundry detergent or frozen pizza, the package must scream or whine or purr or whisper its message of good taste or cheapness or strength or luxury loud and clear enough to grab our interest. (p. 56)

Shell uses the packaging of a cake mix as an example:

> Imagine, for instance, a substance in a clear plastic bag bearing a simple label with its list of ingredients and the words "CHOCOLATE CAKE MIX." Imagine this sad heap slumping on the grocer's shelf in a funk of brown powder, devoid of its promise to bloom into a showy dessert. How many of us would choose to pick up, let alone buy, this pile of dust? (p. 56)

Hine (1995) explained the importance of color use on a package. Orange is "powerful," yellow is "the most visible color," and blue is the "memorable, likable color, which symbolizes softness and mildness" (p. 149). "Natural" foods and those with "whole grain goodness" often use earth tones in their packaging. Hine explained that frozen food packaging requires visually warmer colors to alleviate the "iciness" of the product. Shapes (people prefer circles over triangles on product packaging) and cultures (Americans don't like to pour milk from a plastic pouch) also influence how items are packaged.

We often hear the phrase "brand loyalty." Older children certainly are aware of brand names and can delve deeper into brands and branding. Clifton and Simmons (2004) reported:

> The past few years have seen the apparent triumph of the brand concept: everyone from countries to political parties to individuals in organisations is now encouraged to think of themselves as a brand. At its best this means caring about, measuring and understanding how others see you, and adapting what you do to take account of it, without abandoning what you stand for. At its worst it means putting a cynical gloss or spin on your product or your actions to mislead or manipulate those you seek to exploit. (p. xii)

Clifton and Simmons's collection of essays discusses what makes a brand successful, brand communication, public relations and branding, and more. Psychology approached in this way overlaps well with consumer education.

POLITICAL SCIENCE

Political science is "the study of how human beings think, organize, and act politically" (Welton and Mallan, 1996, p. 59). A convenient, inexpensive resource for developing an interest in political science is introducing children to political or editorial cartoons, which are found in most newspapers. Although political cartoons show only one person's opinion—often through satire and exaggeration—they provide a means to initiate a discussion of current events.

Even young children can create their own political cartoons. First they should identify a problem in the neighborhood such as noise or litter or a more global issue such as climate change. Then they should decide how to portray the problem with minimal illustration. If captions are needed, you can assist them in honing their message so that a few words say a lot. Perhaps your local newspaper would be willing to publish your child's work.

CHARACTER EDUCATION

This chapter would not be complete without the mention of character education, which is a part of the social studies curriculum and often taught as a part of civics and citizenship. Commercial programs that address character education are available in most public schools. An effective way to address character education with young children is through moral dilemmas created by the parent or caregiver.

Moral dilemmas are scenarios that require analysis to determine various courses of action and to identify the consequences of the actions taken. What follows is a simple moral dilemma for young children.

The Missing Toy

Brenda brought a new toy to school and put it in her desk for show-and-tell later that morning. As Brenda left the classroom for recess, Melissa stuck her hand into Brenda's desk, took out the toy, and stuffed it into her backpack. Juan saw Melissa take Brenda's toy. What should Juan do?

After children hear or read the moral dilemma, they can name the various courses of action and the consequences. For example, Juan can say nothing, but then Brenda might not get her toy back. Juan can tell the teacher, but then others might think he is a tattletale. He can confront Melissa and urge her to return the toy, but Melissa might not appreciate his interference. He also can tell Brenda that Melissa took her toy, but she might not believe him. Melissa might feel guilty and return the toy on her own.

Parents can write their own moral dilemmas to illustrate a behavior in their own children that they would like to modify or change without calling attention to the immediate situation. Moral dilemmas can be used with any age group. Here are just a few.

1. You are in a convenience store. You see someone shoplifting. What should you do?
2. A cashier accidentally gives you too much change back after a purchase. What should you do?
3. You see a classmate cheating on a test. What should you do?
4. While waiting in a long line for tickets to a concert, two people sneak in ahead of you. What should you do?

Moral dilemmas present themselves frequently in everyday life, and they are an effective starting point for discussing what we value as individuals—trusting others, the importance of friendship, being patient with others, and so on.

THE MULTIDISCIPLINARY NATURE OF SOCIAL STUDIES

An engaging way for a parent or caregiver to highlight the multidisciplinary nature of social studies is through construction projects. Children can decide what they would like to build: a theme park, a city of the past or future, a mountain village. Projects should not be started without some research. For example, if a medieval castle is going to be constructed, several questions arise: On what type of terrain were castles usually built? What was it like inside the walls? Were there usually other buildings outside the walls? How was water supplied? Were castles ever on a main thoroughfare? What surrounded the castle? How did those outside the castle earn a living? Planning a more contemporary scene involves commercial buildings, residential buildings, transportation considerations such as roads and bridges, government buildings such as fire stations, schools, libraries, and recreation considerations such as parks. Recyclable materials can be used for the project.

Any item, no matter how small or common, can be used as a focus for social studies curriculum, because every item has a history, a geography, and so on. Petroski (1992), for example, has written an entire book on the pencil. Other books have been written on the codfish, salt, and even on the ingredients in a cheeseburger. No item is too inconsequential for study. With your guidance, your children can develop an interest in an aspect of social studies that could last a lifetime. Perhaps they will become Civil War buffs or cartographers. Maybe they will lead archaeological digs. To engage them in the engrossing subject of social studies is to give them a priceless gift.

9

The Myth of Average Intelligence

> I think I differ from those who subscribe to the admittedly foundational belief that we cannot have gifted education without gifted children only with respect to means, not ends.
>
> —James Borland

We conclude our book by arguing that there is no such thing as average intelligence. Although psychometricians have come up with a theoretical construct of average intelligence and have identified possible ways of measuring it, the level of intellectual diversity among those students who are classified as such is so overwhelming that it would simply be a pretense to come up with such an overgeneralization. Many readers at this point might think that we're going out on a limb or that we take an extreme position in stating our thesis about the chimera of average intelligence. But clearly, as we have identified in chapters 3 and 4, others too have challenged conventional thought on the beguiling phenomenon of intelligence and have developed differing views on ability and how to measure it (see Borland, 2005; Dweck, 2006; Johnson & Johnson, 2006; Ness & Farenga, 2007; Nisbett, 2009; Pea, 1993; Perkins, 1992, 1995a; Piaget, 1930; Sternberg, 1985). In fact, some have questioned not only the concept but also the practice of how ability is measured and reported within the American education system.

In his chapter entitled "Gifted Education without Gifted Children: The Case for No Conception of Giftedness," James Borland (2005) argues that divisions of intelligence, such as gifted versus average, do not exist. In fact, contemporary research in psychology and neuroscience seems to conclude that these divisions are more an issue of social class or ethnic difference rather than one of genetic disparity. Richard Nisbett's (2009) view of intelligence corroborates Borland's argument in this regard. In his book, *Intelligence and How to Get It: Why Schools and Culture Count*, Nisbett places a greater emphasis on environmental conditions that are required to take advantage of hereditary potential, suggesting that genetics may account for less than 50 percent of an individual's IQ scores. However, Nisbett does not throw the baby out with the bathwater. He states that IQ tests do measure some level of ability, pointing to the example that siblings with higher IQ scores tend to earn higher incomes than those with lower scores even within the same family. Nisbett compares the differences among adoptive families, higher socioeconomic families, and children who are raised in the same family to support his position on the importance of environmental attributes on cognition. It is precisely Nisbett's argument that we find encouraging and crucial for children labeled as average. Children require a degree of intelligence to take advantage of the appropriate environmental stimuli for maximizing their ability. Nisbett also identifies a similar need noted by Johnson, Johnson, Farenga, and Ness (2008) for very early intervention—prior to preschool—that calls attention to the recognition of varying child-rearing practices by parents and their impact on measures of ability.

Nisbett and others have identified the importance of talking, explaining, and playing with young children in creative ways for supporting cognitive development. In *Knowledge under Construction: The Importance of Play in Developing Children's Spatial and Geometric Thinking*, Ness and Farenga (2007) provide evidence for the idea that a wide range of cognitive environments may have a greater affect on children from lower socioeconomic families. Comparing low, medium, and high socioeconomic families with preschool children, all of whom are in cognitively stimulating environments, the authors found no difference in the complexity of the children's block-building abilities or the development of spatial and geometric thinking. Further, Ness and Farenga point out the importance and need for an enriching curriculum and both early and extended academic interventions in order to increase children's measures of ability.

In Ness and Farenga's (2007) work, young children, regardless of socioeconomic background, were provided the opportunity and the environment for engaging in Lego and block play. Children from low socioeconomic families attended preschools that determined qualification for subsidized day care through the Agency for Child Development Services. These preschools provided the materials and thus enabled these children to engage in an environment conducive to free play. But, indeed, these conditions are not always available in the lives of all children of low-income households. The authors conclude that when ordinary people are offered and take advantage of extraordinary opportunities, exceptional performances are likely. The issue of IQ and its related ability labels does raise the complex issues that confound a number of factors. Nisbett makes an important distinction between two such factors: ethnic and social class IQ differences. He asserts that we can most likely eliminate ethnic IQ differences but probably cannot eliminate social class IQ gaps. Ethnic IQ differences may be due to different customs and values that are not recognized as mainstream and thus are not included on tests. However, differences in IQ scores of individuals in lower socioeconomic classes are more a matter of depravation. But these children are in no way deprived of academic and intellectual potential or social and emotional attachment; rather, depravation occurs as a result of poor nutrition, lack of sufficient health care, and everyday concerns for safety.

In his book, *The Myth of the Deprived Child*, Herb Ginsburg (1972) investigates numerous views of intelligence and research studies during the twentieth century that focus on poor children's intellectual abilities. Nearly all the works that Ginsburg introduces contend that poor children are deprived intellectually and that their language abilities are in many respects deficient in some way. Ginsburg shows that these works are almost entirely without warrant. He succinctly demonstrates how the great majority of these positions on intelligence fail to consider the starkly different environments in which children of varying socioeconomic backgrounds are raised. Ginsburg informs us that intellectual depravation is simply a fallacious construct, basing this position on the very nature of social and environmental diversity of children of low-income households. We would add that many of these children have more pressing issues to be concerned about in their everyday lives than their educational progress. These include the safety of the communities in which they live, adequate health care, food security, and nutrition. Indeed, as suggested by Abraham Maslow, concern about health and safety trumps intellectual pursuit.

We also argue that institutions of education fail average (and other) students, because for the last decade or so, there has been an overwhelming emphasis on meeting benchmarks and standards—as trivial or as complex as they might be—at the expense of student health, creativity, and imagination. This plan ignored the many children of low-income households who are working within a deficit model and are continually caught in a game of trying to reach a moving target. If so-called average- and high-ability children are simultaneously learning, each group advances at their own rate to reach new levels of achievement. In short, the Matthew Effect, a sociological phenomenon that demonstrates an increasingly widening gap between the haves and have-nots (in the present case, nonaverage students and average students), is in full motion in our schools, especially when considering the gross disparities in attention given to low-ability students who have not met state standards. Although the Matthew Effect is used to explain why high-ability students advance beyond other groups of students, it can also be used to explain how average students are held back.

THE UNSPOKEN CONSPIRACY

One of our final claims is that government agencies have initiated a plan to deal with the inequities in society. However, instead of directly addressing the problems, the government has decided to test its way out of achievement differences by focusing on the instrument that identifies the differences. The problem that arises is that in order to raise the scores of a selected group within a system, the other members within that system have to be held constant. Learning is a dynamic process in which students have the opportunity to advance. But one must recognize that in a dynamic setting, *all* students have the opportunity to advance. The only way to change the current setting is to hold some groups constant or create a static situation. This is the educational strategy that we see imposed on average students and used by most schools that spend their instructional time in remedial mode. This remedial strategy takes precedent over all other concerns and is accomplished with the imprimatur of the federal and state governments. The strategy has the greatest negative impact on the average students who could advance but must wait for their peers to catch up. The conspiracy that exists among regulatory and semiregulatory educational agencies advances an agenda that substitutes standards for intellectual ability and propensity.

Through the use of standards, national and state education enterprises, in collusion with professional associations and testing companies, have thwarted the progress of average students. Simply put, governments have outsourced their responsibility to an alphabet soup of organizations in order to establish a national stranglehold on what constitutes appropriate educational achievement. What should be of concern to state and federal governments is that none of the new standards are research- or empirically based (Johnson, Johnson, Farenga, & Ness, 2005). Instead, students are being subjected to curricula that are so-called consensus-driven. The vast majority of the public has no idea of the limited number of people who determine what is appropriate study for the masses. Mindful questions that appear to have been ignored should have been directed to all educational agencies, which would have required them to empirically demonstrate how the new standards are better than past efforts. It is evident that the standards movement has been a boom time for many educational enterprises at the expense of average students and taxpayers. Due to major cutbacks in numerous state departments of education, a lack of oversight allows educational enterprises or nongovernmental agencies to usurp control of curriculum, instruction, and assessment and to establish new norms for students. These enterprises are either autonomous nonprofit or for-profit corporations that parallel the functions of traditional institutions of education. Moreover, their task is to develop, promote, and enforce standards for students in our school systems throughout the country. Our apprehension is that none of these enterprises is an official government entity. One can easily recognize these educational enterprises through the myriad of acronyms used to describe them. Examples include teacher union–related organizations (National Education Association [NEA] and the American Federation of Teachers [AFT]), accreditation enterprises (National Council for the Accreditation of Teacher Education [NCATE] and the Teacher Education Accreditation Council [TEAC]), intergovernmental enterprises (Council of Chief State School Officers [CCSSO], Interstate New Teacher and Assessment Support Consortium [INTASC], and National Board for Professional Teaching Standards [NBPTS]), educational testing enterprises (Educational Testing Service [ETS] and the College Entrance Examination Board [CEEB]), and specialized professional association (SPA) enterprises (International Reading Association [IRA], National Council of Teachers of Mathematics [NCTM], National Science Teachers Association [NSTA], Association for Childhood Education International [ACEI], and National Association for the Education of Young Children [NAEYC]).

To take this a step further, one need only examine teachers' unions (such as the NEA or AFT), which have similar motives for expanding beyond the realm of collective bargaining to managing issues involving curriculum, assessment, professional development, and teacher training. A number of these organizations have coconspired to gain control of education and establish a new order—a goal that in no way benefits the average student. The tools that they have used to accomplish this feat are standards. Each organization has developed a series of standards that attempts to establish what they believe to be an appropriate "level" of education. These nonregulatory organizations are performing regulatory functions by controlling the curriculum in education, thus usurping the authority of traditional educational providers, such as local communities, colleges, and universities. They achieve their regulatory roles through the standards-based reform and accountability movement. Ironically, this movement came about as a result of the purported failure of students in primary and secondary schools (Boyer, 1983; NCEE, 1983; Sizer, 1984), and now they are a major cause of limiting student potential by creating the apparition of average achievement.

Paulo Freire (1970) and Ivan Illich (1972) provide theoretical explanations and perspectives on the present standards movement in education. They suggest that the use of bureaucratic standards and criteria may be viewed as a means by which an enterprise gains control of a given situation. Illich suggests that schooling devoted to achieving consensus-driven benchmarks (i.e., standards) perpetuates hopelessness for the underprivileged. In our investigation, the underprivileged are those who are underserved. Those who are underserved in our case are the silent majority of students who are invisible and ignored by the educational system—the average students. An analysis of the contemporary context places the SPAs and the educational testing enterprises at the heart of what Illich would refer to as the most culpable of the bureaucratic enterprises: organizations that perpetuate the status quo. Gate-keeping is therefore achieved by requiring the majority of students to conform and adhere to a presubscribed conception of average. Extending on Illich's position, the act of labeling students only serves to sectionalize, and not unite, student populations.

An examination of the role of these educational gatekeepers demonstrates Freire's argument in which the haves oppress the have-nots. Groups who receive recognition by federal or state governments are entitled to extra financial and material benefits, thus placing them among the "haves." Being among the "haves" enables these groups to establish a social order of dominance whereby they bestow gate-keeping authority on members of their organization. This method of funding systematically pits groups and their organizations in opposition and establishes an entrenchment mentality that has continually caused educational reforms to fail.

Further, the "standards movement" practice doubly disenfranchises a large number of students, usually from urban and rural areas, who are academically labeled "average" and come from less affluent families. Labeling these students as average avoids the need to provide any additional educational services to maximize their academic potential or to remediate any weaknesses that are not identified so severe as to be a learning disability. The average label is simply a matter of economics—a designation used as a cost-savings measure by local, state, or federal governments to avoid additional funding. In this situation, the social construction of average is buttressed by economic concerns, thus establishing a false pretense of acceptable academic performance. The goal is to eliminate the inequities among various groups in society by demonstrating that they are all average. The solution, however, creates another inequity for a large majority of students. In effect, students' formal education is held hostage at a low level of competence. This is a case of the emperor's new clothes: groups of educators and policymakers agree to advance an educational climate that embraces low-level performance and mediocrity and passes it off to an unsuspecting public that putatively accepts it as "average" ability. This is evidenced by vast discrepancies from most states' high-stakes test results when compared to federal test results. Even superficial comparisons reveal how this low level of knowledge that the states consider "acceptable student performance" develops a false sense of achievement in students. The present educational expectation, then, is based on a minimal competency that is substituted as "average" ability. This practice, when combined with unequal, informal learning opportunities for average low-income students, once again places them at a greater disadvantage than students of more affluent families whose parents are able to provide their children with superior experiences that make up for the deficient formal education. The research is clear that affluent parents have the ability to provide their children with tutors, mentors, educational materials, music lessons, and specialty camps that can both qualitatively and quantitatively increase one's experiences, which, in turn, can be measured as increased academic potential in school (Johnson, Johnson, Farenga, & Ness, 2008).

Again, the Matthew Effect works against children of lesser ability in most comparisons. Even as the low socioeconomic families make gains, they are still at a disadvantage; any gains are usually minimized by poor instruction, summer loss, limited health care, poor nutrition, underfunded community resources, or less parental stimulation. In addition, the assessment industry is dynamic, so any gains that have been made will be erased when new norms are established to redefine "average." In this case, "average" is simply the large number of students whose performance now places them in the 50th percentile when compared to their peers. These arguments make it crucial for parents to recognize the profound effect that they have early in their children's development and the profound effect of social constructs in their lives.

PRIMUM NON NOCERE: FIRST, DO NO HARM

The reasons and arguments presented throughout this book—in addition to the summary arguments made in this chapter—support Borland's (2005) premise concerning the identification of students as average or gifted. There is ample evidence to suggest that Borland's position is correct when he argues that although the notion of the gifted child is spurious, gifted programs and curricula are not. In fact, gifted programs are very much alive—and that's a good thing. In the same light, we argue that although there is no such thing as an average child, average programs and curricula are very real and play an important role in school culture. But unlike gifted programs, the existence of average curricula, especially in its current form, is not such a good thing—in fact, it can thwart student academic progress.

Despite several crises that have erupted in the field of education during the twentieth century, the average curriculum was, for the most part, free from mitigated content. In other words, content-based problems in education such as overemphasis on procedural knowledge at the expense of conceptual knowledge notwithstanding, the average curriculum included content that did not deprive students of what they needed to learn in order to succeed in high school and college-level subjects. In recent years, however, the average curriculum has been eviscerated to the degree that more advanced skills have been replaced with back-to-basics content that leaves most students unprepared for the curriculum that they need to know in order to succeed. In essence, the rigor of the curriculum has been stripped out and replaced with drill and practice skills. In many cases, methodology has replaced content in the curriculum. The algorithm or strategy that was once thought of as a tool to further understanding has become the content to be taught. This practice is only accelerated and exacerbated by the current attitude toward assessment.

At present, then, students have only two options of study: (1) advanced placement courses or accelerated curriculum that were originally meant for individuals who are highly capable in these courses,[1] or (2) watered-down, slow-paced curriculum that is designed to get children to pass high-stakes tests in order to avoid parental, administrative, and community censure. This leaves no option for students in the middle who need strong transcripts in order to attend competitive or highly competitive colleges or universities. They have to either struggle taking classes that are beyond their developmental ability or suffer in classes that are below their developmental level. Students placed in classes in which they do not have the ability to work at the rate of instruction may constantly have to play catch-up, receive tutoring, drop the course, or fail out. We are not saying that students should not work hard or that students should not be allowed to fail; rather, there must be balance in the curriculum to afford students who exhibit the appropriate effort and ability an environment in which the pace of study fosters a greater depth of understanding in any given subject. Students should also have the option to pursue areas of interest in order to increase their motivation. Optional or elective classes are often selected based on students' interests outside of school. These elective classes can provide a bridge between formal and informal learning opportunities, thus increasing students' successful transition from school to everyday life and vice versa. These experiences need to be encouraged so that students are able to experience the practical importance of what they learn in school and its direct impact on societal endeavors.

Many schools offer students the opportunity to self-select classes. The opportunity to self-select is for students who have an undiscovered potential, persistence, and interest in the option to work in a fast-paced setting. Too often, students self-select advanced classes because of peer, parental, or college-related pressures. In some cases, students are pushed into advanced classes so that school administrators can boast about the number of students in advanced or accelerated classes. These are all poor reasons for students to be placed into advanced classes. This practice ignores one of the most important educational questions: what is the appropriate placement for the student? Further, it violates the primary concern when working with students—a concern that was borrowed from the Hippocratic oath and stated succinctly by one of our colleagues Dan Brovey, professor emeritus at Queens College: first, do no harm.

Teachers, administrators, and parents have identified another major concern about students who self-select advanced or accelerated classes and do not succeed: the problem of change in students' schedules. This is especially troublesome for middle school students who are placed on academic teams. In this case, a student's entire schedule may change midyear, thus affecting classes, teachers, and peers. This can add additional pressure to an already stressful situation of stepping down from an accelerated class to a regular class—a situation that can adversely affect one's self-esteem, attitude toward learning, and feelings about school in general. A further concern regarding inappropriate placement in classes is that the student may be pulled from other classes that are considered less-important elective courses—such as music, art, physical education, or technology—to be given the additional academic support required in order to remain in that accelerated mathematics, science, English, or social studies class. The student's broad-field education is curtailed and often the arts and humanities are sacrificed in order to get through the advanced class. What we are suggesting is that there should be an additional option in which the curriculum is sufficiently challenging but by no means remedial or mundane. As stated earlier in this book, the curriculum for all students should be essentially the same and modified only in terms of pace. It should be self-evident that any change in the content changes the course of study. If the objectives of the course are to be met in an intellectually honest manner, then the objectives should be met by all students and measured by equivalent forms of assessment. The current practice of removing prerequisites to many classes and opening them up to all students may be expeditious to administrators and parents, but this solution, despite its egalitarian intentions, has undesirable implications that will adversely affect student learning and success. Opening advanced and honors classes to all students raises numerous concerns, many of which are, surprisingly, raised by students themselves. These criticisms include but are not limited to the following:

- Classes are less rigorous when open to all students, and many of these students require coddling. The content is often truncated or watered-down to accommodate the level of the students.
- Some teachers increase the workload to unreasonable levels in order to get the academically weaker students to drop the class, placing unneeded pressure on all students.
- Some students who work hard and eventually perfect a skill feel that they are alienated and shortchanged when students who have not exerted the same effort are placed in leadership roles.

- The school day is limited and students who may require additional help often have to sacrifice lunch periods, physical education periods, second languages, or fine arts.
- Parents may be overenthusiastic about placing their children in advanced classes, causing unnecessary pressure and stress on their children.

One important question, then, is: what is average curriculum? This question is not that difficult to answer; it is simply the default curriculum—the large part of the curriculum that does not include content and strategies, a number of which are found in chapters 5 through 8 of this book. It is curriculum designed to focus on preparation for high-stakes tests, broad in scope but limited in depth, scripted for teachers who are incapable of preparing appropriate material, and finally a curriculum that lacks creativity.

WHY IT'S NEVER TOO LATE TO SUCCEED
IN SCHOOL AND BEYOND

If a single number is so telling about an individual's intelligence—in other words, an individual's level of intellectual and cognitive ability in comparison to others—our argument that average intelligence is a myth should resonate among those who find it necessary to take a second look at the reasons for being categorized as average. In essence, the reader might infer from our thesis that parents would need to take appropriate measures in the early years in order to ward off the dreaded label of "average" intelligence on their children. From a neuropsychological perspective, research does in fact strongly suggest that the greatest amount of synaptic growth in the brain following birth occurs during infancy and steadily decreases in the second and third year of life. The research also points to a curtailment of neuronal connection—known as synaptic pruning—during adolescent years. Synaptic pruning is simply a weeding-out process that involves the removal of seldom-used connections of neurons for the purpose of making synaptic configurations more efficient. It does not, however, mean that students in their adolescence are unable to learn or succeed in their endeavors or that they are unable to transition from "average" to a higher intellectual level. In sum, it does not mean that they lose intelligence. In fact, they have great potential in gaining it.

THE IMPORTANCE OF FAMILY ON INTELLIGENCE

The importance of family involvement in all levels of a child's education and success cannot be underestimated. For students who are labeled or considered average, family involvement can make the difference between acceptable and exceptional performance. Supreme Court Justice Sonia Sotomayor stated that success like hers is possible when ordinary people are given extraordinary opportunities. We concur with Justice Sotomayor and also suggest that there must be a degree of persistence and the appropriate mind-set toward achievement. The appropriate mind-set must enable the individual to transcend the present and envision a successful future. Nisbett (2009) emphasizes the need for enriching opportunities for children and argues that the racial IQ gap is "purely environmental." A plethora of studies supports the importance of early exposure to out-of-school experiences and increased cognitive potential. Children's early exposure to reading materials, linguistically fluent caregivers, and a variety of manipulative play objects provides fundamental learning experiences that other children who do not have such exposure often fail to receive. Collectively, these experiences provide the student with the necessary opportunities to advance cognitive schema used to interpret future experiences and are measured as a level of intellectual ability.

Wang, Haertel, and Walberg (1993) state that in most instances, parents are the first and most influential teachers. When the home reflects the values of the school and supports the efforts of the school, the child is provided with a continuous experience of education. Support for the school curriculum by parents can help to establish a positive attitude for learning in children. Parents accomplish this task by providing their children with the appropriate out-of-school activities. As far back as 1966, Richard Wolf suggested that the quality of the interaction that parents have with their children has a greater effect on academic achievement than does the socioeconomic background of the family. The experiences that parents create for their children can give rise to a subenvironment that promotes academic ability. Dweck (2006) has supplied ample data to suggest the existence of a positive relationship between an appropriate mind-set and success. Further, she has demonstrated that parents, teachers, and coaches have the ability to promote either a fixed or growth mind-set through their interactions with children.

It is critical to realize that even good intentions that misapply praise can lead to negative consequences. These actions help one to develop the belief that talent is genetic and that success does not require much effort. Individuals with this belief usually view failure as a personal defeat or offense. This is often observed in the student who is thought of as a so-called natural, the one who finds that most challenges can easily be tackled. On the contrary, one with a growth mind-set believes that talent is developed and that effort and persistence increase one's chances to achieve a more successful outcome. A growth mind-set places success outside the limits of one's ego, limiting the effect of failure on one's self-efficacy. This is a particularly significant factor when dealing with failure. Lee Iacocca stated,

"We've lost the value of failure. The first thing some youngsters flunk these days is life itself. That's because they've been passed from one grade to another, and eventually graduated, even though they've been failing at every step. The only problem is, nobody's told them. In attempting to shield these kids from failure, we've guaranteed it" (Seeger, 1994, p. 300). Iacocca has aptly identified the unfortunate phenomenon that has led to the overassessment of one's ability, grade inflation, and the disdain for hard work. Each of these factors has worked against the average student to create both a feeling of entitlement and a learned helplessness that contributes to apathy and failure. Students with a growth mind-set appear to be at an advantage in dealing with failure over those with a fixed mind-set. In fact, the opportunity to fail may provide students with a growth mind-set and a greater probability to learn. Dweck suggests that when these students reattempt the task, they are more focused as they analyze the errors they have made. Now, when students succeed at the task, it can be inferred that they have learned. In behavioral terms, a new response occurs. In cognitive terms, a new schema has developed, and the brains of the growth mind-set students have physically changed. It is important to consider that students with a fixed mind-set never reach the intense level of thought that is demonstrated by their growth mind-set counterparts when they analyze their mistakes.

In addition, effective family involvement is important at all levels of education. Although many parents are actively involved with younger children's education, we often see parents pull back from their level of involvement when their children become adolescents. At this stage, parents try to balance the adolescent's desire for increased independence and their need to monitor the social and academic activities of their children (see table 9.1). Effective parents stay engaged in their children's activities, if only peripherally, in order to be aware of any emerging issues and to prevent minor issues from escalating into larger problems.

Parents who believe their children may not have been provided the appropriate experiences in their early years as outlined by Nisbett (2009) and Ness and Farenga (2007) should not simply give up on providing enriching and rewarding experiences for their families. In fact, the Harvard Family Research Project (HFRP, 2006) investigated numerous research studies showing that family involvement is an essential part of older student and adolescent success in school and college acceptance rates. These studies note a continuum in parenting style, whereby the extremes of this continuum pose a threat to the success of school-age children. On one extreme is the so-called disengaged parent. This parent impedes school success by being uninvolved in their children's everyday lives. Disengaged parents rarely ask their children questions about school and do not attend school functions or participate in school-based activities. On the other extreme

Table 9.1. Suggestions for Parents to Improve Their "Average" Student's Academic Success

Tip	Explanation
1. Encourage your child *not* to cram for exams.	Cramming for an exam forces students to focus on isolated facts that they will more than likely not remember the next day. Moreover, research indicates that cramming makes memories associated with the time that the cramming took place (e.g., 1 or 2 a.m., at the bedroom desk) and not the subject matter. Distributing study over longer periods of time is much more effective.
2. Help your child actively review notes and read chapters by making real-life connections.	Some students who review notes and read chapters based on soon-to-be-tested material don't perform as well on exams as they would have liked. This is because reviewing notes and reading chapters do not fully allow for one's acquisition knowledge of meaningful content. In order to commit this content to memory, reading a chapter text is not good enough. Students need to make connections between class discussion, readings, and even everyday experiences. To do this, put more time into study (say, 1 hour instead of 20 minutes per day for each subject) and consider tips 3 and 4 below.
3. Teach your child to think like the teacher. Encourage your child to create her/his own test questions as exam preparation.	In addition to reviewing material during study, students need to be actively engaged in the content in order to fully understand it and do well. To do this, students need to think of alternative ways to learn the material so that it remains in their memory. One way is for them to develop their own test questions. Create test questions that are similar to those that the teacher uses for exams. In addition, don't create factual questions that can be answered simply with one or two words. Rather than a question such as, "What year was George Washington born?" ask, "What social and political factors were evident during George Washington's youth?" instead.
4. Help your child focus on memorizing concepts—not merely facts and procedures alone.	Students who commit facts and procedures to memory will have a harder time remembering what they need to know for an exam than students who commit concepts to memory. Facts and procedures are important, particularly in certain disciplines. But without connecting those facts to what has been learned earlier or to one's everyday experiences, it will be difficult to ace exams.
5. If possible, have your children study unrelated topics when preparing for tests.	If you can, try to study unrelated subjects when preparing for upcoming tests. In other words, it's better to study English and math concurrently than English and a foreign language. This will help you avoid cognitive interference. In this case, the grammar of one language might interfere with the learning of the other.

(continued)

Table 9.1.   (*continued*)

Tip	Explanation
6. Encourage your child to study more than is necessary.	Students who put little time and effort in studying or preparing for an exam will do poorly on the exam. Students who don't study or who study very little and still do well on an exam probably have familiarity in the subject, most likely from prior experiences. These students probably have thought about the subject more and therefore know the material better. Students who devote at least 20 percent more time than what is expected perform better on exams than do students who put in exactly what is expected of them.
7. Teach your child to use colorful cues to aid in the memory process.	Cognitive researchers agree that most forgetting is a result of missing or ambiguous referents or cues. In order to remember content, mnemonics and pictorial imagery are helpful cues because they make content distinct and purposeful.
8. Ask your child to write the main ideas after reading.	Students are more apt to memorize important material if they write the main ideas of each section or chapter in a notebook or on index cards.

Source: Used with permission by the CERTA Corporation (2006).

is the authoritarian parents, who give children no latitude in decision making and little if any autonomy in both academic and social pursuits. Authoritarian parents often (but certainly not in every case) invoke corporal punishment or other types of punitive measures in an attempt to mold their children's behavior in line with their own values, traditions, and ways of life. Successful parenting style with respect to student success, according to HFRP, is one in which children are given a degree of autonomy, while at the same time parents are highly engaged in their children's education and social involvement. These parents are described as authoritative parents (not authoritarian parents) and fall in the middle of this continuum—they provide a liberal environment for their children and also structure and discipline so that their children develop a concern for education and its intrinsic connections with success later in life.

SCHOOL EFFECTS

Since the Coleman report of 1966, there has been a growing consensus that schooling has little affect on achievement. We would argue with this assumption and suggest that for many average students, schooling has hindered achievement. In fact, much of the variation in students' test scores is not attributed to schooling but family and community factors (Johnson, Johnson, Farenga, & Ness, 2005; Ness & Farenga, 2007; Orfield, Bachmeier, James, & Eitle, 1997; Rothstein, 2004). Although only a small percentage of variation in achievement can be attributed to education, there is still major disagreement in the research community as to the importance of schooling. Some researchers have argued that the effects of schooling have been underestimated (Madaus, Kellaghan, Rackow, & King, 1979; Rutter, 1983). Since all students study similar subjects, and the exposure to these subjects is primarily through school, education would account for only a small percentage of individual variation in achievement scores, whereas the environment outside of school appears to play a greater role in individual variation. This fact could result in an underestimation in the effect of school achievement. There could be an alternate explanation: another group of students, ones identified as average, has even a greater number of common educational experiences that were underwhelming in many circumstances. Again, there would be little variation in achievement scores. If we believe the premise that schools have an effect on student achievement, we need to invest in the silent majority—the average student.

One might draw a parallel between the average student and the average or middle-class taxpayer. The wealthy appear to avoid or to pay a disproportionately smaller percent of taxes, while the poor receive tax breaks and tax credits. Yet the middle class pay the burden of taxes. This is an example of providing for the extremes at the expense of those in the middle, similar to the average in education. The stimulus plan put forth by the Obama administration, despite progressive intentions, continues in the direction of many federal initiatives of the past. A total of $79 billion is put aside to offset education cutbacks, $13 billion for low-income students and $13.5 billion for additional special education funding (Khadaroo, 2009). Again, where is the funding for the average student? What initiatives are planned to assess learning beyond high-stakes examinations? How is informal knowledge being assessed? Is there a composite picture of ability that more accurately measures one's skill both in and out of school?

In *The Best and the Brightest*, David Halberstam (1993) emphasizes the importance of both knowledge and practical experience by concluding that academic ability alone does not often serve as the best criterion in making correct decisions for successful outcomes. Halberstam supports his assertion by referring to decisions made during the Vietnam War by Robert McNamara and the whiz kids of the Kennedy administration. These so-called whiz kids were mostly Ivy League college graduates who had a great deal of intellectual acumen but little in the way of practical government and military experience. Halberstam suggests that their lack of experience is what contributed to the escalation of the Vietnam War. No matter how good their analytical ability in predicting the outcome of a conventional war, it was of little practical use in an unconventional guerilla war in a tropical forest. Clearly, education must better bridge the gap between abstract concepts and everyday life, and it must do it with the same intensity as one would do in practice.

CONCLUSION

This book is about making connections between teachers, parents, and students in order to maximize and increase the potential of average students' learning opportunities. Any person who believes that school has a minimal effect on a child's life has not lived with a child who is attending school. Parents who have experienced a teacher with whom their child has made a connection are ecstatic about the academic and social growth their child makes during that school year. When the opposite occurs, parents sense that it is going to be a long year. Every day becomes a nightmare, the drama unfolds before school and continues after school, and there is no happy ending until the last calendar day.

This scenario occurs annually in so many homes that it creates a dilemma that is almost universally experienced. It seems to occur in every school and sometimes at every grade level. There is a teacher who no parents wish their children to encounter. The parents who are connected with the school—such as members of the PTA, volunteers, or those parents who communicate with teachers, administrators, and among themselves—are quick to send letters to the principal requesting any teacher but this one. Even parents whose children attend schools with policies stating that they do not honor such requests find ways to circumvent the rule. In these schools, parents identify the so-called learning styles or traits of their children and request placement with a teacher who they believe matches their children's learning preferences. The ruse is based on the premise that parents who use the strategy are not selecting their children's teachers; they are merely helping to secure an appropriate educational placement based on their children's learning needs.

So, who gets the teacher that no one seems to want? Not the high-ability students, who require someone on their game to handle such talent. Not the students with additional learning needs, who also require a teacher with additional skills. Indeed, it is the average students who do not have an advocate or advocacy group to avoid such placement. Average students are not protected by educational laws and statutes. These students will be left with this poor placement for at least one year. If the child progresses under these conditions, it is in spite of the situation. Readers may not want to believe this, but it's true, and it occurs more often than many of us in the field want to admit to.

We have suggested what needs to be done to improve education and specifically to improve education for the average student. It seems evident that no one method will work for all students and that a successful method in one environment does not necessarily translate well into a new setting. There needs to come a time, in order to be practical, where we recognize that most students can be successful with an appropriate degree of effort and persistence. Effort and persistence must be valued and cultivated in students. For the most part, the constantly changing curriculum, assessment, and pedagogies to create the illusion of achievement have been a waste of a vast amount of monetary and human resources. Successful teachers are able to manipulate the environment and develop pedagogies and content knowledge in order to assess and evaluate both the performances of their students and themselves. The problem is that many teachers do not have the freedom, support, or expertise to help our average students achieve success. For many teachers, the curriculum has been scripted, the assessments and levels of achievement have been prescribed, and the decisions concerning which students should get attention has been determined by administrative policies. There are no secrets for success at any level. It requires a degree of effort, applied in a consistent manner, over a length of time. This is a realization that has escaped many who seem to need immediate gratification.

Through this book, we hope that we have challenged you—the parent, teacher, administrator, and policymaker—to examine the current conditions of education for average students and to do what needs to be done by refocusing educational priorities for the silent majority of students. We close by revisiting our opening for chapter 1—Garrison Keillor's famous observation regarding the residents of Lake Wobegon, "where all the women are strong, all the men are good-looking, and all the children are above average." We hope that we have convinced you, the reader, that with the right environment, development of personal attributes, as well as parent and teacher input, the children of Lake Wobegon need not merely serve as an idealistic, romanticized model to which our children should aspire, but as a model that can serve as a real, achievable goal. But what price is our society willing to pay to make above-average ability for all children a reality?

Notes

Chapter 1: Average Anyone?

1. In most cases, the "crisis" doesn't end, because the organizations that receive funding to eliminate the crisis wish to perpetuate the problem for additional funding.

Chapter 4: Success for the Average

1. There are three general models of motivation that are readily applied in educational settings. Nevertheless, more than three models can be identified in the literature, and integrations and variations of the three models can be readily observed in school environments.

Chapter 6: Success for the Average: Effort, Ability, or Luck?

1. A manipulative, often referred to in plural form (manipulatives), is a tool used to help teachers present mathematical topics more clearly through the use of sensory stimulation, particularly sight and touch. The ultimate goal in using manipulatives is to connect students' everyday, informal mathematical knowledge with the formal, algorithmically produced (i.e., written) mathematics learned in school.

Chapter 9: The Myth of Average Intelligence

1. Despite our contention of "average intelligence," we argue that a segment of the student population does in fact fall into a category that requires a faster pace of instruction. These students exhibit a natural propensity for the subject matter, prior preparation, or combined effort and interest in the area of study. We also argue in favor of acceleration and that capable students deserve an appropriate educational experience. In most cases, we would argue that the rate of instruction should be changed among the different levels of students. Therefore, all students would be learning the same material, however, at a different rate. Students who are often labeled "high ability" are more than likely to have had certain experiences in early childhood that fostered and encouraged interest, expertise, or genetic predisposition in academic areas. We have elaborated on this issue earlier in our discussion of the importance of environmental factors in cultivating intelligence during the early years.

References

Adler, Mortimer, J. 1982. *The paideia proposal: An educational manifesto.* New York: Macmillan Publishing Company.

Albers, Donald J., and Alexanderson, G. L. 1985. *Mathematical people: Profiles and interviews.* Boston: A. K. Peters Ltd.

Albers, Donald J., and Alexanderson, G. L. 2008. *Mathematical People: Profiles and Interviews.* 2nd ed. Natick, MA: A. K. Peters Ltd (Interview with Gerald Alexanderson).

Alexander, K., Entwistle, D., and Thompson, M. 1987. School performance, status relations, and the structure of sentiment: Bringing the teacher back in. *American Sociological Review, 52,* 665–82.

Altmann, Gerry T. M. 1997. *The ascent of Babel: An exploration of language, mind, and understanding.* Oxford, UK: Oxford University Press.

American Association for the Advancement of Science (AAAS). 1989. *Science for all Americans.* Project 2061: Summary statement. Washington, DC: Author. Retrieved from www.project2061.org/publications/articles/2061/sfaasum.htm

Andrade, H. G., and Perkins, D. N. 1998. Learnable intelligence and intelligent learning. In R. J. Williams (Ed.), *Intelligence, instruction, and assessment: Theory into practice* (pp. 67–94). Mahwah, NJ: Lawrence Erlbaum Associates.

Annenberg Foundation. 2008. *Minds of our own: Lessons from thin air.* Washington, DC: Author. Retrieved from www.learner.org/resources/series26.html#jump1

Ash, Russell. 1995. *The top 10 of everything: 1996.* London: Dorling Kindersley.

Atkinson, John W. 1964. *An introduction to motivation.* Princeton, NJ: Van Nostrand.

Balfanz, Robert. 1999. Why do we teach young children so little mathematics? Some historical considerations. In Juanita V. Copley (Ed.), *Mathematics in the early years* (pp. 3–10). Reston, VA: National Council of Teachers of Mathematics.

Bandura, Albert. 1986. *Social foundations of thought and action: A social cognitive theory.* Englewood Cliffs, NJ: Prentice-Hall.

——. 1994. *Self-efficacy: The exercise of control.* New York: Freeman.

Barchers, Suzanne I. 1994. *Teaching language arts: An integrated approach.* Minneapolis, MN: West Publishing.

Baroody, A. J. 2003. The development of adaptive expertise and flexibility: The integration of conceptual and procedural knowledge. In. A. J. Baroody and A. Dowker (Eds.), *The development of arithmetic concepts and skills: Constructing adaptive expertise* (pp. 1–33). Mahwah, NJ: Lawrence Erlbaum Associates.

———. 2004. The developmental bases for early childhood number and operations standards. In D. H. Clements, J. Sarama, and A. DiBiase (Eds.), *Engaging young children in mathematics: Standards for early childhood mathematics education* (pp. 173–219). Mahwah, NJ: Lawrence Erlbaum Associates.

Baroody, A. J., and Wilkins, J. L. 1999. The development of informal counting, number, and arithmetic skills and concepts. In J. V. Copley (Ed.), *Mathematics in the early years* (pp. 48–65). Reston, VA: National Council of Teachers of Mathematics.

Berk, Laura, and Winsler, Adam. 1995. *Scaffolding children's learning: Vygotsky and early childhood education.* Washington, DC: National Association for the Education of Young Children.

Berliner, D., and Biddle, B. 1995. *The manufactured crisis: Myths, fraud, and attack on America's public schools.* Cambridge, MA: Perseus.

Bettmann, Otto L. 1974. *The good old days—They were terrible!* New York: Random House.

Bloom, Benjamin S. (Ed.). 1956. *Taxonomy of educational objectives: Cognitive domain.* New York: David McKay Company.

Board of Education of the Hendrick Hudson Central School District v. Rowley, 458 U.S. 176 (1982).

Bodrova, E., and Leong, D. J. 1996. *Tools of the mind: The Vygotskian approach to early childhood education.* Englewood Cliffs, NJ: Merrill/Prentice Hall.

Boring, Edwin G. 1923. Intelligence as the tests test it. *The New Republic, 34,* 35–36.

Borland, J. H. 2005. Gifted education without gifted children: The case for no conception of giftedness. In R. J. Davidson (Ed.), *Conceptions of giftedness* (pp. 1–19). New York: Cambridge University Press.

Borland, James H. 1986. IQ tests: Throwing out the bathwater, saving the baby. *Roeper Review, 8*(3), 163–67.

———. 2005. Gifted education without gifted children: The case for no conception of giftedness. In Robert J. Sternberg and Janet E. Davidson (Eds.), *Conceptions of giftedness* (2nd ed., pp. 1–19). New York: Cambridge University Press.

Bouchard, Thomas J., Jr. 1984. Review of *Frames of the mind: The theory of multiple intelligence. American Journal of Orthopsychiatry, 54,* 506–8.

Bower, Bruce. 2003. Essence of g: Scientists search for the biology of smarts. *Science News, 163,* 92–93.

Boyer, E. 1983. *High school: A report on secondary education in America.* New York: Harper & Row.

Bransford, J. D., Brown, A. L., and Cocking, R. R. (Eds.). 2000. *How people learn: Brain, mind, experience, and school.* Washington, DC: National Academy Press.

Braunger, Jane, and Lewis, Jan Patricia. 2006. *Building a knowledge base in reading* (2nd ed.). Newark, DE: International Reading Association.

Brody, Nathan. 1992. *Intelligence.* New York: Academic Press.

———. 2000. History of theories and measurements of intelligence. In Robert Sternberg (Ed.), *Handbook of intelligence* (pp. 16–33). New York: Cambridge University Press.

Brophy, Jere. 1982. *Research on self-fulfilling prophesy and teacher expectations.* East Lansing, MI: Institute for Research on Teaching.

———. 1983. Research on the self-fulfilling prophesy and teacher expectations. *Journal of Educational Psychology, 75,* 631–61.

———. 1987. Synthesis of research on strategies for motivating students to learn. *Educational Leadership, 45*(2), 40–48.

Brown, Ann L., and French, Lucia A. 1979. The zone of potential development: Implications for intelligence testing in the year 2000. In Robert J. Sternberg and Douglas K. Detterman (Eds.), *Human intelligence: Perspectives on its theory and measurement* (pp. 217–35). Norwood, NJ: Ablex Publishing.

Brush, Lorelei, R. 1978. Preschool children's knowledge of addition and subtraction. *Journal for Research in Mathematics Education, 9,* 44–54.

Campbell, Donald T. 1976. Assessing the impact of planned social change. Paper No. 8 from the Occasional Paper Series. Hanover, NH: Public Affairs Center, Dartmouth College.

Campbell, F. A., and Ramey, C. T. 1994. Effects of early intervention on intellectual and academic achievement: A follow-up study of children from low-income families. *Child Development, 65,* 684–98.

Carey, Susan. 1986. Cognitive science and science education. *American Psychologist, 41,* 1123–30.

———. (Ed.). 1987. *Eyewitness to history.* New York: Avon Books.

Carroll, John B. 1993. *Human cognitive abilities: A survey of factor-analytic studies.* New York: Cambridge University Press.

Carruth, Gorton, and Ehrlich, Eugene. 1988. *American quotations.* New York: Wings Books.

Cattell, Raymond B. 1963. Theory of fluid and crystallized intelligence: A critical experiment. *Journal of Educational Psychology, 54,* 1–22.

Ceci, S. J. 1990. *On intelligence . . . more or less: A bioecological treatise on intellectual development.* Englewood Cliffs, NJ: Prentice-Hall.

CERTA Learning Center. 2006. *Metacognitive techniques in improving study skills.* Williston Park, NY: CERTA Corp.

Chapin, Harry. 1979. Flowers are red. On *Legends of the lost and found—New greatest stories live* [CD]. New York: Elektra Entertainment Group, Inc.

Chase, William G., and Simon, Herbert A. 1973. Perception in chess. *Cognitive Psychology, 4*(1), 55–81.

Chi, Micheline T. H., Feltovich, P. J., and Glaser, Robert. 1981. Categorization and representation of physics problems by experts and novices. *Cognitive Science, 5,* 121–52.

Chi, Micheline T. H., and Glaser, Robert. 1981. The measurement of expertise: Analysis of the development of knowledge and skills as a basis for assessing achievement. In Eva L. Baker and Edys S. Quellmalz (Eds.), *Design, analysis, and policy in testing* (pp. 37–47). Beverly Hills, CA: Sage Publications.

Clement, J. 1982. Students' preconceptions in introductory mechanics. *American Journal of Physics, 50,* 66–71.

———. 1987. Overcoming students' misconceptions in physics: The role of anchoring intuitions and analogical validity. In J. D. Novak (Ed.), *Proceedings of the second international seminar on misconceptions and educational strategies in science and mathematics* (Vol. 3, pp. 84–97). Ithaca, NY: Department of Education, Cornell University.

Clark, Eve. 1993. *The lexicon in acquisition.* Cambridge, UK: Cambridge University Press.

Clifton, Rita, and Simmons, John. (Eds.). 2004. *Brands and branding.* Princeton, NJ: Bloomberg Press.

Cobley, John. 1970. *The crimes of the first fleet convicts.* London: Angus & Robertson Publishers.

Colbert, David. (Ed.). 1997. *Eyewitness to America: 500 years of America in the words of those who saw it happen.* New York: Pantheon Books.

Coleman, J. S., Campbell, E. Q., Hobson, C. J., McPartland, F., Mood, A. M., Weinfeld, F. D., et al. 1966. *Equality of educational opportunity.* Washington, DC: U.S. Government Printing Office.

Coles, Robert. 2004. *The story of Ruby Bridges.* New York: Scholastic, Inc.

Conway, Linda. 2000. Quote from "Faculty Center for Excellence in Teaching." Western Kentucky University. Website: www.wku.edu/teaching/db/quotes/index .html

Corbett, Christopher. 2003. *Orphans preferred: The twisted truth and lasting legend of the Pony Express.* New York: Broadway Books.

Council for Exceptional Children. 2008a. CEC's mission and vision. Arlington, VA: Author. Retrieved from www.cec.sped.org/Content/NavigationMenu/AboutCEC/ CECs MissionandVision/default.htm

———. 2008b. Public policy agenda for the 111th United States Congress. Arlington, VA: Author. Retrieved from www.cec.sped.org/AM/Template.cfm?Section=Home& CONTENTID=11301&TEMPLATE=/CM/ContentDisplay.cfm

Crystal, David. 2005. *How language works.* Woodstock, NY: Overlook Press.

Cunningham, H. H. 1958. *Doctors in gray: The Confederate medical service.* Baton Rouge: Louisiana State University Press.

Dahl, Sandra S. 1984. Strategies for creating readers. In James F. Baumann and Dale D. Johnson (Eds.), *Reading instruction and the beginning teacher: A practical guide* (pp. 299–314). Minneapolis, MN: Burgess Publishing.

Daniels, Harvey, and Zemelman, Steven. 2004. *Subject matter: Every teacher's guide to content-area reading.* Portsmouth, NH: Heinemann.

Darwin, Charles. 1859. *On the Origin of Species.* London: John Murray.

———. (1874). *The Decent of Man.* 2nd ed. London: John Murray.

Deci, E. L. 1992. The relation of interest to the motivation of behavior: A self-determination theory perspective. In K. A. Renninger, S. Hidi, and A. Krapp (Eds.), *The role of interest in learning and development.* Hillsdale, NJ: Lawrence Erlbaum Associates.

Deci, E. L., and Ryan, R. M. 1985. *Intrinsic motivation and self-determination in human behavior.* New York: Plenum Press.

———. 1992. The Initiation and regulation of intrinsically motivated learning and achievement. In A. K. Boggiano and T. S. Pittman (Eds.), *Achievement and motivation: A social-developmental perspective.* Cambridge, England: Cambridge University Press.

———. 1995. Human autonomy: The basis for true self-esteem. In M. H. Kernis (Ed.), *Efficacy, agency, and self-esteem.* New York: Plenum Press.

Delandshere, G., and Petrosky, A. R. 1998. Assessment of complex performances: Limitations of key measurement assumptions. *Educational Researcher, 27*(2), 14–24.

———. 1999. Anything can be measured, even colors can be measured: That's not the point. *Educational Researcher, 28*(3), 28–31.

———. 2002. In a contact zone: Incongruities in the assessment of complex performances of English teaching designed for the National Board of Professional Teaching Standards. In C. Dudley-Marling and C. Edlesky (Eds.), *The Fate of Progressive Language Policies and Practices,* 293–325. Urbana, IL: National Council of Teachers of English.

Dickson, Paul. 1990. *Timelines.* Reading, MA: Addison-Wesley.

———. 1996. *What's in a name? Reflections of an irrepressible name collector.* Springfield, MA: Merriam-Webster.

Dillon, Sam. 2005. Students ace state tests, but earn Ds from U.S. *New York Times,* November 26, pp. A1, A10.

Driver, R. 1983. *The pupil as scientist?* London, UK: Open University Press.

Dweck, Carol. 1986. Motivational processes affecting learning. *American Psychologist, 41,* 1040–48.

———. *Foundations of a Psychology of Education,* 87–136.

———. 2006. *Mindset: The new psychology of success.* New York: Ballantine Books.

Dweck, Carol, and Elliott, E. S. 1983. Achievement motivation. In E. M. Hetherington (Ed.), *Handbook of child psychology:* Vol. 4. *Socialization, personality, and development* (4th ed., pp. 643–91). New York: Wiley.

Dweck, Carol, and Leggett, E. L. 1988. A social cognitive approach to motivation and personality. *Psychological Review, 95,* 256–73.

Eccles, Jacqueline, Adler, T. F., Futterman, R., Goff, S. B., Kaczala, C. M., Meece, J. L., and Midgley, C. 1980. *Self-perceptions, task perceptions, and academic choice: Origins and change.* Final Report to the National Institute of Education. Washington, DC: National Institute of Education.

———. 1983. Expectancies, values, and academic behaviors. In J. T. Spence (Ed.), *Achievement and achievement motivation* (pp. 75–146). San Francisco: Freeman.

Eccles, Jacqueline, Adler, T. F., and Kaczala, C. M. 1982. Socialization of achievement attitudes and beliefs: Parental influences. *Child Development, 53,* 310–21.

Eccles, Jacqueline, Wigfield, A., and Schiefele, U. 1998. Motivation to succeed. In N. Eisenberg (Ed.), *Handbook of child psychology:* Vol. 3. *Social, emotional, and personality development* (5th ed., 1017–95). New York: Wiley.

Elias, Cynthia L., and Berk, Laura E. 2002. Self-regulation in young children: Is there a role for sociodramatic play? *Early Childhood Research Quarterly, 17*(2), 216–38.

Elliott, E. S., and Dweck, Carol. S. 1988. Goals: An approach to motivation and achievement. *Journal of Personality and Social Psychology, 54,* 5–12.

Engels, Frederick. 1975. *The part played by labour in the transition from ape to man.* Beijing: Foreign Languages Press. (Original work published 1864)

Farenga, Stephen. J., and Joyce, Beverly. 1999a. Intentions of young students to enroll in science courses in the future: An examination of gender differences. *Science Education, 83*(1), 55–75.

Farenga, Stephen J., and Joyce, Beverly A. 1999b. Science sensibility. *Science Scope, 22*(6), 6–9.

Farenga, S. J., Joyce, B. A., and Ness, D. 2002. Reaching the zone of optimal learning: The alignment of curriculum, instruction, and assessment. In R. Bybee (Ed.), *Learning science and the science of learning*. Washington, DC: National Science Teachers Association.

———. 2006. Adaptive inquiry as the silver bullet: Reconciling local curriculum, instruction, and assessment procedures with state mandated testing in science. In M. McMahon, P. Simmons, and R. Somers (Eds.), *Assessment in science: Practical experiences and educational research*. Washington, DC: National Science Teachers Association.

Fatout, P. (Ed.). 2006. *Mark Twain speaking*. Iowa City: University of Iowa Press.

Feather, Norman T. 1982. *Expectations and actions: Expectancy-value models in psychology*. Hillsdale, NJ: Lawrence Erlbaum Associates.

Fennema, Elizabeth, and Sherman, Julia A. 1976. Fennema-Sherman Mathematics Attitudes Scales: Instruments designed to measure attitudes toward the learning of mathematics by females and males. *Journal for Research in Mathematics Education, 7*(5), 324–26.

Feuerstein, Reuven. 1979. *The dynamic assessment of retarded learners*. Baltimore, MD: University Park Press.

———. 1980. *Instrumental enrichment: An intervention program for cognitive modifiability*. Baltimore, MD: University Park Press.

Feynman, Richard P. 1969. What is science? *The Physics Teacher, 7*(6), 313–20.

———. 2000. *The pleasure of finding things out*. New York: Basic Books.

Finn, Chester E., and Petrilli, Michael J. 2008. Conjuring cut scores: How it distorts our picture of student achievement. *American Educator, 31*(4), 20, 22, 28.

Firestone, W. A., Fairmen, J., and Mayrowetz, D. 1997. *The under-whelming influence of testing on mathematics teaching in Maine and Maryland*. Paper presented at the annual meeting of the American Educational Research Association, Chicago.

Flavell, John. 1982. On cognitive development. *Child Development, 53*, 1–10.

Flexner, Doris, and Flexner, Stuart Berg. 2008. *The pessimist's guide to history*. New York: Collins.

Freire, Paulo. 1970. *Pedagogy of the oppressed*. New York: Continuum.

———. 1996. *Pedagogy of the Oppressed*. New York: Continuum. (Original work published 1970)

Fuson, Karen C. 1992. Research on whole number addition and subtraction. In D. Grouws (Ed.), *Handbook of research on mathematics teaching and learning* (pp. 243–75). New York: Macmillan.

Gallant, Frank K. 1998. *A place called Peculiar: Stories about unusual American place-names*. Springfield, MA: Merriam-Webster.

Galton, Francis. 1869. *Hereditary genius: An inquiry into its laws and consequences*. London: MacMillan and Company.

Gardner, Howard. 1983. Frames of mind. New York: Basic Books.

———. 1993. *Frames of mind: The theory of multiple intelligences*. New York: Basic Books. (Original work published 1983)

Geary, David. 2004. Mathematics and learning disabilities. *Journal of Learning Disabilities, 37*(1), 4–15.

Gelbert, Doug. 1996. *So who the heck was Oscar Meyer? The real people behind those brand names.* New York: Barricade Books.

Ginsburg, Herbert P. 1972. *The myth of the deprived child: Poor children's intellect and education.* Englewood Cliffs, NJ: Prentice Hall.

———. 1989. *Children's arithmetic: How they learn it and how you teach it.* Austin, TX: Pro-Ed.

———. 1997. *Entering the child's mind: The clinical interview in psychological research and practice.* New York: Cambridge University Press.

Ginsburg, Herbert P., Inoue, Noriyuki, and Seo, Kyoung-hye. 1999. Young children doing mathematics: Observations of everyday activities. In J. V. Copley (Ed.), *Mathematics in the early years* (pp. 88–99). Reston, VA: National Council of Teachers of Mathematics.

Ginsburg, Herbert P., Pappas, Sandra, and Seo, Kyoung-hye. 2001. Everyday mathematical knowledge: Asking young children what is developmentally appropriate. In S. Golbeck (Ed.), *Psychological perspectives on early childhood education,* 181–219. Mahwah, NJ: Lawrence Erlbaum.

Gleitman, H. 1992. *Basic psychology* (3rd ed.). New York: Norton.

Goodlad, John. 1984. *A place called school.* New York: McGraw-Hill.

Gopnik, A. M., Meltzoff, A. N., and Kuhl, P. K. 1999. *The scientist in the crib: What early learning tells us about the mind.* New York: Harper Collins.

Gopnik, Alison, and Meltzoff, Andrew. 1997. *Words, thoughts, and theories.* Cambridge: MIT Press.

Gottfredson, L. 1994. Mainstream science on intelligence. *Wall Street Journal,* December 13, p. A18.

Gould, Stephen Jay. 1996. *The mismeasure of man.* New York: W. W. Norton.

Guilford, J. P. 1959. Three faces of intellect. *American Psychologist, 14,* 469–79.

———. 1967. *The nature of human intelligence.* New York: McGraw Hill.

Gustin, William C. 1985. The development of exceptional research mathematicians. In B. S. Bloom (Ed.), *Developing talent in young people* (pp. 270–331). New York: Ballantine.

Halberstam, D. 1993. *The best and the brightest.* New York: Ballantine.

Halloun, I. A., and Hestenes, D. 1987. Modeling instruction in mechanics. *American Journal of Physics, 55,* 455–62.

Hardman, Michael L., Drew, Clifford J., and Egan, M. Winston. 2002. *Human exceptionality: Society, school, and family* (7th ed.). Boston: Allyn and Bacon.

Harvard Family Research Project. 2006. Family involvement makes a difference in school success. Retrieved on May 29, 2009, from Harvard Family Research Project—Publications and Resources, www.hfrp.org/publications-resources/browse our-publications/family-involvement-makes-a-difference-in-school-success

Hayes, J. R. 1981. *The complete problem solver.* Philadelphia: Franklin Institute Press.

Hembree, Ray. 1990. The nature, effects, and relief of mathematics anxiety. *Journal for Research in Mathematics Education, 21*(1), 33–46.

Heider, Fritz. 1958. *The psychology of interpersonal relations.* New York: Wiley.

Helvetius, Claude Adrien. (n.d.). *Quotes.net.* Retrieved October 20, 2009, from http://www.quotes.net/quote/14105

Hertzman, C. 2002. *Leave no child behind: Social exclusion and child development.* Toronto: Laidlaw Foundation.

Hertzman, C., and Weins, M. 1996. Child development and long-term outcomes: A population health perspective and summary of successful interventions. *Social Sciences and Medicine,* 43, 1083–95.

Hillocks, G. 1997. *How state mandatory assessment simplifies writing instruction in Illinois and Texas.* Paper presented at the annual meeting of the American Educational Research Association, Chicago.

Hine, Thomas. 1995. *The total package: The evolution and secret meanings of boxes, bottles, cans, and tubes.* Boston, MA: Little, Brown and Company.

Horn, John L. 1979. The rise and fall of human abilities. *Journal of Research and Development in Education,* 12, 59–78.

———. 1998. A basis for research on age differences in cognitive capabilities. In J. J. McArdle and R. W. Woodcock (Eds.), *Human cognitive abilities in theory and practice* (pp. 57–87). Mahwah, NJ: Lawrence Erlbaum Associates.

Horn, John L., and Cattell, Raymond B. 1966. Refinement and test of the theory of fluid and crystallized intelligence. *Journal of Educational Psychology,* 57, 253–76.

———. 1967. Age differences in fluid and crystallized intelligence. *Acta Psychologica,* 26, 107–29.

Horn, John L., and McArdle, John J. 2007. Understanding human intelligence since Spearman. In Robert Cudeck and Robert C. MacCallum (Eds.), *Factor analysis at 100: Historical developments and future directions* (pp. 205–48). Mahwah, NJ: Lawrence Erlbaum Associates.

Huey, Edmund Burke. 2008. *The psychology and pedagogy of reading.* Whitefish, MT: Kessinger Publishing. (Original work published 1908)

Huinker, D. 2002. Calculators as learning tools for young children's explorations of number. *Teaching Children Mathematics,* 8(6), 316–21.

Humphreys, Lloyd G., Parsons, Charles K., and Park, Randolph D. 1979. Dimensions involved in differences among school means of cognitive measures. *Journal of Educational Measurement,* 16, 63–76.

Illich, I. 1972. *Deschooling society.* New York: Boyars.

Ingram, Jay. 1992. *Talk talk talk.* Toronto, ON: Penguin Books.

Jehlen, Alain. 2009. Is NCLB working: The "scientifically-based" answer. *NEA Today,* 27(4), 30–31.

Jennings, Joyce Holt, Caldwell, JoAnne Schudt, and Lerner, Janet W. 2006. *Reading problems: Assessment and teaching strategies.* Boston, MA: Pearson.

Jensen, A. R. 1969. How much can we boost IQ and scholastic achievement? *Harvard Educational Review,* 39, 1–123.

———. 1980. *Bias in mental testing.* New York: Free Press.

———. 1981. *Straight talk about mental tests.* New York: Free Press.

———. 1983. The nonmanipulable and effectively manipulable variables of education. *Education and Society,* 1(1), 51–52.

———. 1998. *The g factor: The science of mental ability.* Westport, CT: Greenwood Publishing.

Johnson, Bonnie. 1999. *Wordworks: Exploring language play.* Golden, CO: Fulcrum.

Johnson, Bonnie, and Johnson, Dale D. 1996. An oral history project in an integrated reading/language arts/social studies methods class. *The Reading Professor,* 18(2), 43–59.

Johnson, Dale D., and Johnson, Bonnie. 2005. Language development. In Stephen J. Farenga and Daniel Ness (Eds.), *Encyclopedia of education and human development* (Vol. 3, pp. 688–717). Armonk, NY: M. E. Sharpe.

———. 2006. *High stakes: Poverty, testing, and failure in American schools* (2nd ed.). Lanham, MD: Rowman & Littlefield.

Johnson, Dale D., Johnson, Bonnie, Farenga, Stephen J., and Ness, Daniel. 2005. *Trivializing teacher education: The accreditation squeeze.* Lanham, MD: Rowman & Littlefield.

———. 2008. *Stop high-stakes testing: An appeal to America's conscience.* Lanham, MD: Rowman & Littlefield.

Junior League of Monroe, Inc. 2000. *The cotton country collection.* Monroe, LA: Cotton Bayou Publications.

Kaplan, Sandra N. 1981. The should nots and shoulds of developing appropriate curriculum for the gifted. In W. B. Barbe and J. S. Renzulli (Eds.), *Psychology and education of the gifted* (pp. 351–58). New York: Irvington Publishers.

———. 1986. Qualitatively differentiated curricula. In C. June Maker (Ed.), *Critical issues in gifted education: Defensible program for the gifted* (pp. 121–34). Rockville, MD: Aspen Publishers.

Keillor, Garrison. 2009. A Prairie Home Companion with Garrison Keillor. American Public Media. Website: http://prairiehome.publicradio.org/about/podcast

Khadaroo, S. T. 2009. Can't buy me A's: Critics pan schools plan. ABC News Internet Ventures, February 8. Retrieved February 15, 2009, from http://abcnews.go.com/print?=6823320

Kinget, G. Marian. 1975. *On being human: A systematic view.* New York: Harcourt Brace Jovanovich.

Kirschner, David, and Whitson, James A. 1997. *Situated cognition: Social, semiotic, and psychological perspectives.* Mahwah, NJ: Lawrence Erlbaum Associates.

Koretz, Daniel. 2008. *Measuring up: What educational testing really tells us.* Cambridge, MA: Harvard University Press.

Krafft, Kerry C., and Berk, Laura E. 1998. Private speech in two preschools: Significance of open-ended activities and make-believe play for verbal self-regulation. *Early Childhood Research Quarterly, 13*(4), 637–58.

Lemke, Jay L. 1990. *Talking science: Language, learning, and values.* Norwood, NJ: Ablex Publishing.

Lenneberg, Eric H. 1967. *Biological foundations of language.* New York: Wiley.

Levitt, Steven D., and Dubner, Stephen J. 2005. *Freakonomics: A rogue economist explores the hidden side of everything.* New York: William Morrow.

Lin, Chia-ling. 2005. Mathematical operations and functions. In S. J. Farenga and D. Ness (Eds.), *Encyclopedia of Education and Human Development.* Armonk, NY: M. E. Sharpe.

Linn, M. C. 1986. Science. In R. Dillon and R. Sternberg (Eds.), *Cognition and instruction* (pp. 155–204). Orlando, FL: Academic Press.

Losq, Christine S. 2005. Number concepts and special needs students: The power of ten-frame tiles. *Teaching Children Mathematics, 11*(6), 310–15.

Lorge, Irving. 1953. Difference or bias in tests of intelligence. *Proceedings: Invitational Conference on Testing Problems.* Princeton, NJ: Educational Testing Service.

Mabry, L. 1999. Writing the rubric: Lingering effects of traditional standardized testing on direct writing assessment. *Phi Delta Kappan, 80*(9), 673–79.

Macaruso, Paul, and Sokol, Scott M. 1998. Cognitive neuropsychology and developmental dyscalculia. In C. Donlon (Ed.), *The development of mathematical skills*, 201–25. New York: Psychology Press.

Madaus, G. F., Kellaghan, T., Rakow, E. A., and King, D. 1979. The sensitivity of measures of school effectiveness. *Harvard Educational Review, 49*(2), 207–30.

Martin, Bill, Jr. 1966. *Sounds of language readers* (series). New York: Holt, Rinehart & Winston.

Matthews, Jay. 1989. *Escalante: The best teacher in America.* New York: Henry Holt.

McClure, Alexander K. 1901. *Lincoln's yarns and stories.* Philadelphia: J. C. Winston Company.

McLoyd. 1998. Socioeconomic disadvantage and child development. *American Psychologist, 53*, 185–204.

Midgley, C., Eccles, J., and Feldlaufer, H. 1991. Classroom environments and transition to junior high school. In B. J. Fraser and H. J. Walberg (Eds.), *Educational environments: Evaluation, antecedents and consequences* (pp. 113–39). New York: Pergamon Press.

Midgley, C., Feldlaufer, H., and Eccles, Jacqueline. 1989. Change in teacher efficacy and student self- and task-related beliefs in mathematics during the transition to junior high school. *Journal of Educational Psychology, 81*, 247–58.

Mineola Union Free School District. 2009. Letter to the community. Outreach (Spring 2009). Mineola, NY: Author.

Montessori, Maria. 1966. *The secret of childhood.* (M. J. Costelloe, Trans.). New York: Ballantine Books. (Original work published 1936)

Morgan, Harry. 1996. An analysis of Gardner's theory of multiple intelligence. *Roeper Review, 18*, 263–70.

Morrow, Ed. 1995. *Born this day: A daily celebration of famous beginnings.* New York: Citadel Press.

National Association for Gifted Children. 2008. Mission statement. Washington, DC: Author. Retrieved from www.nagc.org/index.aspx?id=661

National Aeronautic and Space Administration (NASA) Glenn Research Center. 2008. *Kite index.* Cleveland, OH: NASA. Retrieved from www.grc.nasa.gov/WWW/K-12/airplane/shortk.html

National Commission on Excellence in Education. 1983. *A Nation at Risk: The Imperative for Educational Reform.* Washington, DC: U.S. Department of Education.

National Research Council (NRC). 1995. *National science education standards.* Retrieved on June 9, 2008, from www.nap.edu/html/nses

National Science Foundation (NSF). 2005. *Systemic reform initiatives.* Retrieved on June 9, 2008, from www.nas.edu/rise/backg3.htm

National Science Teachers Association. 2009. U.S. students "static" in science. *NSTA Reports, 20*(5), 1, 5.

Ness, Daniel. 2002. Helping teachers recognize and connect the culturally bound nature of young children's mathematical intuitions to in-school mathematics concepts. In L. Catelli and A. Diver-Stamnes (Eds.), *Commitment to excellence: Transforming teaching and teacher education in the inner city* (pp. 171–89). Creskill, NJ: Hampton Press.

Ness, Daniel, and Farenga, Stephen J. 2007. *Knowledge under construction: The importance of play in developing children's spatial and geometric thinking.* Lanham, MD: Rowman & Littlefield.

Nicholls, J. G. 1978. The development of the concepts of effort and ability, perception of academic attainment, and the understanding that difficult tasks require more ability. *Developmental Psychology, 49,* 800–814.

———. 1979. Development of perception of own attainment and causal attributions for success and failure in reading. *Journal of Educational Psychology, 71,* 94–99.

———. 1990. What is ability and why are we mindful of it? A developmental perspective. In R. J. Sternberg and J. Kolligian (Eds.), *Competence considered,* 205–25. New Haven, CT: Yale University Press.

Nisbett, R. 2009. *Intelligence and how to get it: Why schools and culture count.* New York: Norton.

Nowicki, Stephen and Strickland, Bonnie R. 1973. A locus of control scale for children. *Journal of Consulting and Clinical Psychology, 40,* 148–54.

O'Keefe, Kevin. 2005. *The average American: The extraordinary search for the nation's most ordinary citizen.* New York: Public Affairs.

Orfield, G. B., Bachmeier, M. D., James, D. R., and Eitle, T. 1997. *Deepening segregation in American public schools.* Cambridge, MA: Harvard Project on School Desegregation.

Palincsar, A. S., and Brown, Ann L. 1984. Reciprocal teaching of comprehension monitoring activities. *Cognition and Instruction, 1,* 117–75.

Parker, Walter C., and Jarolimek, John. 1997. *Social studies in elementary education* (10th ed.). Upper Saddle River, NJ: Prentice-Hall.

Pascual-Leone, Juan, and Ijaz, H. 1989. Mental capacity testing as a form of intellectual-developmental assessment. In R. J. Samuda, S. L. Kong, et al. (Eds.), *Assessment and placement of minority students.* Toronto, ON: Hogrefe & Huber.

Patel, V. L., and Groen, G. J. 1991. The general and specific nature of medial expertise: A critical look. In K. A. Ericsson and J. Smith (Eds.), *Toward a general theory of expertise* (pp. 93–125). New York: Cambridge University Press.

Pea, R. D. 1993. Practices of distributed intelligence and designs for education. In G. Salomon (Ed.), *Distributed cognitions: Psychological and educational considerations* (pp. 47–87). New York: Cambridge University Press.

Perkins, David N. 1992. *Smart schools: Better thinking and learning for every child.* New York: Free Press.

———. 1995a. *Outsmarting IQ: The emerging science of learnable intelligence.* New York: Free Press.

———. 1995b. *Smart schools: Better thinking and learning for every child.* New York: Free Press.

Perkins, David N., and Segal, Judith W. (Eds.), *Informal reasoning and education* (pp. 331–43). Hillsdale, NJ: Lawrence Erlbaum Associates.

Petchesky, Barry. 2007. Salad daze. *Smart Money,* November, 108–11.

Petroski, Henry. 1992. *The pencil: A history of design and circumstance.* New York: Knopf.

Phillips, Meredith. 1997. What makes schools effective? A comparison of the relationships of communitarian climate and academic climate to mathematics achievement and attendance during middle school. *American Educational Research Journal, 34,* 633–62.

Piaget, J. 1930. *The child's conception of the world.* New York: Harcourt.

Piaget, Jean. 1953. *Origins of intelligence in the child.* London: Routledge & Kegan Paul. (Original work published 1936)

Piaget, Jean, and Inhelder, Bärbel. 1975. *The origin of the idea of chance in children.* New York: Norton.

Pinar, W. F. (2003). What is curriculum theory? Mahwah, NJ: Lawrence Erlbaum Associates.

Pinker, Steven. 1994. *The language instinct: How the mind creates language.* New York: HarperPerennial.

Pintrich, Paul R., and Garcia, Teresa. 1994. Regulating motivation and cognition in the classroom: The role of self-regulatory strategies. In D. Schunk and B. Zimmerman (Eds.), *Self-regulation of learning and performance: Issues and educational applications.* Hillsdale, NJ: Lawrence Erlbaum Associates.

Plato. (1937). *The Dialogues of Plato.* 2 vols. Translated by Benjamin Jowett. New York: Random House.

Plucker, Jonathan, Callahan, Carolyn M., and Tomchin, Ellen M. 1996. Wherefore art thou, multiple intelligences? Alternative assessments for identifying talent in ethnically diverse and economically disadvantaged students. *Gifted Child Quarterly, 40,* 81–92.

Popham, W. James, and Baker, Eva L. 1970. *Systematic instruction.* Englewood Cliffs, NJ: Prentice-Hall.

Programme for International Student Assessment (PISA). 2009. A summary of findings from PISA 2006. International Center for Educational Statistics. Retrieved from http://nces.ed.gov/surveys/pisa/pisa2006highlights.asp

Reid, Ivan, and Croucher, Audrey. 1980. The Crandall Intellectual Achievement Responsibility Questionnaire: A British validation study. *Educational and Psychological Measurement, 40*(1), 255–58.

Resnick, Lauren B. 1983. Mathematics and science learning: A new conception. *Science, 220,* 477–78.

———. 1987. *Education and learning to think.* Washington, DC: National Academy Press.

Richardson, Frank C., and Suinn, Richard M. 1972. The mathematics anxiety rating scale: Psychometric data. *Journal of Counseling Psychology, 19*(6), 551–54.

Ritchie, Donald A. 1995. *Doing oral history.* New York: Twayne.

Roe, Anne. 1951a. A psychological study of eminent biologists. *Psychological Monographs, 65*(14).

———. 1951b. A psychological study of eminent physical scientists. *Genetic Psychology Monographs, 43,* 121–235.

———. 1952. A psychologist examines 64 eminent scientists. *Scientific American, 187*(5), 21–25.

———. 1981. A psychologist examines 64 eminent scientists. In W. B. Barbe and J. Renzulli (Eds.), *Psychology and education of the gifted* (pp. 103–10). New York: Irving Publishers.

Roeper, Annemarie. 1988. The early environment of the child: Experience in a continuing search for meaning. In P. F. Brandwein and A. H. Passow (Eds.), *Gifted young in science: Potential through performance* (pp. 121–39). Washington, DC: National Science Teachers Association.

Rogoff, Barbara. 1990. *Apprenticeship in thinking.* New York: Oxford University Press.

Rosenthal, R. 1966. *Experimenter effects in behavioral research.* New York: Appleton-Century-Crofts.

———. 1994. Interpersonal expectancy effects: A 30-year perspective. *Current Directions in Psychological Science, 3,* 176–79.

Rosenthal, R., and Fode, K. L. 1963. The effect of experimenter bias on the performance of the albino rat. *Behavioral Science, 8,* 183–89.

Rosenthal, Robert, and Jacobson, Lenore. 1968. *Pygmalion in the classroom: Teacher expectations and pupil's intellectual development.* New York: Holt, Rinehart, & Winston.

Rothstein, R. 2004. *Class and schools: Using social, economic, and educational reform to close the black-white achievement gap.* Washington, DC: Economic Policy Institute.

Rowe, Mary Budd. 1978. *Teaching science as continuous inquiry.* New York: McGraw-Hill.

Rutter, M. 1983. School effects on pupil progress: Research findings and policy implications. *Child Development, 54,* 1–29.

Sacks, Oliver. (2008). *Musicophilia: Tales of Music and the Brain.* New York: Vintage.

Salomon, Gavriel, and Perkins, David. 1996. Learning in Wonderland: What do computers really offer education? In Stephen T. Kerr (Ed.), *Technology and the future of schooling* (pp. 111–30). Chicago: University of Chicago Press.

Sattler, Jerome. 2001. *Assessment of Children: Cognitive Applications.* San Diego: J. M. Sattler Publication.

Schoenfeld, Alan (1984). Mathematical Problem Solving. Orlando, FL: Academic Press.

———. (1991). On Mathematics and Sense Making: An Informal Attack on the Unfortunate Divorce of Formal and Informal Mathematics. In J. F. Voss, D. N. Perkins, and J. W. Segal, (Eds.), *Informal Reasoning and Education* (pp. 331-343). Hillsdale, NJ: Lawrence Erlbaum Associates.

Seebach, Linda. 1997. In lieu of grades—Applesauce. *Des Moines Register,* April 20, C3.

Seeger, M. (Ed.). 1994. *"I gotta tell you": Speeches of Lee Iacocca.* Detroit: Wayne State University Press.

Shell, Ellen Ruppel. 1996. Package design: The art of selling all wrapped up. *Smithsonian,* April, 54–66.

Siegel, Marvin. (Ed.). 1999. *The last word: The New York Times book of obituaries and farewells: A celebration of unusual lives.* New York: Quill.

Siegler, Robert, S., and Ellis, Shari. 1996. Piaget on childhood. *Psychological Science, 7,* 211–15.

Simpson, John, and Weiner, Edmund (Eds.). 1989. *Oxford English Dictionary.* Oxford, UK: Oxford University Press.

Sizer, T. R. 1984. *Horace's compromise.* Boston: Houghton Mifflin.

Skinner, B. F. 1968. *The technology of teaching.* New York: Appleton-Century-Crofts.

Snow, Catherine E., Burns, M. Susan, and Griffin, Peg. (Eds.). 1998. *Preventing reading difficulties in young children.* Washington, DC: National Academy Press.

Spearman, Charles. 1904. General intelligence: Objectively determined and measured. *American Journal of Psychology, 15*, 201–93.

Spring, J. 2007. American education (13th ed.) [Audiotape]. Boston: McGraw Hill.

Steen, Lynn, A. 2004. *Achieving quantitative literacy: An urgent challenge for higher education.* Washington, DC: Mathematics Association of America.

Sternberg, R. J. 1985. *Beyond IQ: A triarchic theory of human intelligence.* New York: Cambridge University Press.

———. 1996. *Successful intelligence.* New York: Simon & Schuster.

———. 2001. Dr. Jekyll meets Mr. Hyde: Two faces of research on intelligence and cognition. J. S. Halonen and S. F. Davis (Eds.), *The many faces of psychological research in the 21st century* (chap. 6). Website: http://teachpsych.org/resources/e-books/faces/script/Ch06.htm

———. 2005. The WICS model of giftedness. R. J. Sternberg and J. E. Davidson (Eds.), *Conceptions of giftedness* (2nd ed., pp. 327–42). New York: Cambridge University Press.

Sternberg, Robert J., and Kaufman, James C. 1998. Human abilities. *Annual Review of Psychology, 49*, 479–502.

Sternberg, Robert J., Wagner, Richard K., Williams, Wendy M., and Horvath, Joseph A. 1995. Testing common sense. *American Psychologist, 50*, 912–27.

Tannenbaum, Abraham J. 1965. The IPAT culture fair intelligence test: A critical review. In D. Buros (Ed.), *Six mental measurements yearbook* (pp. 721–23). Highland Park, NJ: Gryphon Press.

———. 1983. *Gifted children: Psychological and educational perspectives.* New York: Macmillan.

Terman, Lewis M. (1916). *The measurement of intelligence: An explanation of and a complete guide for the use of the Stanford Revision and extension of the Binet-Simon Intelligence Scale.* Boston: Houghton Mifflin Company.

Thurstone, Louis L. 1938. *Primary mental abilities.* Chicago: University of Chicago Press.

Thurstone, Louis L., and Thurstone, Thelma G. 1941. Factorial studies of intelligence. *Psychometric Monographs,* No. 2. Chicago: University Chicago Press.

Thurstone, Thelma G. 1958. *SRA primary mental abilities.* Chicago: Science Research Associates.

Tobias, Sheila. 1993. *Overcoming mathematics anxiety.* New York: W. W. Norton.

Trends in International Mathematics and Science Study (TIMSS). 2009. TIMSS 2007 results. International Center for Educational Statistics. Retrieved from http://nces.ed.gov/timss/results07.asp

Trigger, Bruce G. 2006. *A history of archeological thought.* New York: Cambridge University Press.

Vygotsky, Lev S. 1962. *Thinking and speech (Thought and language).* Cambridge: MIT Press.

———. 1978. *Mind in society: The development of higher psychological processes.* Cambridge, MA: Harvard University Press.

Wade, Nicholas. 2003. Early voices: The leap to language. *New York Times,* July 15, pp. F1, F4.

Wandersee, J. H. 1983. Students' misconceptions about photosynthesis: A cross-age study. In H. Helm and J. Novak (Eds.), *Proceedings of the international seminar on misconceptions in science and mathematics* (pp. 441–65). Ithaca, NY: Department of Education, Cornell University.

Wang, M. C., Haertel, G. D., and Walberg, H. J. 1993. Toward a knowledge base for school learning. *Review of Educational Research, 63,* 249–94.

Weiner, Bernard. 1974. *Achievement motivation and attribution theory.* Morristown, NJ: General Learning Press.

———. 1976. An attributional approach for educational psychology. *Review of Research in Education, 4,* 179–207.

———. 1986. *An attributional theory of motivation and emotion.* New York: Springer-Verlag.

Weiss, R. 2005. How DNA is influenced. *Washington Post,* July 6, p. A26.

Welsh, Patrick. 2006. Students aren't interchangeable. *USA Today—Education Forum,* September 19. Retrieved from http://blogs.usatoday.com/oped/2006/09/post _17.html

Welton, David A., and Mallan, John T. 1996. *Children and their world: Strategies for teaching social studies* (2nd ed.). Boston, MA: Houghton Mifflin.

White, B. Y., and Frederickson, J. R. 1998. Inquiry, modeling, and metacognition: Making science accessible to all students. *Cognition and Science, 16,* 90–91.

Whitenack, Joy W., Knipping, Nancy, Loesing, Jenine, Kim, Ok-Kyeong, and Beetsma, Abby. 2002. Starting off the school year with opportunities for all: Supporting first graders' development of number sense. *Teaching Children Mathematics, 9*(1), 26–31.

Wilson, Frank T. 1953. Some special ability test scores of gifted children. *Pedagogical Seminary and Journal of Genetic Psychology, 82,* 59–68.

Wissler, Clark. 1901. The correlates of mental and physical tests. *Psychological Review,* Monograph No. 3.

Wolf, R. 1966. The measurement of environments. In A. Anastasi (Ed.), *Testing problems in perspective* (pp. 491–503). Washington, DC: Council on Education.

Yazzie-Mintz, E. 2007. Voices of students on engagement: A report on the 2006 high school survey of student engagement. Bloomington, IN: Center for Evaluation and Education Policy (CEEP), Indiana University. Retrieved on November 12, 2008, from http://ceep.indiana.edu/hssse/pdf/HSSSE_2006_Report.pdf

Index

About the Authors

Stephen J. Farenga is professor of human development and learning at Dowling College in Oakdale, New York. He specializes in science education, gifted education, and human development.

Daniel Ness is associate professor of human development and learning at Dowling College. His specialization is mathematics education and mathematical thinking from the early years through adulthood.

Bonnie Johnson is professor of human development and Learning at Dowling College. Dr. Johnson is the author of numerous publications in the fields of language, civics, and social justice.

Dale D. Johnson is professor of literacy education at Dowling College. He has written fifteen books and more than 100 chapters and journal articles on reading comprehension and vocabulary development.

Breinigsville, PA USA
05 February 2010
232014BV00003B/2/P